THE SKILLS YOU NEED
THE FAITH YOU WANT

SEEKERS WANTED

ANTHONY SWEAT

DESERET BOOK

Salt Lake City, Utah

*To my beloved students and colleagues
at Brigham Young University.*

Thank you for helping me better seek.

Illustrations on pages 9, 69, 71, 107, and 138: © 2019 Bryan Beach, DBA Beachouse Multimedia

Photos on pages 6, 53, and 98: FotoDuets/Shutterstock.com

Page iv: varijanta/Getty Images; p. 2: ciripasca/Getty Images; p. 3: aelitta/Shutterstock.com and varijanta/Getty Images; p. 11: varijanta/Getty Images; p. 15: varijanta/Getty Images and graphixmania/Shutterstock.com; p. 54: ciripasca/Getty Images; p. 60: aelitta/Shutterstock.com and ciripasca/Getty Images; p. 61: graphixmania/Shutterstock.com; p. 65: varijanta/Getty Images; p. 66: graphixmania/Shutterstock.com; p. 75: nanmulti/ Shutterstock.com; p. 85: graphixmania/Shutterstock.com; p. 86: graphixmania/Shutterstock.com; p. 87: phipatbig/Shutterstock.com; p. 87: shum-stock/Shutterstock.com; p. 100: Vector Tradition/Shutterstock.com; p. 111: graphixmania/Shutterstock.com; p. 118 & 122: graphixmania/Shutterstock.com and varijanta/Getty Images; p. 149: uncimo and cTermit/Shutterstock.com

© 2019 Anthony Sweat

All rights reserved. No part of this book may be reproduced in any form or by any means without permission in writing from the publisher, Deseret Book Company, at permissions@deseretbook.com or PO Box 30178, Salt Lake City, Utah 84130. This work is not an official publication of The Church of Jesus Christ of Latter-day Saints. The views expressed herein are the responsibility of the author and do not necessarily represent the position of the Church or of Deseret Book Company.

DESERET BOOK is a registered trademark of Deseret Book Company.

Visit us at deseretbook.com

Library of Congress Cataloging-in-Publication Data

Names: Sweat, Anthony, author.
Title: Seekers wanted : the skills you need for the faith you want / Anthony Sweat.
Description: Salt Lake City, Utah : Deseret Book, [2019] | Includes bibliographical references and index.
Identifiers: LCCN 2019015376| ISBN 9781629725734 (paperbound : alk. paper) | ISBN 1629725730 (paperbound : alk. paper)
Subjects: LCSH: The Church of Jesus Christ of Latter-day Saints—Doctrines—Study and teaching. | Mormon Church—Doctrines—Study and teaching.
Classification: LCC BX8610 .S94 2019 | DDC 230/.9332071—dc23
LC record available at https://lccn.loc.gov/2019015376

Printed in the United States of America
Lake Book Manufacturing, Inc., Melrose Park, IL

10   9   8   7   6   5   4   3   2   1

CONTENTS

Prologue: Seeking God 1

Part 1: Seeking Knowledge

Chapter 1: Studying Church History 7
Chapter 2: Evaluating Church Doctrine 24
Chapter 3: Researching Church History and Doctrine 39

Part 2: Seeking Truth

Chapter 4: Interpreting Scripture 54
Chapter 5: Embracing Ambiguity 71
Chapter 6: Discerning Truth from Error 84

Part 3: Seeking Holiness

Chapter 7: Obtaining Spiritual Gifts 99
Chapter 8: Sustaining Modern Prophets 115
Chapter 9: Inviting the Presence of God 134

Epilogue: Seeking Zion 147

Notes 153
Index 167

"WHAT SEEK YE?"

—John 1:38

"We are seekers, you and I. We are light gatherers. . . . Don't ever stop seeking. Jesus promised that if we seek, we shall find. . . . Even if it takes your entire lives to find the precious light and truth you seek, it will be well worth the effort."

—DIETER F. UCHTDORF

Prologue

SEEKING GOD

 **Seeking Sentence: Honest seekers are wanted, expected, and in the end, always rewarded.**

It's 9:00 a.m. on a Friday morning and I'm at the orthodontist's office. Calm, instrumental music plays in a swanky green and white waiting room filled with iPads and pictures of smiling people with perfect teeth. As the parents of seven children, my wife and I have spent a lot of time and money on orthodontia. Only this time, I am not here for my children. As a 42-year-old man, I'm filling out paperwork meant for teenagers but checking boxes about *my* teeth, which have become problematic because I've put off facing and bracing them for far too long. I only have two teeth that touch as they should. My crossbite and underbite misalign the rest of my mouth. I've been able to hide it fairly well over the years. My teeth themselves don't look too bad. I floss and brush routinely, even doing some whitening strips now and then. On the surface, you wouldn't expect that there were major issues underneath. My mouth is small, and when I talk you only see a small part of my top and bottom teeth. Most of the time I smile with my lips closed. Decades of avoiding misalignment issues, however, have started to catch up. I feel some constant low, dull pain in my jaw. I currently can only chew with one side of my mouth. My back teeth have carried displaced pressure for far too long and are failing. Like misaligned tires, for a while the problem could be overlooked, but now they're wearing out quicker than they should. Something should probably be done.

I'll come back to this story in a moment, but first I have a few questions for you. Have you ever heard someone teach something at church like, "There will be plural marriage in heaven," and wondered if it were really Church doctrine? Have you ever come across something on the internet about Church history, like Joseph Smith translating the Book of Mormon with a stone in a hat, and didn't know if you should trust it? Have you ever desired to research something related to the Restoration more deeply, but you didn't really know where to go other than Google and the Church's website? Has your personal scripture study become somewhat rote, boring, or uninspiring? Do you want to know how to better approach ambiguous concepts, like why black African members of the Church were not allowed the priesthood, that have no seemingly clear answers? Have you ever struggled to reconcile the apparent doctrinal dilemma that we acknowledge that modern prophets are mortal and make mistakes, but we have been promised they will never lead the Church astray? Have you ever questioned whether your personal promptings were from God, just yourself, or from the great deceiver? Do you wonder how you can become more holy, keeping sacred covenants despite repeated personal shortcomings? Do you want to better understand how to live celestial covenants, like the law of consecration, in today's consumer-centric society? Have you ever wished you could contribute to the Restoration, like those who lived in Joseph Smith's time?

If you said yes to any of these questions, then likely you are a latter-day *seeker,* and seekers are wanted.

Seekers Wanted

The English verb *seek* derives from a variation of words that mean to "inquire, search for; pursue" or "to track down."[1] The Lord, as the author of Truth, invites diligent inquiry as it leads to divine answers: "Ask, and it shall be given you; seek, and ye shall find" (Matthew 7:7). But we are not to seek just anything, in any way. During the early School of the Prophets the Lord counseled, "As all have not faith, seek ye diligently and teach one another words of wisdom; yea, seek ye out of the best books words of wisdom; seek learning, even by study and also by faith" (D&C 88:118). For many Saints, however, the question is not *if* to seek learning by study and faith but knowing *how* to effectively do so. This is especially true as the tectonic plates of modern society seismically shift beneath our feet, causing many to feel unsteady on their gospel footing in our rapidly changing world. Addressing our modern religious landscape, President M. Russell Ballard gave a landmark talk to religious educators in February 2016, contrasting past approaches to present needs, saying:

"Gone are the days when a student asked an honest question and a teacher responded, 'Don't worry about it!' Gone are the days when a student raised a sincere concern and a teacher bore his or her testimony as a response intended to avoid the issue. Gone are the days when [learners] were protected from people who attacked the Church. Fortunately, the Lord provided this timely and timeless counsel to you teachers, 'And as all have not faith, seek ye diligently and teach one another words of wisdom; yea, seek ye out of the best books words of wisdom; seek learning, even by study and also by faith' (D&C 88:118). . . . You can help [gospel learners] by teaching them what it means to combine study and faith as they learn. Teach them by modeling this skill and approach."[2]

This book seeks to do just that: to teach and model essential *skills* of seeking learning by study and faith. It aims to increase one's capacity to be a disciple-scholar, giving explicit methods for faithful seekers who want to increase their capacity to learn in a day when opinions, options, and information abound. Using relevant and transparent doctrinal, historical, and contemporary examples—coupled with visual infographics—each chapter teaches models, steps, and frameworks to enhance our ability to seek. Unlike books that address specific issues or doubts, this book will not give doctrinal or historical answers to resolve specific questions. Instead, it aims to provide you with skills and perspectives to help better approach subjects on your own. The book is divided into three sections. Part 1 centers on skills for seeking knowledge. It covers academic study related to learning, researching, and evaluating Church history and doctrine. Part 2 focuses on seeking Truth. It explores seeking learning by faith, addressing how to view and interpret scripture, why ambiguity is a friend of faith, and how to receive revelation and avoid spiritual deception. Part 3 is a culmination of what seeking by study and faith do—they help us seek holiness. These chapters cover crucial, celestial skills and perspectives related to obtaining essential spiritual gifts such as faith, hope, and charity, sustaining modern yet mortal prophets, and keeping celestial covenants that connect us with the presence of God. This book aims to not so much tell you *what* to think, but more *how* to seek. To this end, at the beginning of each chapter you will find a "Seeking Sentence" that helps summarize in one line the major concept to grasp in that chapter. Also within each chapter is a section called "Seekers Wanted!" that encourages personal reflection on how to apply the concepts being discussed. At the end of each chapter is a concluding "Hide or Go Seek" summary that lists common attributes of those who generally hide from true seeking and those who pursue it.

Seeking Sentence

Seekers Wanted!

Hide or Go Seek

Seekers Expected

The title of this book carries a *double entendre.* Not only does God *approve* of those who seek (seekers are wanted), but to please God, we *must* be seekers (seekers are expected). For various reasons, some simply "will not seek after God" (Psalm 10:4). Sometimes we don't seek because we are afraid of what we will find. In Church culture, some associate what is faithful with what is familiar, and thus disapprove of exploring certain corners of inquiry. Others are merely content where they are, sitting comfortably on their current beach of spiritual faith. If you are reading this book, this likely isn't you. We must all be leery of "low-power mode"—that internal setting where we shut down our cellular reach to heaven because it requires energy from our intellectual and spiritual battery. To be a seeker is to be a worker.

Church history and doctrine scholar Steven Harper gave a BYU Women's Conference address called "Seekers Wanted"[3] in which he said: "Seeking is a long, patient, persistent process. . . . Seeking is hard work. It is not for the weak-willed or faint of heart, nor for the intellectually or spiritually lazy. But it will sustain faith in a world intent on destroying it. . . . Seekers are wanted in The Church of Jesus Christ of Latter-day Saints. The first converts were all seekers. Today's converts are seekers. We are all commanded to be seekers."[4]

I can relate to the innate desire to avoid seeking. I sit in front of the orthodontist as he shares his expertise, offering three different approaches to fix my teeth. I came voluntarily seeking this consultation, even a solution, but as I sit there I'm not sure I want to stay there. I am half tempted to just stand up and walk out and forget it, going back to my closed-mouth smile and one-side chewing, saying, "Hey, this has worked for forty-two years, it will probably hold out for forty-two more! This really isn't that big of a deal. And, anyway, *adult* braces? I can't do this. I speak in front of thousands of people. It will affect my speech. I'll look funny. I should just keep doing what I've been doing. It works. I don't want to address this. It's uncomfortable. It's costly. It takes time. I'm out." Even as I write this book, I am not sure what I am going to do. Do you think I should I confront the issue, or avoid it?

Although teeth are incomparable to truth, you can see parallels for seekers. For some members of the Church, the status quo answers suffice. The *Ensign* is everything. The rituals and routines of the Restoration are accepted and repeated without rigorous analysis. Basic Church history is good enough (we don't want to hear things we are unsure about anyway). Answers are accepted that are cut and dry, black and white. Joseph and living prophets are infallible. The Church is true because it is perfect. The doctrine brings security because it never changes. Every word in scripture is inerrant. Pleasing thoughts and feelings are from God, and difficult ones from the devil. Our relationship with God means crossing off the checklist: pray (check!), read (check!), church (check!).

Every now and then, however, there is some spiritual dissonance—misalignment with these simplicities that we know needs addressing. A low, dull ache arises when we listen to a podcast or learn on the internet about Church history we've never heard; our theological bite reveals that certain Church doctrines have shifted and changed over time. A conversation with a loved one exposes that some typical explanations are tenuous, and we try to cover up the uncertainty with a confident, closed-mouth smile. Despite doing our dutiful routine checklist, we yet feel disconnected from God, even with some occasional repenting. We realize our personal touchpoints of faith, hope, and charity, obedience, sacrifice, and consecration have noticeable gaps. We're placing too much pressure on a few thoughts and feelings instead of displacing answers across a wider spectrum of truth. We know there's a better version of ourselves that can be brought out by the Savior. Overall, there's some major work to be done that will take significant time, effort, discomfort, and personal cost. Even though we know we will come out stronger and on a better path in the end, we are tempted to retreat to what is comfortable and familiar. What should we do?

Let us seek! Seekers don't run away. Seekers don't put their head in the sand. Seekers face the reality that is in front of them and desire to be fully aligned with God. "Honest seekers"[5] don't pretend everything is fine and give a half smile. Truth seekers are confident and unafraid. Seekers willingly wrestle with the uncomfortable ideas that God always has placed, and will place, at their feet to help them continue to grow. Seekers "open the door" when there is a knock, no matter what the time of day or phase of life, and invite Truth to "come in" (Revelation 3:20). Honest seekers are wanted, expected, and in the end, always rewarded.

I just called the orthodontist to schedule my braces.

PART 1

Seeking Knowledge

We are told to "seek learning, even by study" (D&C 88:118). Therefore, using our mind is an essential exercise—not an antithetical one—to religious education. Joseph Smith taught, "Thy mind O man, if thou wilt lead a soul into salvation, must stretch as high as the utmost heavens, and search into and contemplate the darkest abyss, and expanse of eternity."[1] The following three chapters focus on using our minds as we seek—one on studying Church history, one on evaluating Church doctrine, and one on researching Church subjects. These chapters aim to provide skills and perspectives necessary to facilitate celestial, cerebral stretching to seek knowledge by study.

Chapter 1

STUDYING CHURCH HISTORY

 Seeking Sentence: There is no such thing as objective history.

When a friend of mine learned I was in the preliminary stages of composing a new painting of the First Vision—one that better harmonizes details from the various accounts—he excitedly asked me, "So, are you going to paint God the Father touching Joseph Smith's eyes?"

"What do you mean?" I asked him.

"Well, you know, there is that one account that says God touched Joseph's eyes in the grove, and after He touched them, then Joseph saw Jesus." I had never heard that before, so I looked it up. Turns out that in 1893, a Latter-day Saint named Charles Walker attended a testimony meeting at which one of the local elders, John Alger, bore his testimony. Walker recorded in his diary that Alger testified when he was a teenage boy he heard Joseph Smith "relate his vision of seeing the Father and the Son. That God touched his eyes with his finger and said 'Joseph this is my beloved Son hear him.' As soon as the Lord had touched his eyes with his finger he immediately saw the Savior." At the close of the meeting, Walker and others questioned the speaker. Charles Walker recorded in his journal that day, "He [Alger] told us at the bottom of the meeting house steps that he was in the House of Father Smith in Kirtland when Joseph made this declaration, and that Joseph while speaking of it put his finger to his right eye, suiting the action with the words so as to illustrate and at the same time impress the occurrence on the minds of those unto whom He was speaking."[1]

So, if you were me, would you paint God touching Joseph's eyes or not? Do you think that happened? Would you teach it in a Church class or share it in a talk?

On another occasion, I was listening to someone who criticized the veracity of the Book of Mormon, claiming, "Joseph Smith's friend said Joseph didn't even have real plates. All he had was a bag of sand that he put in a box for people to lift to trick them." *Where did he get that from?*, I wondered. There is a historical source by a man named Peter Ingersoll. Ingersoll had known the Smiths in Palmyra since 1822, and in 1827 he traveled with Joseph Smith Jr.

from Palmyra, New York, to Harmony, Pennsylvania, to help Joseph move to his father-in-law's. Ingersoll swore the following affidavit before Judge Baldwin of the Wayne County Court in New York. He remembered Joseph having told him the following about the gold plates:

"[Joseph said,] 'As I was passing, yesterday, across the woods, after a heavy shower of rain, I found, in a hollow, some beautiful white sand, that had been washed up by the water. I took off my frock, and tied up several quarts of it, and then went home. On my entering the house, I found the family at the table eating dinner. They were all anxious to know the contents of my frock. At that moment, I happened to think of what I had heard about a history found in Canada, called the golden Bible; so I very gravely told them it was the golden Bible. To my surprise, they were credulous enough to believe what I said. Accordingly I told them that I had received a commandment to let no one see it, for, says I, no man can see it with the naked eye and live. However, I offered to take out the book and show it to them, but they refuse to see it, and left the room.' Now, said Jo, 'I have got the damned fools fixed, and will carry out the fun.' Notwithstanding, he told me he had no such book, and believed there never was any such book, yet, he told me that he actually went to Willard Chase, to get him to make a chest, in which he might deposit his golden Bible. But, as Chase would not do it, he made a box himself, of clap-boards, and put it into a pillow case, and allowed people only to lift it, and feel of it through the case."[2]

What do you make of that? It is to be believed? Or, how about this one: In 1844, Joseph's mother, Lucy Mack Smith, dictated her history to Martha Coray. She recalled that some few days after bringing the plates home in 1827, Joseph called his mother to come down from her upstairs work on some oil cloths. Lucy reported:

"I finally concluded to go down, and see what he wanted, upon which he handed me the breast-plate spoken of in his history. It was wrapped in a thin muslin handkerchief, so thin that I could see the glistening metal, and ascertain its proportions without any difficulty." Lucy proceeded to describe the breastplate: "It was concave on one side, and convex on the other, and extended from the neck downwards, as far as the centre of the stomach of a man of extraordinary size. It had four straps of the same material, for the purpose of fastening it to the breast, two of which ran back to go over the shoulders, and the other two were designed to fasten to the hips. They were just the width of two of my fingers, (for I measured them,) and they had holes in the end of them, . . . to be convenient in fastening. After I had examined it, Joseph placed it in the chest with the Urim and Thummim."[3]

To begin this chapter, I've provided you with three remarkable sources that, if true, could influence our understanding of Church history and doctrine. One source claims that God touched the young Seer's eyes; another claims there were no gold plates; and another describes an ancient American prophetic relic. What do you make of these claims? To quote Elder Bruce R. McConkie, "What histories shall we believe where Mormon history is concerned?" That is a great question for seekers. Some related questions are, do you trust these historical sources? Why, or why not? How can you more objectively evaluate them? And why does it matter?

Why Does Church History Matter?

Latter-day Saint history matters because our doctrine is inextricably tied to our history. Beyond the historical events of Jesus's ministry and Resurrection, for many Protestant faiths, their founding history doesn't much change their church's doctrine. If you are a Lutheran or a Methodist, for example, what did or didn't happen to Martin Luther or John Wesley doesn't alter your position, because your beliefs are mainly centered in a *theological* movement (grace, sanctification, the supremacy of scripture, etc.), not a *historical* claim.

But for Latter-day Saints, history and doctrine are very intertwined. The historical narrative drives the doctrinal viewpoints. Joseph Smith had a vision (historical event) in which God and Jesus appeared to him as separate beings and told him there had been an Apostasy (doctrinal truth). Joseph went to a hill and removed gold plates (historical event), consequently bringing forth the new scripture called the Book of Mormon (doctrinal truth). The New Testament Apostles Peter, James, and John appeared to Joseph Smith and Oliver Cowdery and laid their hands on the two men's heads (historical event) to give them necessary priesthood authority to organize the Church (doctrinal truth). However, what happens if Peter, James, and John didn't appear to Joseph Smith until a year *after* the Church was restored, as some claim?[4] Now what happens to our doctrine? In the latter-day body of Christ, the bones of history give support for the muscle of our doctrine to move. History matters to members of the restored Church of Jesus Christ.

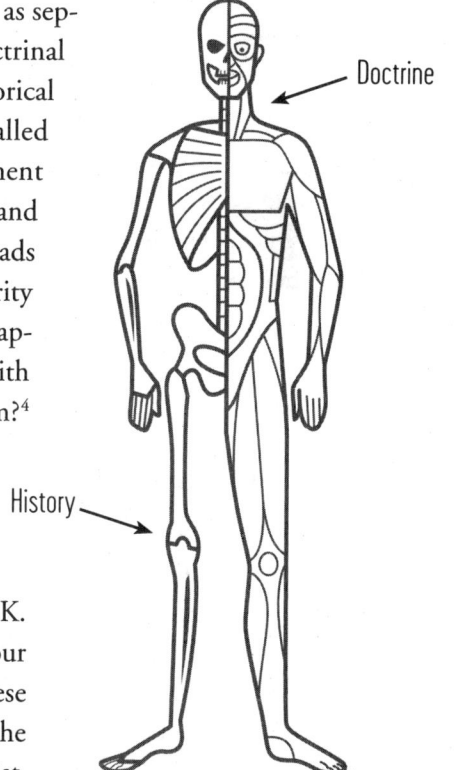

Thus, as Seventy and former Church Historian Marlin K. Jensen said, "It is important that we become familiar with our Church's history, especially with its founding stories. These stories—Joseph Smith's First Vision, the coming forth of the Book of Mormon, angelic visitations by John the Baptist,

Peter, James, John, Elijah, Elias, and others—contain the foundational truths upon which the Restoration is based."[5]

Effectively knowing and studying Church history is important to seekers not only because our history informs much of our doctrine but because people's faith can be affected—for good and bad—by what and how they learn about Church history. Not long ago, my cell phone buzzed with a new text message. It was from a family friend who had a loved one who was having issues with Church history and whose faith was suffering as a result. The text said the issues were raised by a letter posted online with, in my friend's words, "the most objective takes on the Church's historical documents that I have ever read. I was at a complete loss of words as to how I should respond. . . . He just can't get past all the historical discrepancies."

I looked at the website with the historical issues and responded in a text later that night. The website causing the problems, however, was NOT an objective historical take, nor was it good scholarship. It would be shredded by a peer-reviewed academic process. I counted a dozen or so errors, hearsay claims, secondhand or thirdhand sources, mis-statements, half-truths, unbalanced arguments, and quotes taken out of context in the first few pages alone. The problem was that this family friend, and his loved one whose faith is faltering, *lacked the ability to evaluate those historical claims themselves.* This is not an isolated or unique example. As you read this, you will likely think of immediate family members or close friends who have been bogged down intellectually and spiritually in similar historical mudholes, plowing their spiritual two-wheel drive Honda Accord into ten feet of muddy Church history and not knowing how to get out. Due to the flood of muddied information that surrounds us from internet and social media sources, the essential skill of a latter-day seeker is not to be an information finder, but an intelligent information filterer, having the ability to navigate difficult historical roads and push through sticky areas on the path of faith. If we lack the capacity to effectively evaluate information today, we may, in the prophetic words of Paul, get stuck "ever learning, and never able to come to the knowledge of the truth" (2 Timothy 3:7).

Factors to Evaluate Church "History"

So how can we evaluate historical sources and claims? Admittedly, I am not a professional historian. My PhD is in educational theory, not in history. As I have applied my academic training to teaching Church history and doctrine at Brigham Young University, however, I have gleaned from brilliant colleagues who are formally trained historians, picking up a few precious kernels about the historian's craft. Over the years I have learned some about "source criticism"—the process of evaluating the reliability of historical claims and the sources from which they are derived.

Like scientific studies, historical claims must be evaluated for their reliability, or trustworthiness. Nobody should trust a singular scientific study that claims drinking 64 ounces of Coca-Cola each day is good for your body—particularly if the research was sponsored by the Coca-Cola company, if there were only two research participants in the sample, and if the survey had consisted of only one question (Don't you agree that drinking a Coke makes you feel better? Yes/No). In scientific research, these are called threats to validity and reliability. Studying Church history is no different. Seekers shouldn't take a historical source at face value any more than they would take scientific claims at face value.

One day while walking across BYU's campus, I heard a student call out, "Professor Sweat!" The young man quickly jogged over to me and said, "I'm so glad I bumped into you because I have something I wanted to ask you." And then, without almost any hesitation, he blurted out, "So what's up with Fanny Alger? I heard that Joseph Smith had some sort of an affair with her in a barn and Emma saw them together. Is that true?" I stopped and asked him where he had heard that. He said, "Well, I don't know. My roommate read it on a website" (that's code for *he* read it on a website).

I told him I was aware of that source, and that it was from a letter written by William McLellin (who, after being excommunicated from the Church for the third time in 1838, participated in the persecution of the Saints in Missouri[6]), who wasn't present at the event (passing on second-hand hearsay), and who was writing forty-plus years after the supposed event (when memory confounds, even inadvertently). I said to this student, "While all accounts should be considered, you need to realize you are trusting a second-hand, late reminiscent account by an embittered apostate. There are many reasons why his claims could be questionable."

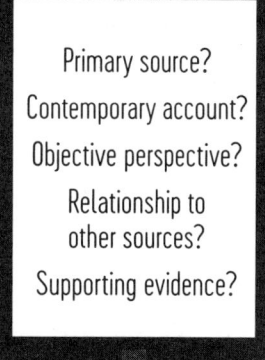

Primary source?
Contemporary account?
Objective perspective?
Relationship to other sources?
Supporting evidence?

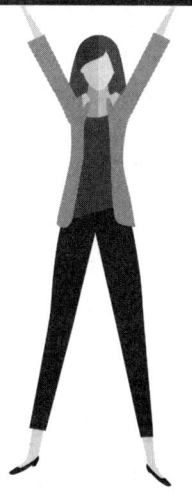

The student said, "I never thought of that!" and thanked me. The thought to do any historical source criticism simply hadn't crossed his mind.

So how can we do some historical source criticism? The following are five areas I suggest should be considered. I don't pretend this framework to be all-inclusive or without flaw, but it has proven helpful for me and many others in studying and evaluating Church history. Five questions to ask about any historical source are

1. Is it a **primary source**?
2. Is it a **contemporary account**?

3. Does it have an **objective perspective**?
4. What is its **relationship to other sources**?
5. Are its claims **supported by evidence**?

Primary Source

A primary source is produced by a participant or observer of the event. It comes from someone who was there, firsthand, whereas a secondhand source or account is by a nonparticipant in the event, usually relating or summarizing what that person learned from a firsthand participant. It's obvious why one carries more reliability than the other. A secondhand or thirdhand source can introduce miscommunication, factual errors, reinterpreting of events, or other discrepancies because the source was not an actual participant. It's the historical difference between being at the game and learning about the game through ESPN highlights. One is direct, the other filtered. For example, Willard Richards kept Joseph Smith's Nauvoo journals in 1843 and 1844, however, as the *Joseph Smith Papers* historians note in their introduction to this journal, "Though Richards appears to have either participated in or witnessed most of the events he documented, he at times wrote retrospectively or from secondhand information. Occasionally, such practices resulted in factual error."[7]

When I was a young full-time seminary teacher for the Church, I received a phone call from a concerned parent who asked me why I had taught that God the Father and Heavenly Mother had been married in the Salt Lake Temple. That was a revelation to me! I had never taught that (is it even feasible?). Turns out that when my student learned in my class that prophets have taught we have a Heavenly Father and a Heavenly Mother who have a celestial marriage (I *did* teach that), she superimposed *her understanding of eternal marriage onto my words.* She happened to live very near the Salt Lake Temple and associated it with eternal marriage. An understandable mistake that made what I said untrue. Similarly, Joseph Smith's four primary accounts of the First Vision—written or overseen by Joseph Smith himself—are more reliable than the five secondary accounts produced by people who wrote what they remembered hearing Joseph Smith say. Of all the First Vision accounts, Alexander Neibaur's 1844 secondhand journal account is the only one that gives certain physical descriptions of God. Neibaur claims Joseph said that he "saw a personage in the fire light complexion blue eyes." It may very well be that God has a light complexion or even blue eyes and that Joseph related that unique aspect on this occasion, or it may be that Neibaur interpreted God through his own lens and unconsciously superimposed details in his recollection that Joseph never directly claimed.[8]

Contemporary Account

Another major factor that influences the validity of a historical source claim is *when* the source was recorded. A contemporary account is one that is recorded at or relatively near the time of the events discussed. It is well established that memories change over time, even inadvertently. Details become lost, events confounded, and experiences reinterpreted through new lenses.

When my wife and I were married, our temple sealer asked me, "What are the three most important words you can say to your wife each day to keep a happy marriage?"

I answered, "I love you?" He smiled and told me I was wrong, and that the three most important words to say to your wife each day to keep a happy marriage are, "You're probably right." That memory is a great one for me and my wife, until we recently told the story at a family gathering. My sister-in-law, who married my brother in the same temple two weeks after our wedding, turned and said, "That wasn't said at your wedding. That was said at *ours!*" My mother confirmed it. My grandfather did too. To this day, I can't sort out the story. Perhaps it was said at their wedding and I unconsciously conflated events due to our weddings being so close and in the same temple, or perhaps they have done the same. Either way, one of our memories is inadvertently mistaken. If only we had written it down when it had happened. A contemporary record, like a journal entry from that day or soon thereafter, would help immensely to prove my sister-in-law, mom, and grandpa are inevitably mistaken. We often can't keep our own personal histories straight. What does that say for the reliability of contested and public histories that form legacies?

Not only do details of events diminish over time, but so does our *interpretation* of details. The more that time passes, the more likely we are to see our memories through new lenses, and then our new memory replaces the old. In a scientific experiment testing the ability to remember the location of items on a computer screen, if participants misplaced an item and put it where it didn't belong, the next day the participant tended to place the object *in the same wrong location again.* Why? The researchers concluded, "Our findings show that incorrect recollection of the object's location on day two influenced how people remembered the object's location on day three," said the lead author of the study published in the *Journal of Neuroscience*. "Retrieving the memory didn't simply reinforce the original association. Rather, *it altered memory storage to reinforce the location that was recalled at session two.* . . . When you think back to an event that happened to you long ago—say your first day at school—you actually may be recalling information you retrieved about that event at some later time, not the original event."[9] Just ask embattled news anchor Brian Williams about how memory can be unintentionally confounded.[10]

Historian Steven C. Harper has written extensively about memory in relation to Joseph Smith's accounts of the First Vision. Why do some of the accounts differ from others in certain details, like Joseph's age or the exact wording of God to Joseph? Remember, Joseph didn't record the event until at least a decade after it happened (in 1832), with his latest account recorded twenty-two years after the First Vision (in 1842). Harper writes, "Joseph may have purposely or unconsciously conflated events. Such compression or blurring is common when people remember and tell their histories. Joseph may have had a hard time remembering exactly when the vision occurred and, thus, how old he was at the time. Some of his accounts use the word 'about' to describe his age or when his father moved to Palmyra or later the Manchester farm or other details of the story. As we all do, Joseph may have mixed information from his explicit episodic memory (the kind that consciously recalls events from the past) with semantic memory (the kind that knows what it knows without remembering how it knows, as in remembering one's name or phone number)."[11]

For these reasons, when we analyze historical documents, the more contemporaneous the account, generally the more trustworthy are the details surrounding the event: the who, what, when, where, how, and why. The more time passes and historical accounts become late reminiscences, the more likely these details are to be forgotten or reinterpreted through current contexts. Earlier I called an aspect of Alexander Neibaur's First Vision account into question, but one factor supporting the reliability of Neibaur's account is that he recorded it in his journal the same day he heard Joseph Smith relate the vision. The words were fresh. To be clear, for something to be considered a solid contemporary account it does not have to be recorded the day of the events. The principle of the matter is that the nearer to the events it is recorded, generally the more likely the account is to be factually accurate.

Objective Perspective

Another factor influencing the validity of a historical document or claim is the potential for implicit bias in the claims made by the teller of the events. A bystander who sees a car accident will likely give a less biased report to police than the drivers involved in the crash. The drivers have potential motive for bias, whereas the objective observer, less so.

Generally, when something of import is at stake, bias naturally rears its protective head. Hence, discussions about religion, politics, finances, family, gender, power, etc. can become contentious and are often full of partiality. Participants can look at the same facts and data and come to completely different conclusions, depending on their agendas and perspectives. The latest tax reform? "A celebration!" says one political party. "A travesty to justice!" says another.

Think of the latest argument you with had with your spouse or a family member. There would not only be differences in perspective but likely some slight bias in how you each interpret who is at fault.

To understand bias, we also must understand that there is no such thing as objective history. History isn't made by events; it is made by those who *record and interpret events*. "Historians do not discover a past as much as they create it," say the authors of *An Introduction to Historical Methods*. "They choose the events and people that they think constitute the past, and they decide what about them is important to know."[12] Thus, we must "always consider the conditions under which a source was produced—the intentions that motivated it"[13] and the context in which it was created. Notable LDS historian Dean C. Jessee wrote, "The sources are not the past but only the raw materials whence we form our conception of the past, and in using them we inherit the limitations that produced them."[14]

Another historian wrote: "What is distasteful is to present historical facts as historical truths. Each historian interprets historical facts, mostly primary sources, and constructs a narrative and analysis around them. However, we often forget to explicitly state that the facts we present are facts as we see them. We omit some and highlight others. . . . There will always be bias in history. We need to be more open about it."[15]

Thus, in this category of analyzing the objective perspective of the source, we are not looking for a complete lack of bias. That doesn't exist. *We are looking for the motivations and degree to which the author may introduce bias.* Does the author have a lot at stake? An obvious, or perhaps a hidden agenda? Bias can be detected through selective omissions of facts and details and a lack of balance in perspective that continually favors one side or perspective. Additional indicators of bias are judgmental words that seek to influence the reader—trigger words like "deranged" or "ridiculous" on the negative side or "phenomenal" or "wondrous" on the positive. Look at the tone of the writer. Does the writer seem to be more neutral, balanced, candid, and open, or more polemical, one-sided, critical, evasive, and defensive? These questions and more help us spot overt bias.

 **Seekers wanted!**

Here is a great example of bias. When the Church published the Gospel Topics essay "Plural Marriage in Kirtland and Nauvoo" in 2014,[16] various media outlets reported on the essay with varying degrees of bias. One prominent headline read:

MORMON CHURCH FINALLY ADMITS FOUNDER JOSEPH SMITH WAS POLYGAMIST WITH 40 WIVES[17]

What do you notice about that headline? What words indicate bias?

Relationship to Other Sources

The next factor to examine for the reliability of a historical source is to compare and contrast the account with other sources dealing with the same events. Are the dates, facts, details, and claims consistent with other sources? What are the major similarities and differences? Why might those exist? For example, in Joseph Smith's First Vision accounts, there clearly are different elements emphasized in each source, but each source also consistently tells the same essential event: a young boy in his mid-teens, confused over religion, consulted the scriptures, went to a grove of trees behind his home to pray, and had a vision in which heavenly beings ministered to him. Those details are consistent, while others vary.[18]

As an artist and a professor of Church history and doctrine, some of my research has to do with how the Book of Mormon translation has been depicted in Church art over the years.[19] Notably, until recently there were no known paintings produced by Latter-day Saint artists or published in Church materials that depicted Joseph Smith translating the Book of Mormon by using a seer stone(s) placed in a hat. I decided to attempt to create this image, as I felt it was important to have this historical visual. The painting was later published in the book *From Darkness unto Light: Joseph Smith's Translation and Publication of the Book of Mormon.*

After the painting was published and began to be circulated, I received an email from someone who had been a mentor to me as I began my career in LDS religious education. His email asked, "Can you help me understand the purpose in teaching that the Prophet translated in this manner [using the hat]?" His email showed good scholarship, asking why I would choose to rely on sources for my painting from disaffected members of the Church who have potential for bias, such as David Whitmer or Emma Smith. Unfortunately, Joseph Smith is relatively silent on the mechanics of translation, saying only that the translation was done "by the gift and power of God"[20] and sometimes adding the line "by means of the Urim and Thummim" (Joseph Smith—History 1:64). To understand the process of the Book of Mormon translation, we are left to rely on those who *saw* Joseph Smith translate (a type of primary source because they can relate what they personally observed of the translation process) or heard him tell about it. In my email reply to my friend, I sent the following accounts, and I share them here with you. The questions are: What is *consistent* across each account? What *differs*?

First, an early contemporary account (1829) of the translation by an antagonistic source, Jonathan Hadley, a local printer who declined to print the Book of Mormon when he was approached with the offer by Joseph Smith. Hadley published the following in *The Palmyra Freeman* on August 11, 1829:

"It was said that the leaves of the [Gold] Bible were plates, of gold about eight inches long, six wide, and one eighth of an inch thick, on which were engraved characters or hieroglyphics. By placing the spectacles in a hat, and looking into it, Smith could (he said so, at least,) interpret these characters."[21]

This is a secondhand account, as Hadley would have been told the details of the translation by someone else (assumedly Joseph Smith, Hyrum Smith, Martin Harris, or Oliver Cowdery). However, it is a strong contemporary account from 1829, the earliest on record and before the Book of Mormon was published.

Here is another secondhand, contemporaneous account (1831), this time by a less antagonistic Shaker man who had heard Oliver Cowdery preach, saying that the Book of Mormon was translated by "two transparent stones in the form of spectacles" through which the translator "looked on the engraving & afterwards put his face into a hat & the interpretation then flowed into his mind."[22]

Here are some more moderate translation sources, by individuals who believed in the Book of Mormon but did not remain faithful to or come westward to Utah with the Church. Near the end of her life, in an 1879 interview with her son Joseph III, Emma Smith recalled scribing for her husband while he translated, with Joseph "sitting with his face buried in his hat, with the stone in it, and dictating hour after hour with nothing between us."[23]

A late 1887 reminiscence by David Whitmer explained: "Joseph Smith would put the seer stone into a hat, and put his face in the hat, drawing it closely around his face. . . . A piece of something resembling parchment would appear, and on that appeared the writing. One character at a time would appear, and under it was the interpretation in English."[24]

And now, some more faithful translation sources by those who witnessed the translation and were still faithful in the Church when recounting the translation. Joseph Knight Sr. wrote: "Now the way he translated was he put the urim and thummim into his hat and Darkned his Eyes then he would take a sentance and it would apper in Brite Roman Letters. Then he would tell the writer and he would write it. Then that would go away the next sentance would Come and so on. But if it was not Spelt rite it would not go away till it was rite, so we see it was marvelous. Thus was the hol [whole] translated."[25]

In an 1881 interview with Edward Stevenson, Martin Harris said "that the Prophet possessed a seer stone, by which he was enabled to translate as well as from the Urim and Thummim, and for convenience he then used the seer stone." According to Stevenson, Martin explained the translating as follows: "By aid of the seer stone, sentences would appear and were read by the Prophet and written by Martin, and when finished he would say, 'Written.'"[26]

I've presented six sources that give details about the Book of Mormon translation. All of them are tainted in various ways through bias, or secondhand nature, or late reminiscence. Independent of one another, however, what do they each consistently claim? After laying out these sources I replied in my email to my mentor/colleague, "I do think there is enough consistent mention of Joseph using a hat to translate to logically deduce he may have done so. In my opinion there are just too many independent sources that mention the hat in the translation to try to explain it away or ignore it. Thus, in the painting I did, I wanted to faithfully show Joseph using the hat to translate, as we (Church members) didn't have any images showing the hat process that many documents seem to support." When analyzing historical accounts, we should not carelessly dismiss unique claims in various historical narratives, but as good seekers, we should weigh those details with other accounts, looking for consistency. Consistency is the friend of surety.

Supporting Evidence

In our modern day of "fake news," this last factor in evaluating a historical source can't be overstated in its importance. A good seeker isn't interested only in who the person is who gave an account or when that person said it but also whether the person has evidence to support the claims and conclusions. Are the claims grounded in logical evidence, or are they mere hearsay, conjecture, subjective opinion, or blatantly false information? I remember when in my PhD program, while analyzing studies in my statistics classes, the professor would often ask, "Are the authors drawing their conclusions based on the actual data?" or, "Does the data support what they are claiming?" Surprisingly, sometimes it didn't.

We all do this at times, our perceptions getting the better of objective reality. Returning to another example with my older brother, we played high school basketball together. We were the "Sweat Brothers." *Sweat* may not be the most romantic last name, but it made great basketball headlines. As we have aged and our athletic feats have faded into distant glory days, the question has come up at family get-togethers, "Who was the better basketball player?" I like to think we were equally good. Recently, however, my brother dug up an old stat sheet from his senior year and my junior year. In region play, I averaged 10 points a game, and he averaged 15. I shot 30% from the field; he shot 44%. I was 76% from the foul line; he was 86%. He averaged 5 rebounds a game; I averaged 3. He had twice as many blocked shots, steals, and assists as I did. The only statistical category where we were even was in turnovers—turnovers! Not something to gloat about. As time passes I can construct my own reality in my mind, but data doesn't lie. In every statistical category, my brother was a better basketball player than I was in region play that year (but what about in the preseason, or playoffs, or comparing our senior years head-to-head? The debate continues!).

Thus, when we analyze historical claims, we need to check the claim against the known data. It is not uncommon to hear people make various claims about Joseph Smith's practice of plural marriage. But we need to exercise caution. Due to the secretive nature of Nauvoo polygamy, careful historians know less about Nauvoo polygamy than Utah polygamy. As editors for the *Joseph Smith Papers* point out: "Most of the information on the practice [of polygamy] during this [Nauvoo] period comes either from later affidavits and reminiscences or from reports of disaffected members of the church at the time—none of which, for a variety of reasons, can be considered entirely reliable historical sources for delineating how plural marriage was understood and practiced by those involved at the time."[27] The reliable information on Joseph Smith's practice of plural marriage is sparse, and thus those who make bold claims related to it ("Joseph Smith invented polygamy to justify his sexual promiscuity!" or, on the flip side, "Joseph Smith never had any conjugal relationships with his polyandrous wives!") often lack solid supporting evidence and are stepping out on the shaky ledge of conjecture, supposition, and personal opinion. It may be plausible. It could be possible. It could logically be deduced. It may be inferred. But is it supported by reliable, factual sources? That is the question.

History Evaluators Wanted!

The following visual summarizes the preceding five factors that should be considered when a seeker evaluates the reliability of a historical LDS source.

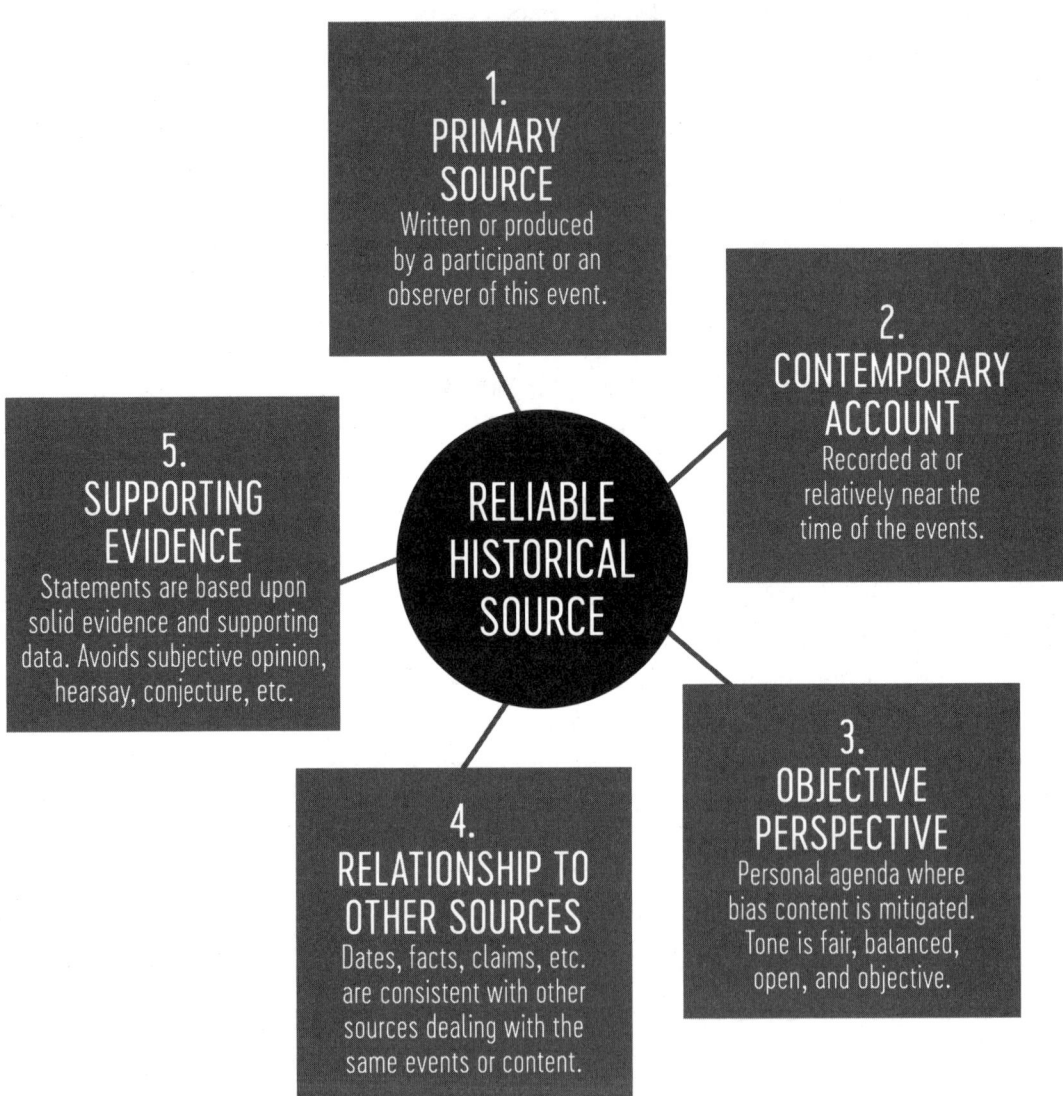

Taking these five intuitive measures together, at times I find it useful to ascribe a ranking to each category to provide an overall reliability level for a historical source, as follows:

	Yes	Somewhat	No
Primary source?	2	1	0
Contemporary account?	2	1	0
Objective perspective?	2	1	0
Relationship to other sources?	2	1	0
Supporting evidence?	2	1	0

Total Points: ____

8–10 Points = A Reliable Source
4–7 Points = A Somewhat Reliable Source
0–3 Points = Not a Very Reliable Source

Although these categories are not hard and fast, this general scoring metric helps give a basic evaluation of a historical source. To see how it can be used, let's evaluate together some of the historical sources listed at the beginning of this chapter. Let's start with Charles Walker's reported account of John Alger's version of the First Vision, in which he claimed God had touched Joseph's eyes. Here is my ranking and explanation on each aspect of that source:

	Yes	Somewhat	No	
Primary source?	2	1	(0)	This is a thirdhand account. Charles Walker is reporting what he heard John Alger say he heard Joseph Smith say.
Contemporary account?	2	1	(0)	John Alger reported this in 1893, some 60 years after the event supposedly was related to him when he was a young boy in Kirtland, Ohio, in the 1830s.
Objective perspective?	2	(1)	0	There is some potential for bias here, given that John Alger may be playing to a Utah crowd who didn't know Joseph Smith personally, as he did. But his motive to contrive the story seems limited.
Relationship to other sources?	2	(1)	0	Alger's claims that the Father and Son appeared to Joseph Smith, and that God appeared first, saying, "This is my beloved Son," are consistent with other First Vision sources. But his unique claim that God touched Joseph's eyes is not reported in any other of the nine contemporary accounts of the First Vision, a detail that seems likely to be mentioned.
Supporting evidence?	2	(1)	0	Alger's claims could be supported by other visionary experiences, such as when God touched Enoch's eyes. But, other than his own claim, there is no JS documentary evidence to support this assertion.

Total Points: __3__

8–10 Points = A Reliable Source
4–7 Points = A Somewhat Reliable Source
0–3 Points = Not a Very Reliable Source

Thus, overall, I would rank this source as a 3/10, or "Not a Very Reliable Source." In answer to my friend's question, no, I will not be doing a painting of God touching Joseph Smith's eyes in the Sacred Grove. To be sure, my ranking herein is not in any way definitive, and my own reasonings may be flawed. But the point is not to affix my conclusion as correct, but to help provide a useful framework for you to personally evaluate sources and come to your own conclusions as to their reliability.

What about Lucy Mack Smith's 1844 report about the breastplate in her personal history? I ranked it as follows:

	Yes	Somewhat	No	
Primary source?	②	1	0	Lucy Mack Smith is reporting her own, personal experience here. She handled, she touched, she felt.
Contemporary account?	2	①	0	Joseph Smith brought the breastplate home in September 1827, and Lucy records this in 1844, about 17 years later. Earlier would have given more credibility, but inordinate time hasn't passed.
Objective perspective?	2	①	0	Lucy's report is candid and straightforward. She is not introducing a lot of opinion or subjective hearsay. However, Lucy Mack Smith has a lot riding on her son's report of angels, plates, seer stones, and breastpates. The family's reputation and her son's prophetic ministry are tied to these claims.
Relationship to other sources?	②	1	0	Lucy's description of a breastpate is consistent with Joseph Smith's, D&C 17's, and David Whitmer's later testimony that he saw the breastplate.
Supporting evidence?	②	1	0	Lucy's description is straightforward, like a factual report. She gives dimensions, details, and material descriptions. Her account is devoid of opinion, conjecture, or hearsay.
Total Points: __8__				

8-10 Points = A Reliable Source
4-7 Points = A Somewhat Reliable Source
0-3 Points = Not a Very Reliable Source

Now, how would you rate the Peter Ingersoll account at the beginning of the chapter, claiming there were no plates, just a bag of sand? Or what about the William McLellin/Fanny Alger account? What about some of the Book of Mormon translation sources I cited? Take a minute and create a reliability chart of your own to come to your own conclusions. I know what I personally think about those sources. The question is, what do you think, and why?

Conclusion

No historical source is perfectly reliable, as all are degraded to some degree by participation, time, bias, consistency, and facts. The issue isn't whether something is perfectly reliable but the degree to which we can perfectly assess the reliability of a historical claim. This holds true for sources in favor of the Church, those that claim neutrality, and those that are decidedly hostile against it. To uncritically quote a source so long as it supports the message we desire is not good seeking, nor will it lead us to truth, and thus is inconsistent with God and the spirit of the Restoration. This is true for the Church critic as well as the apologist. "The historian's basic task is to choose *reliable* sources, to read them *reliably*, and to put them together in ways that provide *reliable* narratives about the past," says a basic historian's craft textbook.[28] The same can be said for latter-day seekers. If we are to understand our beliefs, we must understand our history, as our doctrine and history are intertwined. Yet those events alone do not create our history. History is constructed by people interpreting events. We learn true Church history only to the extent that we can evaluate the sources and stories of those who create and shape it.

 Hide or Go Seek

Hide

I don't think studying Church history is important.
If it is said or written, it must be true.
I don't question historical sources.
I think history is purely objective.

Go Seek

I understand that history is subjective.
I evaluate whether something is a primary or secondary source.
I examine whether something is a contemporary account or late reminiscence.
I look for evidence of whether a source has potential for bias.
I compare what multiple sources say on the matter to check for consistency.
I am leery of claims that are based on hearsay or conjecture rather than evidence.

Chapter 2

EVALUATING CHURCH DOCTRINE

🔍 **Seeking Sentence: In a living Church, doctrine can change.**

Have you ever heard something and wondered, "Is that Church doctrine?" For example, suppose you were in a Church class studying the passage where God teaches Moses there are "worlds without number . . . and by the Son I created them, which is mine Only Begotten" (Moses 1:33). Someone asks, "If Jesus created multiple worlds, did Jesus's infinite Atonement redeem God's children on other earths?" What would you say? Is that true? Is it a sanctioned Church teaching? How would you know? Or, as another example, have you ever heard the teaching that Latter-day Saints are supposed to take the sacrament with their right hand?[1] Is that correct? (All in favor, raise your right hand!) Perhaps you are reading a volume of teachings from a past Church leader and you come across some statements that are very different from what the Church teaches now. If doctrine never changes, how do we handle that? Were past leaders wrong for teaching it, or are we wrong for altering the teaching? Maybe you have heard someone say something like, "I once heard that [fill in a General Authority's name here] said that [fill in a reported teaching here], so that makes it doctrine." Is that how doctrine is determined? If not, how do we view individual statements by General Authorities? How can we differentiate between an official position of the Church and an individual "opinion" of one of its leaders? How do we handle statements by General Authorities that seem to contradict one another, such as statements by Spencer W. Kimball[2] and Joseph Fielding Smith[3] saying there is no progression between kingdoms in the next life, but Brigham Young[4] and J. Reuben Clark[5] saying it is possible? Questions such as these and many others are important for seekers who desire to accurately learn, understand, and articulate Church teachings.

There are many other teachings that can cause someone to wonder whether or not they are sanctioned by the Church, or whether they are considered "doctrine" at all. Instinctively we have metrics in our mind that we use to answer such questions. Perhaps some think: *Is it in the scriptures? Has a Church leader taught it? Is it an eternal, unchanging truth?* In this chapter, I will propose two models to help seekers evaluate LDS doctrine, which I have developed in conjunction with two of my BYU colleagues, Drs. Michael MacKay and Gerrit Dirkmaat.[6] The first model helps to evaluate varying *types* of doctrine, and the second helps to evaluate official *sources* of doctrine. We have found these models to be helpful frameworks by which seekers can analyze and discuss the nuances and complexities of Church doctrine.

Expanding the Definition of "Doctrine"

The simplest definition of "doctrine" is "something that is taught" or "teaching, instruction."[7] Based on this premise, any endorsed Church teaching is a Church *doctrine*. Authorized teachings can come in various types, from the eternal, to the personal, to commandments, to policies, to explanatory teachings. The Church itself seems to suggest that there are different types of "doctrines" in its 2007 essay "Approaching Mormon Doctrine": "Some doctrines are more important than others and might be considered core doctrines. For example, the precise location of the Garden of Eden is far less important than doctrine about Jesus Christ and His atoning sacrifice."[8] Modern prophets sometimes use adjectives before the word *doctrine,* such as "essential doctrine" or "fundamental doctrine," inherently implying there are central doctrines but also doctrines of a different nature.[9]

This general understanding of the term is often the way the word *doctrine* is used in scripture. For example, Matthew records that when Jesus finished the Sermon on the Mount, "the people were astonished at his doctrine: for he taught them as one having authority" (Matthew 7:28–29; see also Matthew 22:33). The word *doctrine* in this verse derives from the Greek *didachē,* meaning "teaching" or "the act of teaching."[10] In the Sermon on the Mount, Jesus taught eternal, timeless truths of the plan of salvation, such as the command to be perfect like God our Father, but He also taught timely cultural applications specific to His hearers, such as the importance of not appearing sad-faced while fasting and responding to lawsuits properly. All these teachings, whether eternal or dispensation-specific, were part of the Lord's doctrine because they each encompassed part of what He taught (see also Mark 2:27, Mark 11:17–18, Mark 12:38, Luke 4:32).

Historically, the early restored Church used the word *doctrine* more in line with this biblical usage of "something that is taught" or "teaching, instruction." The Prophet Joseph Smith and his associates, when printing the *Lectures on Faith* from the School of the Prophets, classified them as "Theology" and subtitled them "On the Doctrine of the Church of the Latter Day Saints,"[11] including them in the 1835 printing of the Doctrine and Covenants. The "doctrinc" was the *Lectures on Faith,* and the "covenants" were Joseph's revelations. These lectures "on the doctrine," however, covered a vast array of topics that included not only eternal, unchanging, simple truths of the gospel but also history, rational theology, elaborative ideas, and pedagogical precepts.

Although some in the modern Church are accustomed to defining *doctrine* only as an "unchanging truth of the gospel,"[12] this is a more recent historical movement. That definition of doctrine is, itself, a new doctrine. Defining Church doctrine only as *eternal truths of the gospel* is very helpful in some situations, but it can also unintentionally negate authoritative doctrines that have changed, such as the sacrament, baptisms for the dead, the Word of Wisdom, or the gathering to Missouri in Joseph Smith's time. It can also omit how to categorize noneternal, explanatory Church teachings such as the Great Apostasy, the sealed portion of the Book of Mormon, the Urim and Thummim, miracles, the gathering of scattered Israel, Aaronic Priesthood, intelligences, the Second Comforter, Zion in Independence, or Christ's Second Coming. Thus, it may be helpful to organize different types of doctrines in our seeking related to authorized Church teachings.

Types of LDS Doctrine

The following images provide a suggested framework to help understand different types of LDS doctrine:

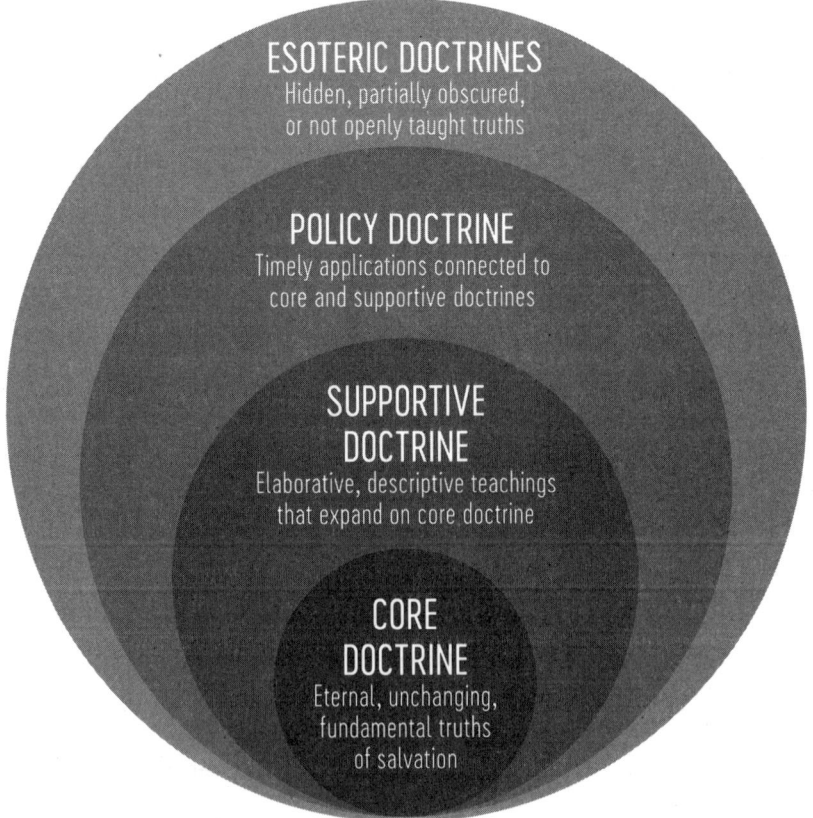

Let's seek to understand each of these categories of Church teachings, or doctrine.

Core Doctrine

Using the same phraseology of the Church's 2007 statement on doctrine, there are teachings that could be termed "core doctrines" or "eternal doctrines." In the words of Elder David A. Bednar, these are "gospel doctrines [that] are eternal, do not change, and pertain to the eternal progression and exaltation of Heavenly Father's sons and daughters."[13] When we sometimes say the "doctrine" never changes, what is often meant is that *the gospel* never changes—meaning faith in Christ, repentance, baptism, receiving the Holy Ghost, and enduring in the covenant to the end (see 3 Nephi 27:13–21 and D&C 33:11–12). This unchanging gospel is sometimes referred to as "the doctrine of Christ" (see 2 Nephi 31:21, 3 Nephi 11:32–35; 3 Nephi 27:13–21, D&C 33:11–12). The doctrine of Christ, or His gospel, was taught as an unchanging doctrine of the Church early in the Restoration.[14]

Other eternal truths that do not change may include the nature of God, the eternal makeup of the Spirit, the universal Resurrection, and the work and the glory of God to bring to pass the immortality and eternal life of His children (see Moses 1:39). The Church's founding "Articles and Covenants," found in Doctrine and Covenants 20, contain a succinct declaration of core, timeless doctrines, beginning in verse 17 with, "There is a God in heaven, who is infinite and eternal," who "created man, male and female, after his own image" (v. 18) and "gave unto them commandments" (v. 19). However, by departing from His ways, humankind "became fallen" (v. 20). "Wherefore, the Almighty God gave his Only Begotten Son" (v. 21) so that through belief in the Savior's divine sacrifice and through the covenant of baptism, mankind "should be saved" (v. 25). Those that "worship the Father in his name, and endure in faith on his name to the end" (v. 29) will receive both "justification" (v. 30) and "sanctification through the grace of our Lord and Savior Jesus Christ" (v. 31). Such truths are at the heart of what has been taught, is taught, and will yet be taught in all dispensations. Such plan-of-salvation truths are what President Boyd K. Packer referred to when he said there are "doctrines" which "will remain fixed, eternal."[15]

Supporting Doctrines

Many doctrines strengthen our belief in and elaborate on the core doctrines. For example, if a core doctrine is that God exists, understanding His corporality will help us better comprehend His nature and, in turn, deepen our faith in Him. While understanding and believing in Christ's Atonement is core and essential for salvation, teachings that discuss the details of how He suffered (like bleeding from every pore) and what He suffered (all the pains and sicknesses of humankind) are not necessary to know in order to be saved, but they serve to expand upon the core concept of Atonement and redemption. Supporting doctrines help us elaborate on the eternal doctrines of salvation, often providing explanations of "how" such teachings function.

An example of a core, eternal doctrine is that Jesus Christ will return to earth and reign as its rightful king and lawgiver. It has been further revealed as a supporting doctrine that a righteous city of New Jerusalem will be built, and Christ's people will be gathered to prepare for His return. Other supporting doctrines related to the Second Coming are that there will be a great gathering in Adam-ondi-Ahman to prepare for Christ's millennial rule, that when Jesus returns to the earth the Mount of Olives will split, that the Jewish people will recognize the Lord as the Messiah (see D&C 45:51–53), that Satan will be bound, and that there will be a thousand-year period of peace. These teachings may not be essential for salvation, nor have they been taught in all dispensations, but they elaborate upon, expand our understanding about, increase our faith in, and provide potential "hows" to the core doctrine of Christ's return to reign over earth. This supporting ring of doctrine has the potential to include many explanatory doctrines of the Church.

Policy Doctrines

Policy doctrines are Church teachings related to the application of core or supportive doctrine. Gathering to Missouri in Joseph Smith's time, paying ten percent tithing in our time, the current role of Seventies, or mission ages can all be considered policy doctrines. Church policy is always authoritative, but it inevitably changes as the Church gives new teachings that adjust, expand, and react to the situations of the membership. These are "the organization, programs, and procedures [that] will be altered as directed by Him whose church this is," as President Boyd K. Packer said.[16]

Policies are sanctioned teachings of the Church, and therefore a type of doctrine. They cannot be lightly dismissed as "just a policy." They can, and sometimes do, affect salvation and exaltation. One could not dismiss Abraham's command to circumcise all his male family as a sign of the covenant as "mere policy." This wasn't an eternal, unchanging teaching. In fact, it was done away with by the New Testament Church. However, if one of Abraham's male household wasn't circumcised, he wasn't part of the covenant, and was "cut off from his people" (Genesis 17:14). The same argument can be made for nearly the entire law of Moses, particularly its rituals and sacrifices, that were necessary to adhere to for proper standing before God but were later done away by Christ.

In our day, the Word of Wisdom is a modern example of a binding policy doctrine that affects salvation. Restrictions on tea, coffee, and wine have not been in effect in all dispensations, yet because the Lord foresaw "evils and designs which do and will exist in the hearts of conspiring men in the last days" (D&C 89:4), He provided a new doctrine for the "benefit" (D&C 89:1) of the Saints. This doctrine has taken many shifts in expected implementation, and eventually by 1933 the Church Handbook of Instruction required members to strictly follow the Word of Wisdom to be able to enter the temple.[17] Today, persons cannot be baptized unless they "live the Word of Wisdom."[18]

There are other policy doctrines that have a spiritually binding effect on Church members, such as saying the sacrament prayer word for word or paying ten percent tithing. Other policy doctrines that are authoritative teachings but more subjective to personal implementation may be Church doctrines such as family home evening on Monday nights or the recommendation to wear a white shirt while administering priesthood ordinances. Each of these, however, is an authorized teaching of the Church centered on application of core and supportive doctrines. Through their priesthood keys, prophets have the authority to create binding Church policies on earth that are honored in heaven (see D&C 128:9). The Church Handbook of Instructions 1 and 2 contain many policy doctrines of the Church (each member has access to Handbook 2 through the gospel library or online).

Esoteric Doctrines

Esoteric doctrines are truths that are only partially known or revealed. The word *esoteric* implies teachings that are understood by only a small group of people. Its synonyms are words such as *obscure* and *ambiguous*. Not all doctrines have been revealed, and there are also doctrines no longer taught that may be true but are not necessary for our understanding now. The Prophet Joseph Smith explained, "It is not always wise to relate all the truth. Even Jesus, the Son of God, had to refrain from doing so, and had to restrain His feelings many times for the safety of Himself and His followers, and had to conceal the righteous purposes of His heart in relation to many things pertaining to His Father's kingdom."[19] Joseph himself lamented, "I could explain a hundred fold more than I ever have, of the glories of the Kingdoms manifested to me in the vision, were I permitted, and were the people prepared to receive it."[20]

As M. Gerald Bradford and Larry E. Dahl stated about "doctrine" in the *Encyclopedia of Mormonism*, "There are many subjects about which the scriptures are not clear and about which the Church has made no official pronouncements. In such matters, one can find differences of opinion among Church members and leaders. Until the truth of these matters is made known by revelation, there is room for different levels of understanding and interpretation of unsettled issues."[21]

There are greater doctrines that were and are known to prophets, that are not known to us, such as those contained in the sealed portion of the Book of Mormon (see Ether 4:2–4).

These esoteric doctrines are true but are not declared openly. In some cases, esoteric doctrines are referred to as "deep doctrines" in a somewhat negative tone. Yet we are told that one day we will read the sealed portion of the gold plates in hopes that it will bring us closer to Christ (see Ether 4, 5). The Lord promises that to the obedient He will "give the mysteries of my kingdom" (D&C 63:23), even to the point of giving "things which have never been revealed" (Alma 26:22). Indeed, the Lord says it is His "delight" to give faithful seekers "the hidden mysteries of my kingdom" (D&C 76:5, 7). Generally, we seek and contemplate esoteric doctrines in private. We do not proclaim them publicly or officially, although they may be true. Seekers rely upon prophetic keys to declare the Church's official, authorized doctrine.

Look at the following image to see how this model of different "types" of LDS doctrines can be used, in this instance, to better understand and teach about baptism:

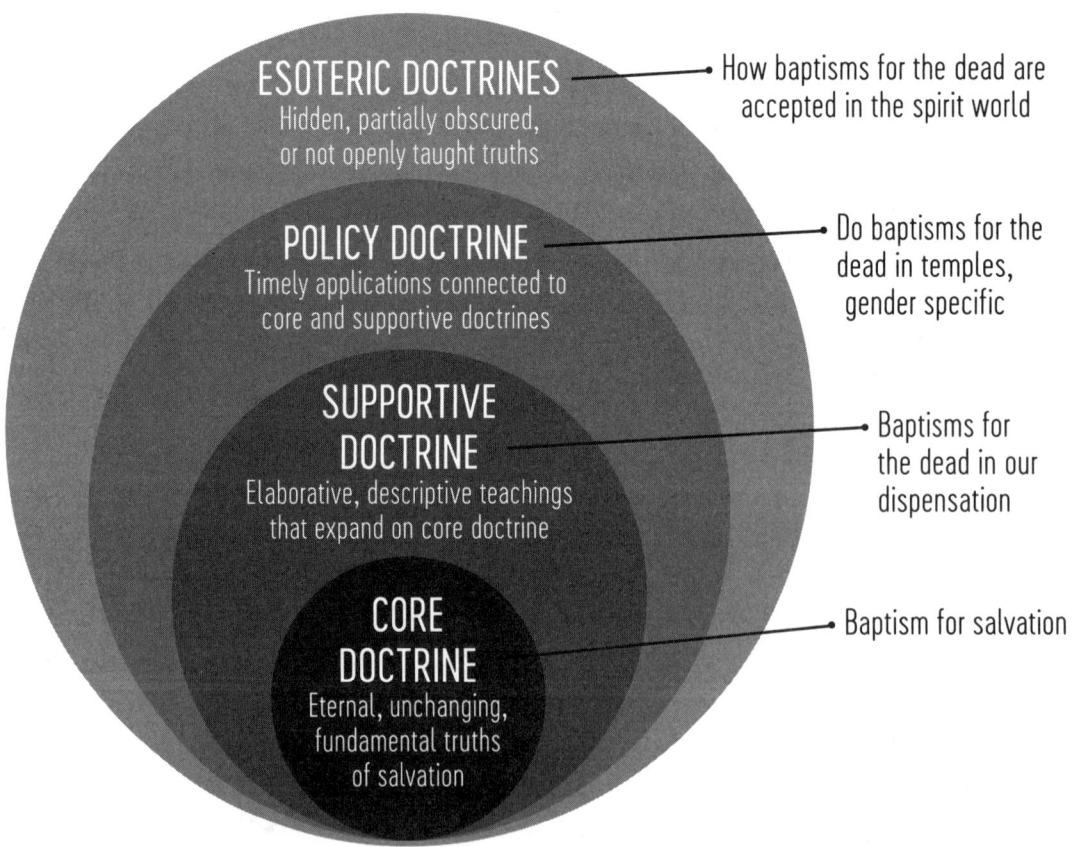

 **Seekers wanted!**

Now that I have explained different types of Church doctrine, look at the following list of Church teachings and ask yourself in which category—core, supportive, policy, or esoteric—you would place each doctrine:

- Satan being bound for 1,000 years during the Millennium
- The division of paradise/prison in the spirit world
- Calling and election made sure
- God as the Father of our spirits
- Deacons passing the sacrament
- The priesthood office of elder
- Two-hour Sunday church
- Heavenly Mother
- Eternal marriage

In all types of doctrine—whether core, supportive, policy, or esoteric—the Lord can always reveal more. We believe that God "will yet reveal many great and important things pertaining to the Kingdom of God" (Articles of Faith 1:9). This implies that new ideas, altered concepts, expanded teachings, and additional knowledge will be given, thus requiring doctrine to be flexible. This does not mean that some doctrines cannot be eternal or immovable, just that certain concepts have yet to be revealed and may alter as new perspectives are gained. The very notion of a living Church and continuing revelation suggest that most authorized teachings reflect current understanding and expediency, not eternal finality.

Sources of Doctrine

Since I am using the definition of an "authorized teaching" to be synonymous with "doctrine," it raises the question: how do we know if a teaching is institutionally "authorized" by the Church as one of its doctrines? The following four questions[22] are designed to help guide us as we seek for official, institutionally sanctioned teachings of the Church:

- Is it repeatedly found in the scriptures?
- Is it proclaimed by the united voice of the current Brethren?
- Is it consistently taught by current General Authorities and General Officers acting in their official capacity?
- Is it found in recent Church publications or statements?

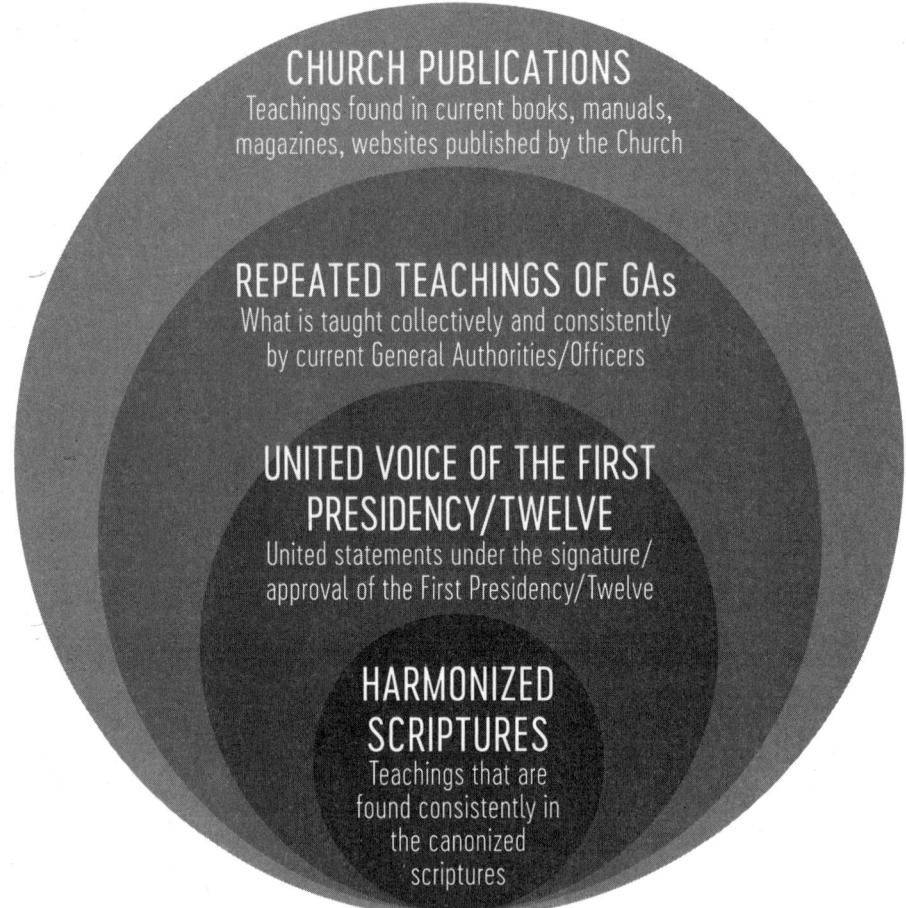

Let's analyze each of these four potential sources of official Latter-day Saint doctrine.

The Harmonized Scriptures

The officially accepted Latter-day Saint scriptures (the Bible, the Book of Mormon, the Doctrine and Covenants, and the Pearl of Great Price) are primary sources that seekers should search when identifying doctrine. Indeed, these books are often colloquially called the "standard" works, implying "accepted," or a benchmark criterion for doctrine. Elder B. H. Roberts of the Seventy taught, "The Church has confined the sources of doctrine by which it is willing to be bound before the world to the things that God has revealed, and which the Church has officially accepted, and those alone. . . . These have been repeatedly accepted and endorsed by the Church in general conference assembled, and are the only sources of absolute appeal for our doctrine."[23] Elder D. Todd Christofferson said, "The scriptures are the touchstone for measuring correctness and truth."[24]

It should be noted, however, that simply because something is found within the pages of canonized scripture does not mean that it represents the Church's current official doctrine (see Articles of Faith 1:8). When using scripture to define official doctrines, we are also to seek truths that are *often repeated and internally consistent.* Although the statement is found in the New Testament, for example, we would not proclaim as our doctrine that "no man hath seen God at any time" (1 John 4:12), because this singular verse conflicts with many other harmonized examples of those who have seen God face to face (see Exodus 24:9–10, 33:11; Genesis 32:30; Acts 7:55–56, Joseph Smith—History 1:16–17). President Russell M. Nelson taught, "In the Bible we read this important declaration: 'In the mouth of two or three witnesses shall every word be established' (2 Corinthians 13:1). This assures God's children that divine doctrines are confirmed by more than one scriptural witness. . . . Scriptural witnesses authenticate each other."[25] As we would with statistical data, we look for consistency in scripture, replicating truth harmoniously in multiple instances. Individual outlier scripture references should be guarded with caution as the basis for doctrinal conclusions.

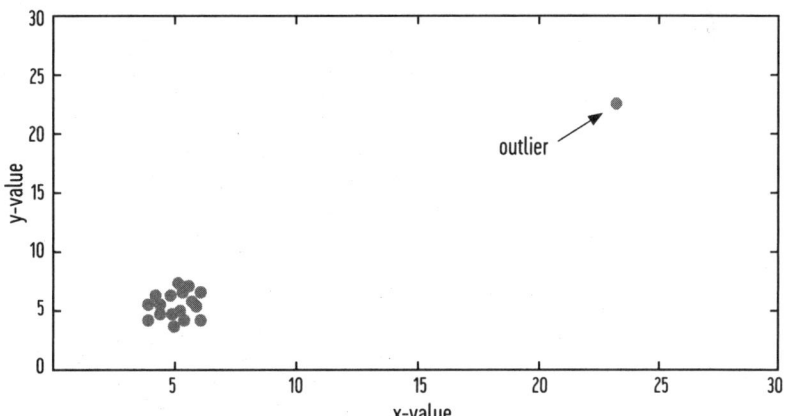

Additionally, some doctrines in scripture, like the performances of the law of Moses or policy doctrines such as requiring missionaries to leave without purse (money) or scrip (food), have been superseded by later revelation or prophetic direction (see Galatians 6:15; 3 Nephi 9:17; 3 Nephi 15:8). Thus, we should look to see if a scriptural teaching is confirmed by modern revelation or supplanted by it.

The United Voice of the Current Prophets

Because the words of the Lord never cease, we look to modern prophets to declare His current voice to His Church and people. One of the roles of the prophet, as President Gordon B. Hinckley said, is to "declare doctrine."[26] Those who also hold all the keys of the kingdom, namely the First Presidency (see D&C 81:2), "receive the oracles for the whole church" (D&C

124:126). Sustained by the key-holding Quorum of the Twelve Apostles (see D&C 112:30), "with divine inspiration" these two highest governing bodies of the Church "counsel together to establish doctrine."[27]

This is consistent with the scriptural injunction to the First Presidency, Quorum of the Twelve Apostles, and others in Doctrine and Covenants 107:27 that "every decision made by either of these quorums must be by the unanimous voice of the same; that is, every member in each quorum must be agreed to its decisions, in order to make their decisions of the same power or validity one with the other" (D&C 107:27). President Gordon B. Hinckley expounded on the point of prophetic unanimity, relating that "no decision emanates from the deliberations of the First Presidency and the Twelve without total unanimity among all concerned."[28] More recently, President M. Russell Ballard taught, "When the First Presidency and the Quorum of the Twelve speak with a united voice, it is the voice of the Lord for that time."[29] Although "the objective is not simply consensus among council members but revelation from God,"[30] as Elder D. Todd Christofferson reminded, prophetic unanimity cannot be lightly overlooked, as with it there is "power or validity" (D&C 107:27) in united doctrinal pronouncements.

Examples of doctrine proclaimed by the united voice of the current First Presidency and Twelve Apostles can include statements such as letters from the First Presidency, official declarations and proclamations, and official handbooks of instruction. There are other books, manuals, publications, or documents released under the approval or sanction of the united voice of the current prophets, such as *Preach My Gospel*.[31] Additionally, there are official announcements made or released under the united voice of the prophets, such as changes to the ministering program or the two-hour Sunday block meeting.[32]

Repeated Teachings from the Current General Authorities and Officers

An additional method to evaluate whether something may be considered part of official Church doctrine is to determine if something is being taught collectively by the current General Authorities and Officers acting in their official capacity. Although there may not be a formal united statement from the First Presidency or the Twelve on a matter, consistent teachings by many individual leaders on individual occasions can indicate cohesive support of a concept. Venues of delivering authorized Church doctrine by Church officers include general conference addresses, worldwide leadership trainings and broadcasts, regional conferences, and trainings and seminars for ecclesiastical leaders.

As with the harmonized scriptures, there is more doctrinal reliability in the cumulative teachings of general Church officers than there is in singular, individual statements. As the LDS Newsroom article "Approaching Mormon Doctrine" reminds, "A single statement made by a single leader on a single occasion often represents a personal, though well-considered, opinion, but is not meant to be officially binding [doctrine] for the whole Church."[33] As Elder Neil L. Andersen said, "True principles are taught frequently and by many. Our doctrine is not difficult to find."[34]

Current/Recent Publications of the Church

While not carrying the same weight of harmonized scripture or the united voice of the Brethren, official doctrine for the Church is also taught via the Church's authorized publications. An LDS Newsroom statement reminds us that "[Church doctrine] is consistently proclaimed in official Church publications." While much of the content contained within official Church publications is written by curriculum personnel, scholars, and lay members alike, "All of the [Church publications] . . . are reviewed and cleared . . . before they are published and issued to the Church."[35]

Examples of official Church publications that publish authorized doctrine include current Church magazines such as the *Ensign* or *New Era;* seminary and institute manuals; priesthood and Relief Society manuals; items published by Intellectual Reserve/the Corporation of the President of The Church of Jesus Christ of Latter-day Saints, such as the *Addiction Recovery Program;* scholarly publications such as *The Joseph Smith Papers* or *Saints,* from the Church History Department; and content on official Church websites.

Applying the Models

It is hoped that understanding *types* and *sources* of LDS doctrine in the two proposed models here can help seekers better evaluate, understand, and articulate various Church teachings. Think, for example, how you could use these models to address some of the questions posed at the front of this chapter (What *type* of teaching is the idea that Jesus is the Savior of other worlds? What *sources* support that teaching?). To conclude, I want to illustrate how these models could address two doctrinal points related to family that are sometimes discussed: Jesus's marriage status and Heavenly Mother.

Jesus's Marriage Status

The question of whether Jesus was married sometimes arises not only out of curiosity and doctrinal assumption (some deduce that if eternal marriage is required for exaltation, and surely the Lord is exalted, He must be married) but also due to the teachings of some early Latter-day Saint Apostles. Elder Orson Hyde taught in the October 1854 general conference that Jesus married Mary Magdalene and that the wedding at Cana of Galilee was Jesus's own,[36] to which President Brigham Young arose and gave an "amen."[37] Apostle Orson Pratt also wrote in *The Seer* that the Savior was married, suggesting that perhaps He had more wives than one.[38] There is also evidence of Joseph F. Smith teaching in 1883 that Jesus was married.[39]

Does this make Jesus's marriage status an authorized Church teaching? Using our proposed models to evaluate doctrine, Jesus being married could be described as a doctrine of the Church in the mid- to latter-nineteenth century based on the cumulative teachings of General Authorities of the time. However, there is no known revelation on the subject, nor is there a united statement from the First Presidency and the Twelve, and the cumulative standard works seem to evade the issue. Like other early doctrines, Jesus's marriage status faded from public teaching over the next decades and moved into the realm of the unknown or undeclared. In 1912, President Charles W. Penrose, then a member of the First Presidency, broached the subject in the *Improvement Era* and said: "We do not know anything about Jesus Christ being married. The Church has no authoritative declaration on the subject."[40] Decades later, a 1997 *Ensign* article suggested that the question, "Was Jesus married?" was "inappropriate to discuss in a classroom setting."[41] In 2006, due primarily to the popularity of the novel *The DaVinci Code*, which posited that Jesus was married and had children, the Church officially released a statement through its spokesperson, saying, "The belief that Christ was married has never been official church doctrine. It is neither sanctioned nor taught by the church."[42] Thus, while once perhaps promoted in the mid-nineteenth century, using the model of *official sources* of doctrine, Jesus's marriage status is no longer an authorized teaching of the Church. It's absent in the Church's current official publications, it is not taught cumulatively by the modern General Authorities, and it is not declared by the united voice of the modern First Presidency and Apostles. Using our model of *types* of doctrine, Jesus's marriage status now seemingly belongs to the esoteric ring of doctrine—something once known or taught by others and that one day may be taught again, but is not known, taught openly, or declared authoritatively today. It is now an unauthorized, esoteric teaching.

Heavenly Mother

Many wonder about teachings on Mother in Heaven. What does the Church officially say about Her? Are teachings about Her also esoteric or unauthorized, like Jesus's marriage status? Recently, the Church released an official essay addressing the Church's fundamental doctrines related to Heavenly Mother, declaring, "All human beings, male and female, are beloved spirit children of heavenly parents, a Heavenly Father and a Heavenly Mother."[43] Teachings confirming Her divine existence are found also in our current published hymnal.[44] Many recent Church authorities have also spoken of Heavenly Mother in official settings such as general conference.[45] The phrases "Mother in Heaven," "Heavenly Mother," or "Heavenly Parents" have been said over one hundred times in general conference settings. The 1995 united statement of the First Presidency and Quorum of the Twelve "The Family: A Proclamation to the World" declares, "Each [person] is a beloved spirit son or daughter of heavenly *parents*, and, as such, each has a divine nature and destiny."[46] Specifically, the First Presidency in 1909 unitedly declared, "All men and women are in the similitude of the universal Father and Mother, and are literally the sons and daughters of Deity."[47] However, the harmonized scriptural record does not specifically address Mother in Heaven, only providing implied or indirect evidence (see Genesis 1:27; Moses 2:27; Abraham 4:27).

Applying the first model, what *type* of doctrine may our belief in Heavenly Mother be? The Church's official essay says, "The doctrine of a Heavenly Mother is a cherished and distinctive belief among Latter-day Saints."[48] While not using the word "core" or "essential," clearly the doctrine that exaltation is predicated upon the eternal sealing of a man and woman is central to our theology (see D&C 131:1–4; D&C 132:19–22). Teachings about Heavenly Mother may be considered as supportive doctrine to this core teaching related to eternal marriage and godhood. Considering who our deified Mother may be, or how She attained Her exalted station, or what Her specific influence or mission may be in our quest for salvation seems to fall into the realm of esoteric doctrine. Clearly, She loves us,[49] and we await further revealed knowledge on the subject, to be received with gladness. Until then, as the official essay on the subject emphasizes, "Our present knowledge about a Mother in Heaven is limited."[50] Using the second model on authorized *sources* of doctrine, teachings about our divine Mother are openly and authoritatively declared by the united voice of the modern prophets, their cumulative teachings, and in official Church publications, thus supporting our belief in and expressions related to Her divine status as an official doctrine of the Church.

Conclusion: Growing in Doctrine

These are but two examples of how the models proposed here may help us better understand Latter-day Saint doctrinal teachings. As you continue to seek learning of Church doctrine by study, it is hoped that these models can help facilitate understanding and provide a starting point for evaluating and discussing other doctrinal subjects, whether the subject is fairly benign, like Jesus's birth date, or more sensitive and potentially controversial, such as priesthood restrictions or same-gender attraction.

My colleagues and I who developed these models make no pretentions that they are definitive. Ironically, these models on doctrine are not official Church doctrine. We have attempted to use words of prophets and scriptures in creating them, but the models proposed herein—like the nature of doctrine itself—are meant to be flexible and only to aid in coming to a clearer understanding of truth. Seekers should question whether something is an eternal doctrine or a supportive doctrine or whether it is considered policy or esoteric doctrine. Some seekers may come to differing conclusions not only about in which category of doctrine a certain teaching may be placed but with the categories themselves.

Whatever their method, seekers must have the skills to discuss different types of Church teachings and clearly discern what is and isn't Church doctrine. We must be able to evaluate whether something is part of the core doctrine of Christ and essential for salvation, or a more explanatory, policy, or only partially known teaching. We must know how to handle individual declarative statements by Church leaders, acknowledge past teachings that are no longer endorsed, and be able to understand why Church teachings have changed and will yet change. These evaluative skills surrounding Church doctrine are an absolute necessity for those who seek learning by study and faith.

 Hide or Go Seek

Hide

I think Church doctrines never have changed and never will change.
Anything said by General Authorities is official Church doctrine.
Everything taught in the past that we no longer teach today is wrong.
Policy teachings aren't that important because they aren't doctrine.

Go Seek

I evaluate whether something is core, supportive, policy, or esoteric doctrine.
I believe that the first principles and ordinances of the gospel never change.
I understand that policy doctrines change based on timely needs of God's children.
I am open to the idea of esoteric doctrines and new doctrines being revealed that clarify current understanding.
I evaluate whether something is an official Church doctrine by seeking for evidence in the harmonious scriptures, united statements of the Brethren, cumulative teachings of modern General Authorities and Officers, and current Church publications.

Chapter 3

RESEARCHING CHURCH HISTORY AND DOCTRINE

 **Seeking Sentence: There are more powerful ways to search than just Googling it.**

In a world full of information, seekers need to be both conscious of what resources are available and wise about what sources they trust while learning Church history and doctrine. Some don't know where to turn other than the Church's website or Google to research subjects on a deeper level. For example, suppose I wanted to answer the following questions: Are Church leaders talking about Zion in general conference more or less than in the past? What about the Word of Wisdom, or grace? How can I learn how prophets and apostles have interpreted a particular verse of scripture over the years? What is Oliver Cowdery's "gift of Aaron" referred to in Doctrine and Covenants section 8? How could I learn the historical context of that revelation? Where can I go to read peer-reviewed research on how the Church has implemented the law of consecration over its history? How can I find reliable and faithful academic/scholarly articles on Church subjects? What book publishers should I read, and why? Welcome to the need for this chapter.

The scriptures and words of the prophets are the central "best books" from which D&C 88:118 tells us to seek wisdom, along with other officially published Church materials. All seekers should have the Church's Gospel Library app downloaded onto their digital devices, if they have them, and should use its myriad of content frequently. Seekers of these best books, however, can also benefit from using research methods and databases to enhance their study of them, employing modern means to seek learning on unprecedented levels compared to previous generations. Databases can incredibly augment our study of the scriptures and help us see trends and patterns in general conference. There are also historical databases available to help us gain access to primary historical documents and understand crucial history and context related to the Restoration. In addition, there are websites with search bars ready to spew out scores of peer-reviewed scholarly research articles. In this chapter, I will introduce you to six powerful databases available to all seekers to conduct in-depth research of LDS teachings: two databases to research doctrinal/scriptural items, two databases to research historical items, and two databases to research scholarly articles related to Church history and doctrine:

> BYU General Conference Corpus: https://www.lds-general-conference.org
> LDS Scriptures Citation Index: http://scriptures.byu.edu
> Joseph Smith Papers: http://www.josephsmithpapers.org
> Church History Library Catalog: http://churchhistorycatalog.lds.org
> Religious Studies Center: https://rsc.byu.edu
> BYU Studies: https://byustudies.byu.edu

BYU General Conference Corpus: https://www.lds-general-conference.org

This is one of my favorite doctrinal research websites. The BYU General Conference Corpus allows you to quickly and easily search talks from general conference from 1851 to present. This database enables you to search certain key words from general conference and to use collocates (words next to other words) to refine searches in a particular context and compare how words are being used in general conference by analyzing the words around them. The interface is easy, clean, and friendly. One of the reasons why this database should be known and used is to see how teachings in the Church have developed and changed over time. I rely heavily on this resource in my research, teaching, and writing for this purpose. Take, for example, the question I mentioned earlier. Do you think Church leaders are now placing more or less emphasis on grace than they have in the past? Let's go to the website and consult the database to find out.

On the main tab, I click the "Chart" tab and then type "grace" into the search bar, and then click "See frequency by section" to search all of general conference.

Holy guacamole. Look what it returns:

SECTION	ALL	1850s	1860s	1870s	1880s	1890s	1900s	1910s	1920s	1930s	1940s	1950s	1960s	1970s	1980s	1990s	2000s	2010s
FREQ	1819	111	100	63	70	106	85	68	84	60	81	90	96	116	107	173	148	261
WORDS (M)	24	1.7	1.3	1.8	1.5	1.5	1.2	1.5	1.6	1.3	1.4	1.5	1.6	1.7	1.3	1.4	1.5	1.2
PER MIL	74.98	66.44	76.79	35.12	47.52	78.96	68.85	44.19	51.68	47.24	56.23	61.37	58.44	69.28	81.53	123.27	96.93	223.84

You don't have to be a statistician to understand this chart. It is a simple histogram, showing how many times the word *grace* has been said in general conference each decade by frequency (1,819 in all, as of this writing) and how many times it is said in words per million (PER MIL) so you can compare content by decades more equitably. If that is confusing you, just look at the bars and the decades to see the trends. In this current decade, we have already heard the word *grace* about three times as much as in the 1970s or 1980s. The 1910s–1960s were more minimal on references to grace, with the 1930s taking the prize for being lowest: sixty references in ten years, or only three times per conference, compared to 261 times in this decade just through 2018 (224 words per million), or fifteen times per conference thus far—four times more often than it was said in the '60s. Indeed, the Church is beginning to "grow in grace" (D&C 50:40; 2 Peter 3:18).

One great feature of this database is that you can simply click on the decade from which you want to see references, and it will list the talks where the word is given, who gave the talk, and when. Even better, I can then click on any of the individual lines and it will give me a broader context of the quote.

This is waaaay better than searching Google, or—dare I say it?—ChurchofJesusChrist.org (Don't get me wrong. I love the Church's website, but their search engine is not nearly this advanced.)

Want to see talks and trends about how Church leaders are addressing contemporary issues, like pornography? Search for that term and you'll see a rise in the 2000s as the internet and smartphones hit the mainstream. I could click on every decade with results to see what is being taught and by whom. Imagine how I could use this to pull together an amazing study or lesson on what Church leaders have taught on this subject.

Speaking of cultural issues, I mentioned Heavenly Parents in the prior chapter on doctrine. When I searched that phrase, I found a recent surge in occurrences. "Heavenly Parents" has been mentioned 43 times in the 2010s, compared to four times in the '80s, nine times in the '90s, and ten times in the 2000s. Why the rise in the 2010s? It could be for a number of reasons. One may be the changing political climate and legalization of same-sex marriage (legalized in 2015 in the United States), and the Church's renewed emphasis on marriage between male and female as the divine, exalting pattern set by our Heavenly Father and Mother. Another may be an increased desire by women to learn about and feel a connection with their Mother in Heaven.

The LDS General Conference Corpus also has other search features that can be useful, such as Collocates, Compare, and KWIC. "Collocates" allows you to see which words appear near other words, giving better results and insights. For example, let's say I want to find conference talks that mention the promise that the "prophet will never lead us astray." If I use only that exact phrase, I may be limited and missing results. Thus, I put the word "prophet" in the top search window and "astray" in the collocate window, and then click the + sign to the right until it is on 9 (the highest it will go) and the + sign on the left to 9. What this does is say, "Find when 'astray' has been said up to nine words before or after the word 'prophet.'" You can adjust those as needed. My search returned twenty results, of which here are a few:

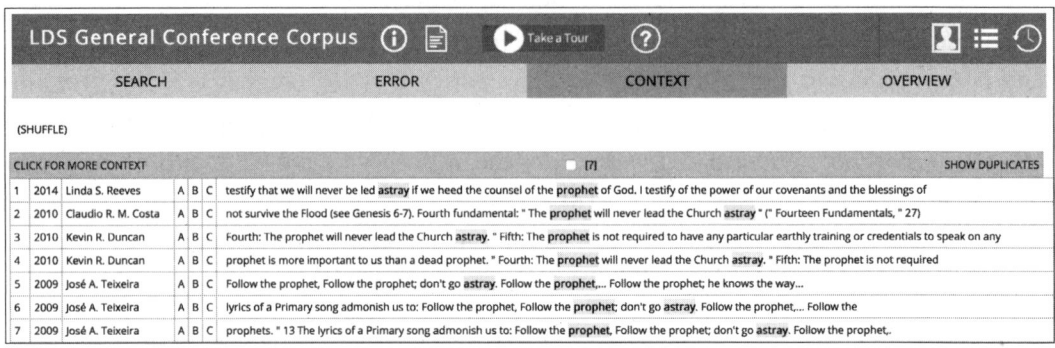

May this database never lead us astray! The BYU LDS General Conference Corpus is a simple yet powerful tool to aid in your seeking and studying of general conference talks.

 Seekers wanted!

Go to the LDS General Conference Corpus and do a simple "chart" search of words you are interested in to see how they have been emphasized or de-emphasized over the history of general conference. Here are five "C" words to try if you'd like: charity, chastity, consecration, constitution, and conversion.

LDS Scriptures Citation Index: http://scriptures.byu.edu/

Another extremely useful tool that is related to the BYU LDS General Conference Corpus is the LDS Scriptures Citation Index. I have found this site superior in some ways to the Corpus website. The Corpus website is limited in that it doesn't provide full-text access to general conference talks (only portions) due to copyright. Scriptures.byu.edu includes the entire talk. Along with containing the text of general conference, this site also enables you to search the *Journal of Discourses* and the *Scriptural Teachings of the Prophet Joseph Smith* (which is beneficial because the BYU Corpus begins in 1851, after Joseph's death). And, as the title implies, this database allows you to search the entire standard works of the LDS scriptures with a powerful tool that connects them to general conference, which I will discuss in a moment (hang tight; it's amazing). Their search tool also allows you to limit your results based on the speaker and/or a range of years.

For example, if I wanted to learn more about Brigham Young's views of Adam (as questions about the Adam-God theory sometimes arise for seekers), here I can limit my search to include only Brigham's talks from general conference and *Journal of Discourses*.

The database search yielded 134 results. I can then click on a result and see the entire discourse with the search word highlighted.

This would provide me a great method as a seeker to personally understand a broad range of Brigham Young's public teachings on Adam, and not leave me dependent upon another scholar's position or perspectives on the matter.

Under the "Library" tab, this database also has a "Topical Index" to the *entire Journal of Discourses*, which proves useful for studying how the early Church leadership understood various topics.

As its name implies, this database is also an excellent resource to study and search the scriptures. It has a search tool similar to the one available on the LDS Tools app, which lets you digitally search each book of scripture for words and phrases—in this case, words related to *endow** (search hint: similar to the BYU Corpus, adding an asterisk at the end of a word finds and includes all the words that begin with that phrase, such as *endows, endowed, endowment*).

In addition, there are sophisticated ways to search this database using the Lucene syntax that yield amazing results. For example:

> +justice +mercy +law finds all matches mentioning justice *and* mercy *and* law.
> -justice +mercy finds any match mentioning mercy but *not* justice.
> "justice mercy" ~5 finds any match where justice and mercy are separated by at most five words.

The most powerful and unique feature of this database, however, is that *it links the scriptures to when they have been referenced or explained in general conference.* If I want to know what the Brethren have said about any particular scripture, this is my go-to website. You can click on any scripture and it has a number listed to the side, and that is how many times that scripture has been mentioned in conference. For example, if I go to Moses 6:9 I can see what may have been said about the phrase that God "called their name Adam"—both male and female—when He created them. There is an [8] next to Moses 6:9, indicating eight times this verse has been cited in general conference.

If I click on Moses 6:9 [8], and it loads all eight conference talks that mention it, and I can read them in context to see how this verse has been interpreted by Church leaders. This yields some great insight.

This is perhaps the single most excellent resource for scriptural interpretation from Church leadership that is available currently. It is a source that seekers should use to learn the words of prophets who have been commissioned with the keys to interpret scripture and doctrine for the whole Church.[1]

Joseph Smith Papers: http://www.josephsmithpapers.org/

There is no way to emphasize strongly enough the impact that the Joseph Smith Papers project is having upon our ability to study primary documents related to the life and ministry of the Prophet Joseph as well as the history of the early restored Church. It is monumental. As content is published, it is made available online, for free. With the click of a few buttons, you can be analyzing primary source materials, reading Joseph's own handwriting in his journals, looking at the earliest versions of his revelations, and analyzing his earliest drafts of his history, all the while being guided by a team of expert historians who provide context and annotation for each document. This is a Church historical seeker's playground.

As the website summarizes, "The Joseph Smith Papers Project is an effort to gather together all extant Joseph Smith documents and to publish complete and accurate transcripts of those documents with both textual and contextual annotation."[2] One reason the website is so powerful and essential to use has to do with reading early versions of the Doctrine and Covenants revelations. As will be discussed in a later chapter, as they prepared the revelations for publication, Joseph Smith and his associates edited Doctrine and Covenants revelations for clarity, grammar, or mistakes in transcription, or to take into account additional revelations on a given subject. Seeing the early versions can unlock clearer original intent of certain scriptural passages. Take D&C 8:6, for example. Our current edition of the Doctrine and Covenants says that Oliver Cowdery had "the gift of Aaron" that "has told you many things." Regarding this gift, Oliver is told, "Hold it in your hands," and "whatsoever you shall ask me to tell you by that means [the gift of Aaron], that will I grant unto you" (D&C 8:6–9). What is this gift of Aaron? Going to the Joseph Smith Papers to see the original illuminates its potential meaning. To go there, I click on the "Documents" tab and go to the year of the revelation (1829), and it populates all the 1829 Joseph Smith documents. Any document that became a Doctrine and Covenants section has a bracket to the side, and I can see the document from April 1829 that became D&C 8.

When I click on the document, up comes the earliest version, with a transcript on the right and a high-res image of the document on the left, which lets me zoom in closely.

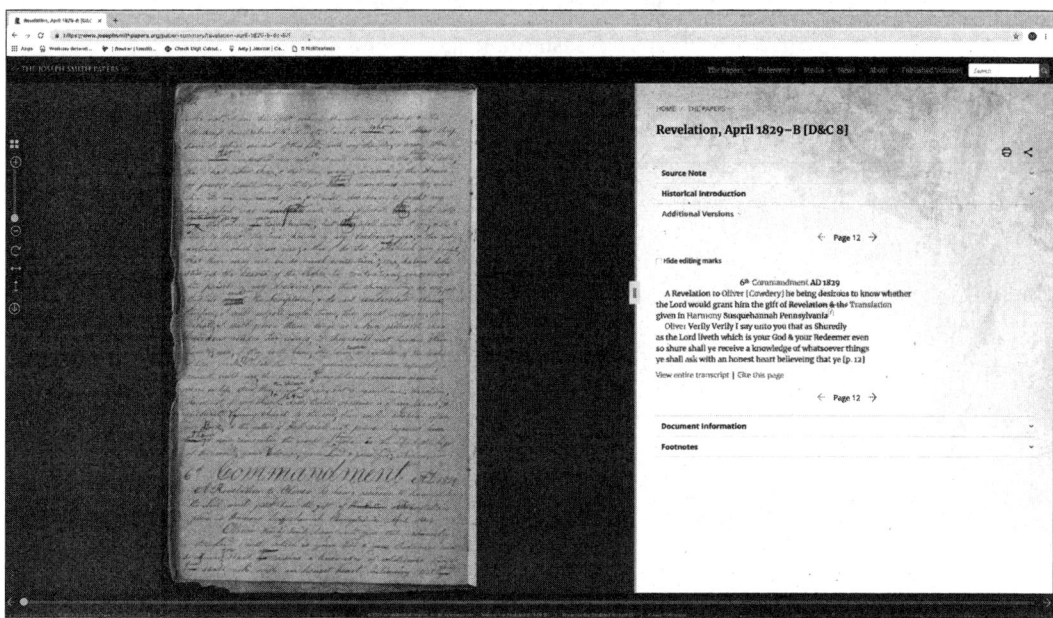

When I go to the verses about Oliver's gift that has told him many things, it does not call it the "gift of Aaron," but instead, look:

RESEARCHING CHURCH HISTORY AND DOCTRINE

The original says that Oliver's gift is "working with the sprout," and then clarified above is "rod." A few lines later it says that God can "cause this ~~thing of nature~~ rod" to work in Oliver's hands. That is fascinating! Likely Oliver's "gift of Aaron" was his ability to work with divining rods to obtain divine direction. The Old Testament has several accounts of people using rods or staffs to perform miracles and obtain the Lord's will.[3] In later editions of the Doctrine and Covenants, this phrase of "the rod" or "the sprout" was changed for publication to "gift of Aaron," likely to connect Oliver's divining gifts with sacred, ancient works and phrases of old found in the scriptures.

Another highly useful feature of the Joseph Smith Papers is that with each document (including each revelation) there is a "Historical Introduction" dropdown option. Click on that dropdown and you get a wealth of carefully reviewed, professional, historical commentary situating the document and providing context to its creation. I use this feature often when I study the Doctrine and Covenants sections, as it provides amazing scholarly insight and context that aids in understanding the intent and subtle contextual teachings within many of the Doctrine and Covenants revelations. The Historical Introduction for each document is a treasure.

This site has much, much more to offer. Another key feature is the "References" dropdown arrow on the top of the website's search bar.

This gives you a list of People, Places, and Events, a Glossary, and much more to search. If I want to learn more about anyone mentioned in Joseph's papers, say, Shadrach Roundy (hey, he's my third great-grandfather through my mom's side!), I can click on his name and up pulls a referenced history of his life, complete with direct links to anywhere he is mentioned in the Joseph Smith Papers. You can do this for hundreds of early Church history people. Unreal!

The same holds true for places mentioned in the Papers. I can click on any place, say, Adam-ondi-Ahman, and it will bring up a summary of the place and provide links to anywhere in the Joseph Smith Papers that place is mentioned and events that happened there. What early seekers wouldn't have given to have access to this kind of knowledge and information!

Church History Library Catalog: http://churchhistorycatalog.lds.org

I won't spend quite as much time on this database as I did on the Joseph Smith Papers website, as the Papers website is centered on Joseph Smith and his revelations, provides helpful scholarly annotation and commentary, and is more user-friendly to the average seeker than the Church History Library's catalog. The Church History Library, however, has a vast array of information available to search at your digital fingertips, but you are on your own a bit more to navigate and make sense of its content. The documents are available but lack helpful scaffolding to give support to non-historians.

As you know, there are thousands of LDS history documents available to you at the Church History Library. With their search tool, which was released in 2012, you can search through the library's catalog without having to visit the actual library. Many of the documents have been digitized (although some have not) so you can view them right on your computer. "The catalog allows easy access to material available in the Church History Library, including 270,000 books, pamphlets, magazines, and newspapers and 240,000 collections of original, unpublished records such as journals, diaries, correspondence, and meeting minutes . . . [and also] 13,000 collections of photographs and 23,000 audiovisual items."[4]

Let's look at something together, shall we? Since I mentioned researching Adam-God, in a matter of a few minutes I clicked on the database of "Brigham Young Letters." I typed in "Adam-God" in the search window, and it returned two hits of letters that were written to Brigham Young inquiring on the subject:

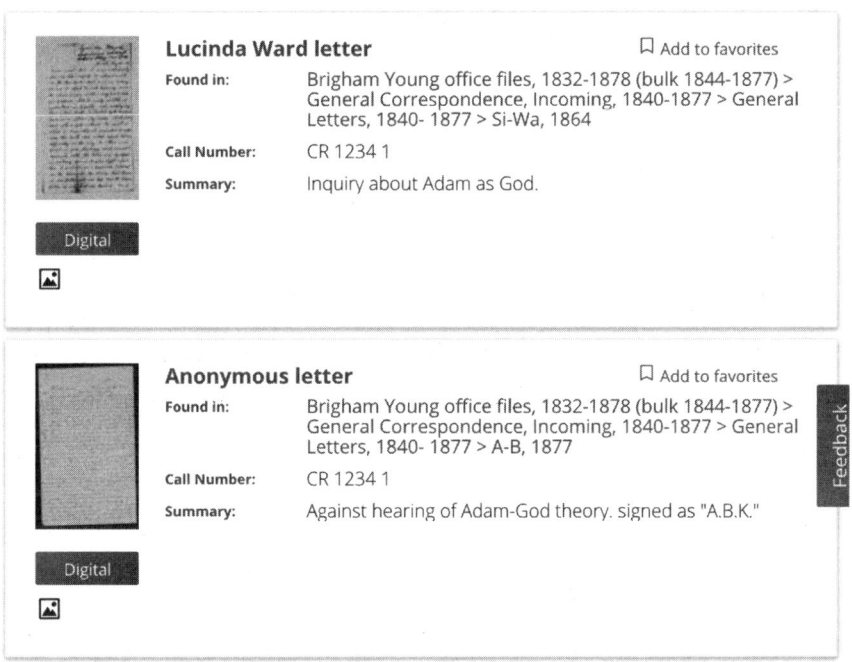

I clicked on the link, which took me to a digital scan of the document (I had to navigate to the date, as other letters were also included in the file). I found the letter of a dubious questioner of the doctrine, who wrote to Brigham "as a stranger" from Niagara County, New York, expressing how "shocked [he] was to learn" about items related to Adam-God. The anonymous man (he only gave his initials) seems not to be a Latter-day Saint but some type of Protestant Christian. He wondered how people could believe that "the sinner in the garden of Eden [Adam] was the Creator of all things. Could he who was formed from the dust of the earth, make that dust? Could he who *sinned* be still a god? Sinful man would be too selfish, to provide a world of beauties for the human family, unless he could sit enthroned in the [unreadable], and think you, a sinful God would do more? I tell you Nay! . . . But do not think you can rob God of his glory, though you have taken passages from his holy word, and added, or subtracted as you saw fit. . . . Repent and turn to God, not to Adam, before it is too late."[5]

This letter provides fascinating historical and contextual insight into how people outside of Utah were understanding Brigham's teachings. I wonder how President Young responded? Thanks to the Church History Library, I can search his letters and other databases to find out, and so can you.

BYU Religious Studies Center: https://rsc.byu.edu/

The Religious Studies Center was formed under the direction of then-Dean of Religion at BYU, Jeffrey R. Holland. It is "a vital research and publications arm of Religious Education. It exists to seek out, encourage, and publish faithful gospel scholarship through sponsoring symposia and seminars; awarding research grants; and producing and disseminating high quality, peer-reviewed works."[6] Many of these past peer-reviewed works are available for free through their search bar.

Coming from an academic this sounds self-serving, but there is great value in works being peer-reviewed and accepted for publication from credentialed journals and presses. This contrasts with websites, blog posts, and entries on social media platforms that Google search results often return. Websites are unvetted and unchallenged for academic integrity and accuracy. If you think a web/blog/social post is great, it very well may be. Having it blindly reviewed, however, by three to five academics credentialed in that field helps certify that it is trustworthy work, or it exposes the writing's lack of rigor, integrity, and scholarship that some laypersons may not be equipped to discern. Seekers should remember that there's inherent worth in most peer-reviewed, critically published works.

Suppose I wanted to read faithful, peer-reviewed, scholarly articles to better understand the law of consecration. In one simple search of "consecration" in the Religious Studies Center's search tool, I returned multiple excellent articles with direct links to read on the subject, from BYU scholars (Steven Harper and Craig Ostler) and Elder Stephen B. Oveson of the Seventy and his wife, Dixie Randall Oveson.

Many of these articles come from the *Religious Educator,* a volume with "a focus on the restored gospel of Jesus Christ, Latter-day Saint scriptures, and Latter-day Saint history. Its goal is to provide carefully prepared, inspirational, and informative articles that will benefit a broad range of Latter-day Saints who love the gospel and its teachings."[7] You can access all of the previous years' *Religious Educator* articles for free from their website.

Other articles come from the annual Church History, Sperry, and BYU Student symposiums and the annual Easter Conference. You can even search articles by author, if you have a favorite few you know by name—or, perhaps, if you have any you may want to avoid!

I assume that if you are reading this book, you are academically minded. But to those who may be skeptical about turning to academic scholars for religious learning, I share the following from President M. Russell Ballard: "Consult the works of recognized, thoughtful, and faithful LDS scholars." In addition to counseling us to seek words from Church leaders, President Ballard said, "We should ask those with appropriate academic training, experience, and expertise for help. This is exactly what I do when I need an answer to my own questions that I cannot answer myself. I seek help from my Brethren in the Quorum of the Twelve and from others with expertise in fields of Church history and doctrine."[8]

BYU Studies: https://byustudies.byu.edu/

Like the Religious Studies Center, BYU Studies is an academic outlet for scholarly work related to the Church. They publish books and journal articles and provide study resources for Latter-day Saint audiences. As their explanatory note in the *BYU Studies Quarterly* journal cites, they strive to "publish articles that reflect a faithful point of view, are relevant to subjects of interest to Latter-day Saints, and conform to high scholarly standards . . . [including] poetry, personal essays, reviews, and never-before-published documents of significant historical value."9

BYU Studies is a highly regarded and reviewed journal. Again, I won't spend much time here, as their site offers similar features to that of the Religious Studies Center, but it offers other types of articles not available through the RSC. For example, say I wanted to read research related to Book of Mormon geography. I simply typed it in their search bar, and the search yielded thirty-four results, which I can refine using their search features to the right. Whether you lean to a Book of Mormon Baja, Heartland, Central America, South America, or New York geography (or, like me, are fine with wherever!), these articles and many more would be worthwhile to study.

Of course, there are many other sites and places, journals and databases from which to seek learning by study. The six mentioned herein have been highly useful to me in my seeking and studying, are easily accessible, and are trustworthy, which is why I wanted to share and show how they can be of help to you.

Other trustworthy places to seek and search are
- Book of Mormon Central, https://bookofmormoncentral.org/
- Harold B. Lee Library collections, https://lib.byu.edu/collections/
- The BYU Maxwell Institute (where you can get past editions of *Mormon Studies Review, Journal of Book of Mormon Studies, Studies in the Bible and Antiquity*), https://publications.mi.byu.edu/
- Mormon Historical Studies, http://mormonhistoricsites.org/publications/
- Journal of Mormon History, http://www.jstor.org/journal/jmormhist

Paying Attention to Publishers

Obviously, book publishers are another source of knowledge for seekers. Books about Latter-day Saint history and doctrine are often published by Deseret Book, perhaps the largest publisher and distributor of Latter-day Saint works. They also distribute many books of interest to Saints published by many other presses. You can digitally gain access to search and read from a vast array of their published works through their Deseret Bookshelf app subscription.

It is wise to pay attention to who is publishing a work, as certain presses cater to certain audiences. Deseret Book is owned by the Church, and therefore vetted closely by their board to ensure that published content is in harmony with the Church's doctrine and mission. At times, however, Deseret Book is limited in what they can and will publish. Thus, turning to other presses and publishers can be helpful, particularly scholarly ones. Published books by Oxford, Yale, Harvard, or other university presses usually indicate works that have been rigorously reviewed and critiqued for academic integrity. These works, however, take on the culture of academia seeking to mitigate bias and don't have building or sustaining the faith of Latter-day Saints as their primary goal. This doesn't mean they should be overlooked or frowned upon by latter-day seekers. On the contrary, even-handed academic work without a faith-based agenda can often expand your understanding of truth and increase faith. It's a false dichotomy to set academic work against building faith. They are not mutually exclusive. The reader should be mindful when reading an academic press book, however, that defending the Church or building faith is usually not the goal of the text.

Richard Bushman's seminal and critically acclaimed work from 2005, *Rough Stone Rolling* (published by Knopf), is an excellent example of a book related to LDS history and doctrine geared with more of an academic approach. Both Richard Bushman and Jed Woodworth (who assisted Bushman) are highly trained historians and members of the Church who support the faith in other ways (both are major contributors/editors of the Joseph Smith Papers). When it was released, however, *Rough Stone Rolling* greatly shook the faith of some Church members, all the while greatly strengthening the faith of other Church members. Why the diverse reaction? It's difficult to say. My anecdotal conversations indicate that some Latter-day Saints were surprised to read a book that didn't seek to *convince* the reader of Joseph's prophetic ministry and discussed directly and without apology various uncomfortable topics. Some felt betrayed by this information and approach, while others gleaned wonderful cultural and historical insights to Joseph Smith and grew in their understanding and faith in the Prophet. The outcome may have been more of a result of what was *expected* from the content, rather than the content itself.

There are and will be many other presses that deal with The Church of Jesus Christ of Latter-day Saints, to be sure. More devotional publishers include Covenant Communications, Cedar Fort, and Millennial Press. Greg Kofford Books often seeks devotion but balances it with a more academic tone. Academic presses that focus on Church-related subjects also include the University of Utah, Utah State University, Illinois, and Farleigh Dickinson. More neutral (and sometimes non-mainstream) publishers can be Signature Books, Dialogue, and Sunstone. Wise seekers should know and be conscious about who is publishing a work, the publisher's general audience and agenda, and the publisher's reputation. This doesn't mean we immediately discard any one publishing outlet, but being "wise as serpents, and harmless as doves" (Matthew 10:16), we are mindfully conscious consumers of the purposes of various publishers.

The Lord has greatly blessed our generation to have access to unprecedented amounts of doctrinal and historical information about the Church. True seekers use the gifts and resources given by God to augment their study from the best books, the best databases, the best websites, the best journals, and the best publishers. Every good seeker of Church history and doctrine should know there's so much more to search than Google, and where to go to do so.

 **Hide or Go Seek**

Hide

When I want to learn about something more deeply I just Google it.

I will only read things about the Church that come from the Church.

I don't go to the Joseph Smith Papers or Church History website because they are confusing and take effort.

I trust what is published on websites and blogs equally to what is published in peer-reviewed books and articles.

Go Seek

I analyze trends in prophetic teachings to understand prophetic priorities and historical emphases.

I search to understand how prophets have interpreted scriptural passages to help my interpretation of scripture.

I search the Joseph Smith Papers and Church History websites to better understand and learn Church history.

I seek after high-quality, peer-reviewed books and articles to learn more about Church history and doctrine.

I pay attention to who is publishing a piece about Church history and doctrine.

PART 2

Seeking Truth

We are not only to seek learning by study, but importantly, we are to "seek learning . . . also by faith" (D&C 88:118). Sister Chieko Okazaki likened learning by study and faith to rowing a boat: "What happens if you try to paddle a boat using only one oar? You go around and around in circles. If you paddle hard, you go fast. If you paddle slowly, you turn gently. But you still just go around in circles. It's the same with trying to make study replace faith or trying to exercise faith but without study. . . . Row, row, row your boat and use both oars!"[1] If we use only our minds, but not our faith, like Jesus told the faithless Pharisees, "Ye shall seek me, and shall not find me" (John 7:34). Learning by faith centers on learning by the Spirit.[2] The Spirit is the Spirit of Truth (see John 14:17). Therefore, Part 2 articulates skills and perspectives to help seek the Spirit of Truth through interpreting scripture, embracing ambiguity, and discerning truth from error by the power of the Holy Ghost.

Chapter 4

INTERPRETING SCRIPTURE

 Seeking Sentence: There are no perfect expressions of revelation.

Words have power. Recorded words have *staying* power. The spoken word may momentarily inspire. The written word is a constant heavenly messenger, resurrecting itself daily in black-and-white text each time you reopen the page. Although Nephi lamented that he didn't write as powerfully as he spoke (see 2 Nephi 33:1), paradoxically it is his written words that have carried the Spirit into the hearts of millions. Alma wished he were an angel and could lift his voice as a sound of a trump to the ends of the earth, yet his wish was fulfilled not through his speaking, but through his writing. His voice is heard in Australia, Japan, and remote corners of the Amazon, like an angel gliding across the globe thundering repentance through printed text (see Alma 29:1–2). Moroni seemed to think he was a great speaker and a poor writer (see Ether 12:23), but it is the *book* he shepherded that has brought millions to the Lamb of God. Books cross oceans, traverse mountains, and sit patiently on shelves for hundreds of years, waiting like hidden pearls of great price for their pages to be read and wisdom revealed.

The most sacred writings we call *scripture*—the written mind, will, and voice of the Lord that leads us to salvation (see D&C 68:4). Of all recorded text, scriptures contain the most Truth and the most power. They are like a modern-day Liahona, revealing anew God's voice each time we pick them up. Scriptures are your own personal Urim and Thummim. If you peer into them with strong enough faith, they will show you God, open His mysteries, and launch you into personal revelations about heaven.[1]

Although scriptures carry such power, paradoxically, to extract the maximum from their revelatory potency we need to acknowledge

REVELATORY DEVICES TO CONNECT TO GOD'S WORDS

Scriptures

Urim and Thummim

Liahona

their weakness. Scripture isn't perfect. It can contain errors and omissions. It can be biased by culture and tainted by time. Like a romantic filled with indescribable love, scripture is sometimes constrained by human language—limited expressions seeking the right words to communicate the ineffable. The written word of God, like mankind in general, must be viewed as a weak vessel before it can be made strong by Jesus's grace (see Ether 12:27). Although we must "study" scripture (D&C 11:22), "search" it (Alma 33:2), and "liken" it (1 Nephi 19:23), one of the most essential skills for seekers to learn is how to properly *view* it and then *interpret* it. When something is seen correctly, it can be more powerfully understood, studied, searched, and applied. The goal of this chapter is to first help seekers properly view scripture and then to provide a four-step approach to interpreting the word of God so its full spiritual power to reveal Truth can be more fully unlocked in our lives.

The Weakness of Language

"All scripture is given by inspiration of God, and is profitable for doctrine, for reproof, for correction, for instruction in righteousness," Paul reminded Timothy, so "that man may be perfect" (2 Timothy 3:16–17). Although scripture can lead us to be perfect, the language of scripture can be far from it. Language strives but cannot always give adequate expression to human experience, feeling, and ideas. Anyone who speaks two languages knows that dialects are inherently limiting, as there are some phrases in one language that communicate certain ideas better than in another. From my mission I learned the Spanish word *sobremesa*. In eight letters and one word, it communicates the intimate experience of a discussion over the dinner table after the meal is eaten when you sit back and talk for a while. See? It took me two dozen words to summarize what is understood in one Spanish word, of which there is no English equivalent. All languages have their robust expressions to communicate ideas, and their feeble ones.

If languages sometimes struggle to express human experience, they struggle even more to express the divine. The first time Joseph Smith wrote about the First Vision, he said he saw a "a piller of ~~fire~~ light."[2] He couldn't find the right word to describe what he experienced (fire, or light?) and would spend the rest of his life seeking appropriate words to express the heavenly. In a November 1832 letter to his friend W. W. Phelps, Joseph concluded with a prayer for the time when the two of them should "gaze upon eternal wisdom engraven upon the heavens" and then prayed, "Oh Lord God deliver us in thy due time from the little narrow prison almost as it were totel darkness of paper pen and ink and a crooked broken scattered and imperfect language."[3] Perhaps that is why the Prophet developed a fascination with the Adamic language, which he called a "pure" language, in which ideas can be perfectly communicated.[4] Joseph wanted Adam's language because he felt confined by his own.

Thus, when the Prophet Joseph recorded revelations, he wasn't writing God's language, but the English words that tried to express what God had given him. As scholar Steven Harper taught, "Records of such revelations are not the revelations themselves; they are but representations captured in our language so that we might come to understand them if we consider the words carefully and solemnly, in light of experience and the Holy Spirit. We make no claim that any scripture is inerrant or infallible."[5] *Records of such revelations are not the revelations themselves.* That is a key concept to grasp about viewing and interpreting scripture. "The revelations were not God's diction, dialect, or native language," historian Richard Bushman has written. "They were couched in language suitable to Joseph's [understanding]."[6] Even God acknowledged that the written revelations that came to Joseph were not in perfect, final form. In the preface to the Doctrine and Covenants the Lord reminds the reader, "These commandments [i.e., revelations] . . . were given unto my servants in their weakness, after the manner of their language, that they might come to understanding" (D&C 1:24).

Joseph Smith and his associates therefore considered the language that expressed God's revelations as malleable, changeable, and editable. They weren't written with an iron pen. For example, D&C 20:40 originally said that priesthood holders are "to administer the flesh and blood of Christ"[7] according to the scriptures. It was later amended in the 1835 edition of the Doctrine and Covenants to read that they are "to administer bread and wine—the emblems of the flesh and blood of Christ,"[8] which is how it stands today. Why the change? Perhaps to clarify the intent of the revelation and avoid misinterpretation of the original statement, such as suggesting an unintended doctrine of transubstantiation.

If you go to the Joseph Smith Papers website and look at the earliest written version of the revelations, as Chapter 3 taught you how to do, you will see numerous ~~strikethroughs~~, ∧ insertions, and amendments. Much of the text is unchanged, but the point is that there *are* changes. Our dialect is not God's—the words used in scripture are but mortal expressions trying to convey heavenly concepts clearly, which is not always possible or perfect in limited human language, with or without words like *sobremesa*.

The Weakness of the Bible and Book of Mormon

To the chagrin of many Christians who believe in the infallibility of the Bible, members of the restored Church often point out biblical errors and problems. We recite our article of faith that the Bible is the word of God "as far as it translated correctly" (Articles of Faith 1:8). In the Book of Mormon, we learn that there have been "many plain and precious things taken away from the [Bible]" causing people to "stumble" over the gospel (1 Nephi 13:28–29). We know, for example, that God doesn't harden people's hearts, as Exodus 10:20 says. The Lord won't cause evil in cities, as Amos 3:6 declares. We don't leave the principles of the doctrine of Christ to be perfected, as Hebrews 6:1 suggests. The Bible has personal opinions, such as

Paul's counsel in 1 Corinthians 7:14 about whom to marry (cross-reference with D&C 74:5) and cultural constructions, such as women having long hair and men having short hair (see 1 Corinthians 11:14–15). While yet believing in the Bible's divinity, we recognize it has its deficiencies.

Lest we get high-minded and heavy-handed toward the Bible's imperfections, we must remember that *all* scripture has limitations. When we say the Bible has issues, the conservative Christian shouts back, "Blasphemy!" When we say the Book of Mormon also has shortcomings, the conservative Latter-day Saint shouts back with equal vigor, "Heresy!" The very title page of the Book of Mormon, however, undercuts its infallibility premise, forewarning, "If there are faults they are the mistakes of men; wherefore, condemn not the things of God." When Joseph Smith said that the Book of Mormon was the "most correct" book[9] of any on earth, he wasn't talking syntax, grammar, adverbs, or expression. By "most correct" he likely meant that its precepts articulate the gospel of Jesus Christ in clarity and lead a reader to "get nearer to God," not that there weren't some limitations to the expressed content. While largely the same as its original, the Book of Mormon text has nevertheless had hundreds of words amended and thousands of grammatical changes made over the years of its subsequent printings.[10]

We must also recognize that Book of Mormon authors, while prophets, were human. They, like biblical writers, were affected by culture, opinion (see Alma 40:20 for that very word), perspective (a male-centric view of things), and memory. The principal writers of the Book of Mormon made conscious decisions (and likely subconscious ones) about what to include and not include in their record.

Grant Hardy, author of *Understanding the Book of Mormon*, has written insightfully on the construction of the Book of Mormon. He says: "[Book of Mormon authors like Nephi, Mormon, and Moroni] reveal their identities from the beginning and exercise strict control over their material. They write from limited, human perspectives—that is, they give us their personal view of what happened and why it is important (though for those within the faith, the prophetic authority of these men makes them uniquely qualified to render such judgments). They do not hesitate to address readers directly to explain their intentions, their writing processes, their editorial decisions, and their emotional responses to the events they recount. . . . They even admit the possibility of human error."[11]

Translating Scripture

At this point, you may be wondering why I've spent the previous pages pointing out some of the weakness of scripture. It is not to undermine faith in the written word of God. Just the opposite. It is to get us *into* the word of God so we can connect to the power it contains. If we don't understand that scripture can be limited by language, influenced by perspective, inserted with opinion, and constructed through human weakness, we will not understand the need to *translate* scripture by the power and inspiration of the Spirit.

When you read the word *translate*, you may have in mind the process of rendering from one language to another—from Greek to French, or English to Spanish. When I say *translate*, however, I have something else in mind. To understand, read the following text message, sent at 7:41 p.m.:

> Hey! what are you doing right now?

This text message may seem straightforward enough. Yet it isn't. It needs to be *translated*. If this is from a young man who is interesting in dating a girl, "Hey, what are you doing right now?" at 7:41 p.m. means, "Hey, if you are up for it I would like to go somewhere with you." If the girl is interested (and translates the text correctly), she will likely message back something like, "Nothing! Why?" Likely she actually is in the middle of something, but interpreting the message correctly, she wants to convey that she is interested in spending time with him and will drop whatever she is doing. "Nothing" says something. You must be able to *translate intent*. Yes, even English to English.

We do the same with scripture. Look at the following verse from Jesus's bread of life sermon and ask yourself what it means:

"Whoso eateth my flesh, and drinketh my blood, hath eternal life" (John 6:54).

Notice how quickly you interpreted the intended meaning of that verse. If I asked what Jesus meant, you probably would say something about the need to take the sacrament. Is that what it says? No, it doesn't directly say a word about the sacrament. That is what it *implies*. It is likely that you immediately grasped that message, perhaps unconsciously. You *translated*. Look at the following sentence to see how different meanings can be inferred from it:

"I never said she stole my money."

It is written in English, but just what does it mean? It has many possible interpretations depending on the emphasis you give different words, as shown in *italics* below:

"*I* never said she stole my money" suggests that I never said it, but someone else did.

"I *never* said she stole my money" suggests that I never said that at all.

"I never *said* she stole my money" suggests that I implied it even if I didn't directly say it.

"I never said *she* stole my money" suggests that I didn't say this girl stole it, but some other girl did.

"I never said she *stole* my money" suggests that I never said she stole my money, but maybe she borrowed it.

"I never said she stole *my* money" suggests that she stole someone else's money, not mine.

"I never said she stole my *money*" suggests that she stole something else, but not my money.

As illustrated above, emphasis changes meaning—sometimes a lot. The same is true in translating scripture. The following is Alma's summary of why the children of Israel, when bitten by poisonous serpents in the wilderness, would not look to Moses holding the brazen serpent on a pole to be healed:

"Now the reason they would not look is because they did not believe it would heal them" (Alma 33:20).

The emphasis changes the doctrinal meaning. If you say, "Now the reason they would not look is because they did not *believe* it would heal them," that is a FAITH issue (they didn't believe it or trust it). If you emphasize it this way: "Now the reason they would not look is because they did not believe it would heal *them*," it now becomes a HOPE issue (they believed it would work for others, but not for them personally). Which reading is right? I can't say. The language is limited. It is up to correct interpretation by the illumination of the Spirit.

When Joseph Smith "translated" the Bible from the summer of 1830 to the summer of 1833, this is what he was doing. There is no historical documentation that supports that Joseph Smith sat down with a Greek or Latin or Hebrew Bible at that time and tried to retrofit the Bible back to its original form. It was an English-to-English revelatory translation. The 1828 Webster's dictionary defines *translation* as "the act of turning into another language," but also "interpretation."[12]

Joseph Smith's Translation of the Bible restored lost doctrines, clarified existing passages, corrected errors, and added information to clarify the intent and meaning of the text. It was a revelatory experience to tap into the voice and mind of the original writer and the text's possible interpretation and application for seekers in our day.[13] Thus, although Joseph technically finished the Bible translation (calling it "finished"[14] in the summer of 1833), if we understand what is meant by *translation*, he could never finish translating the Bible. The Joseph Smith Translation, though extensive, was not exhaustive. Because Joseph Smith's biblical translation implies a revelatory interpretation, it is possible that additional changes would have been made by Joseph Smith if he had lived longer and new needs arose for Joseph to render plainer translations for the Saints (see D&C 128:18). Brigham Young once said Joseph Smith could translate the Bible 40,000 different ways.[15] Forty thousand JSTs? Yes—and that's where you and I enter in.

Personally Interpreting Scripture

The Joseph Smith Translation of the Bible displays a pattern to follow for personal scriptural study interpretation. Once we begin to understand that scripture is from God but limited by mortal constraints, we begin to see the necessity of reaching to heaven to receive grace to understand its potential truths and express them clearly. We see the task of scripture study in fresh light: our job is to get in tune with the same Spirit that revealed the concept, properly interpret the concept in the language and conditions in which it was written, and then by inspiration render the verse in a way we understand. The following graphic shows this process:

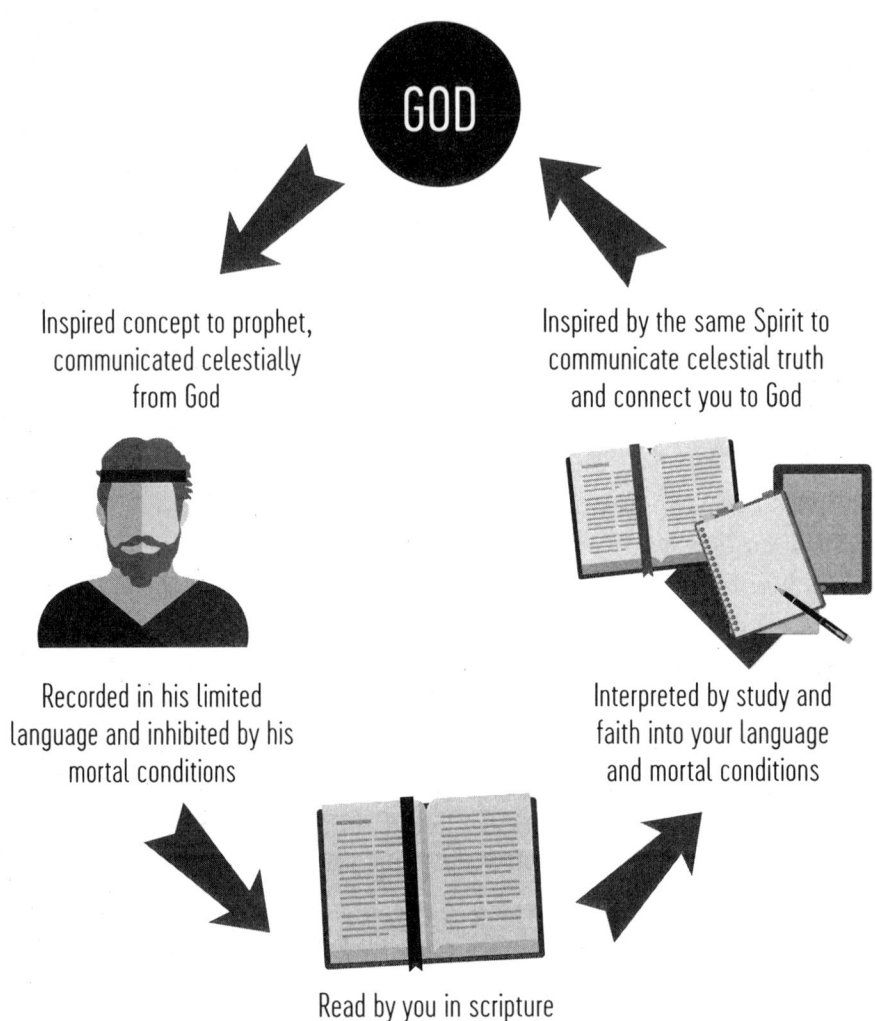

Using Joseph Smith's Bible translation as a model, scholar Adam Miller wrote insightfully on this process of translating or interpreting scripture ourselves: "Joseph produced, as God required, the first public translations of the scriptures we now share. But that work, open-ended all along, is unfinished. Now, the task is ours. When you read the scriptures, don't just lay your eyes like stones on the pages. Roll up your sleeves and translate them again. . . . With a prayer in hand, finish what Joseph started. . . . You and I must translate these books again. Word by word, line by line, verse by verse, chapter by chapter, God wants the whole thing translated once more, and this time he wants it translated into your native tongue, inflected by your native concerns, and written in your native flesh. To be a Mormon is to do once more, on your own small scale, the same kind of work that Joseph did."[16]

Some may read that statement and hesitate, saying that translating scripture is for prophets, not regular people (see 2 Peter 1:20). Don't shy away from your opportunities or your capabilities to let God give you words. Scriptures are lying there at your feet, like a Liahona, waiting for you to pick them up and decipher through faith the words written therein.

Four Keys to Interpreting Scripture

To personally interpret scripture, I suggest a four-step process:

This process flows naturally as we seek God's grace to translate scriptural text in its weakness and in ours: we read the text with care; as we read, we try to listen to the Holy Ghost's whisperings to reveal truth through the words; we then re-write the text in our own language and understanding by inspiration; then we check our interpretation with other sources to help substantiate our rendering of scriptural truths.

PERSONALLY INTERPRETING SCRIPTURE

 1. Read *mindfully*

 2. Listen *reverently*

 3. Restate *personally*

 4. Substantiate *externally*

Read mindfully

Reading the text is somewhat self-evident if we are to interpret or translate it. The key here is to *mindfully read*, however, or to read with concentrated focus, seeking understanding. Digital technology has created an increase in those who don't read the printed copies of scripture—they either listen to audio versions of them or view them digitally on a screen. While it's in vogue to embrace all things tech, and digital text has its advantages (mainly accessibility, portability, searchability, and linkability), research suggests that reading from printed pages is superior in many ways to digital reading, such as increased comprehension,[17] concentration,[18] and time spent in the text.[19] This isn't a comprehensive review of the literature, but I'm trying to make a point: don't just do what is convenient or in vogue; do what allows you to *mindfully read* the words.

Read when you can be relatively uninterrupted by others. Read where it's quiet. Don't try to multitask, a word that in reality means "not paying full attention to anything." For mindful study, read the text more slowly, as Elder Jeffrey R. Holland has pled.[20] To slow down, perhaps read for a set amount of *time* rather than trying to check off a certain number of chapters.[21] Pay closer attention to what is written and how it is expressed—stopping to ask questions and consider implications of words, phrases, and sentences. Reading mindfully also means you pay attention to seemingly insignificant things like punctuation. YES, seemingly, insi-gnificant things like; *punc*tuation. See how that reads? (Or was that: See! How that reads!) Most scriptural punctuation has been added over time. Who is to say that the commas, hyphens, or semicolons are in the right place, or should be there at all? They may change how words and phrases are expressed (!)(.)(?) Seekers who want to *interpret* scripture must read "in concentrated study," as President Howard W. Hunter once said, not just with convenience or for "mere casual reading."[22]

Listen reverently

As we read mindfully we simultaneously seek to listen to the Spirit. This is key because "holy men of God" who wrote scripture "spake as they were moved by the Holy Ghost" (2 Peter 1:20). While scriptural text can be limited due to the constraints of language, interpretation of scriptural text can come directly from the Spirit to our spirit despite confusing sentence structure or archaic grammatical expressions. Thus, to properly interpret scripture, we must get to its spiritual essence. And the only way to do that is to get in tune and hear the voice of the same Spirit that revealed the scriptural concepts in the first place. "The things of God knoweth no man, but the Spirit of God," said Paul directly (1 Corinthians 2:11). Or as educator Joseph Fielding McConkie once wrote, "It takes the spirit of revelation to understand revelation."[23] Like Nephi, to those who mindfully read and diligently seek, "the mysteries of God shall be unfolded unto them, *by the power of the Holy Ghost*" (1 Nephi 10:19; emphasis added). Without the Spirit, "[w]e do err, not knowing the scriptures" (Matthew 22:29), as Jesus accused the Sadducees.

With the "Spirit of Truth" we will "understand" and be "edified" as we read the words of truth (D&C 50:21–22). As you read the holy scriptures carefully, pay attention to the flashes of insight, the ideas to your mind, the messages that press upon you. Begin your study with a prayer that the Holy Ghost will speak to your mind and heart and give you understanding. As you listen reverently, messages will come to you personally.

Restate personally

As you read the written word of God mindfully and listen reverently to the Spirit, the next step is to write down what you are understanding in your own words. This is perhaps the single greatest exercise I could encourage for seekers to deepen scripture study. I suggest two approaches: *summarize* and *paraphrase*.

Summarize. To summarize means to condense the content down to its essence. For example, you may read D&C 89, about the Word of Wisdom. I summarized that section this way:

God gave Joseph Smith a revelation for the benefit of all the Saints to help them avoid evil (vs. 1–4). He teaches us to avoid substances common in society such as tobacco and alcohol (vs. 5–9), to limit meat consumption (vs. 12–13), and to intake other substances such as fruits and grains wisely and gratefully (vs. 10–11, 14–17). He promises His Saints both physical and spiritual blessings for adhering to this disciplined consumption code (vs. 18–21).

This summary digested a revelation of 581 words to 76 words of its main ideas. Summarizing helps clarify understanding and discern patterns and purpose. It helps focus central ideas and express the core concepts of scriptural blocks. As educator Robert Marzano said, "At its core, comprehension is based on summarizing—restating content in a succinct manner that highlights the most crucial information."[24] Read the text carefully yourself, listen to the Spirit, and then summarize verses and scriptural chunks in your own groupings and expressions. Make personal summaries of verses in a notebook or the margins of the scriptures. There are several journaling editions of the scriptures available to help people study and learn from the scriptures in this way.

Paraphrase. Paraphrasing is a powerful way to translate or interpret scriptural text to enhance your study. Paraphrasing is restating the text in your own words without losing essential ideas or details. You aren't condensing; you are rephrasing. Let me illustrate with a scriptural example from John 8:12:

"Then spake Jesus again unto them, saying, I am the light of the world: he that followeth me shall not walk in darkness, but shall have the light of life."

What is the text saying? How could you rephrase it in your own words and retain its essence and details? Here is how I did it in my scripture study journal:

"Then Jesus said: I am the source of truth in the world. Whoever does what I say won't walk around confused about what is right or wrong, or what they should or shouldn't do. But they will have the truth to guide them into joy and eternal life."

Isn't that fun? It was fun for me to do that rendering. It caused me to engage with the text, compare words, look at punctuation, consider synonyms and verbs, ponder on intent, and examine cross-references (for example: what did Jesus mean by "light" in this verse? I interpreted it as "truth," as D&C 93:28–29 uses *light* and *truth* as synonyms).

Paraphrasing is something people of all ages can and should do. Recently our family scripture study had been lacking. It had become rote and somewhat boring—a checklist. Neither my teenagers nor my little kids were thinking and engaging with the text. Thus, my wife and I decided to get journals and have our children render scripture in their own language. We take a set block (usually of ten to fifteen verses) and we each summarize the scripture block or paraphrase one or two verses. We all read the verses silently on our own (my wife and I help our younger kids grasp the harder English words). Then everyone writes for a few minutes, and we share which verse or verses we picked and how we expressed it. It has transformed our family scripture study overnight, as it has caused our children to personally engage with and try to decipher the message of the inspired text. Here's the original of John 2:19–21, and next to it, my eleven-year-old daughter's paraphrase:

ORIGINAL KING JAMES	VIVIAN SWEAT'S PARAPHRASE
"Jesus answered and said unto them, Destroy this temple, and in three days I will raise it up. Then said the Jews, Forty and six years was this temple in building, and wilt thou rear it up in three days? But he spake of the temple of his body."	"Jesus said, 'Destroy the temple and in three days I will put it back up.' And they said, 'It took them 46 years and Jesus is going to do it in three days?' But he meant his resurrection."

Here's my sixteen-year-old daughter's paraphrase of John 3:36:

ORIGINAL KING JAMES	JANE SWEAT'S PARAPHRASE
"He that believeth on the Son hath everlasting life: and he that believeth not the Son shall not see life; but the wrath of God abideth on him."	"He that has a testimony of Christ will have eternal life; and he that doesn't have a testimony will not see eternal life, but see God's anger."

And one more, from my seven-year-old, of John 4:48:

ORIGINAL KING JAMES	CALVIN SWEAT'S PARAPHRASE
"Then said Jesus unto him, Except ye see signs and wonders, ye will not believe."	"If you won't see things you won't believe."

I share these to merely illustrate that translating scripture does not require special circumstances or advanced degrees, just a willingness to engage personally with the text and something to write with.

 ## Seekers wanted!

To practice, consider how you would interpret one of the following three passages. Take a minute and read the verse in context, listen to the Spirit's insights, and then paraphrase them into your own language and understanding:

ORIGINAL SCRIPTURE	YOUR PARAPHRASE
Matthew 16:19 "And I will give unto thee the keys of the kingdom of heaven: and whatsoever thou shalt bind on earth shall be bound in heaven: and whatsoever thou shalt loose on earth shall be loosed in heaven."	
Mosiah 4:27 "And see that all these things are done in wisdom and order; for it is not requisite that a man should run faster than he has strength. And again, it is expedient that he should be diligent, that thereby he might win the prize; therefore, all things must be done in order."	
D&C 88:68 "Therefore, sanctify yourselves that your minds become single to God, and the days will come that you shall see him; for he will unveil his face unto you, and it shall be in his own time, and in his own way, and according to his own will."	

Here are some general summary tips for effective scriptural paraphrasing:

USE YOUR OWN WORDS AND PHRASES

- Find synonyms to replace key words.
- Reorder the text sequence in ways that make sense to you.
- Write in the tense of the text, including first person (don't retreat into third person).
- Bring all your prior knowledge and insights to bear on the text.
- Read between the lines for tone, omissions, and veiled meaning and express it explicitly.

You may hesitate to personally paraphrase because of the sacredness of the text and your own perceived weakness. Don't. Remember, records of revelations are not the revelations themselves. They are human expressions of heavenly concepts in mortal language. Don't worry if you aren't "good" at it. The translation process will teach and connect you to heaven through re-rendering the text—that is what's good. On the other hand, don't err on the other side of thinking that your translation is the *only way* to render a verse. Don't assume your interpretation is so correct that everyone should hear and agree with it (and that those who don't are ignorant or apostate, or both). Lest any be deluded, when we paraphrase scripture into our own words to help us understand, we are not declaring our paraphrase to be a standard for any others. Only the prophets have authority to create and interpret scripture for the Church. As President Dallin H. Oaks once taught, there are two types of scriptural interpretation, "public and private." "An open canon," he taught, "includes private revelations to individual seekers of the meaning of existing scriptures," but "public revelations on the meaning of [canonized] scriptures come through those we sustain as prophets, seers, and revelators."[25] (See Chapter 2, "Evaluating Church Doctrine," and Chapter 6, "Receiving the Spirit," for some checks and balances.)

A major question you may ask as you experiment with both written summary and paraphrase is whether your scriptural ideas are on point. Biblical professor Daniel Wallace said that "each Christian has the right to his own interpretation" of scripture but that each also "has the responsibility to get it right."[26] To try to get our translations in harmony with truth, we should substantiate our scriptural renderings with other external sources.

Substantiate externally

To substantiate externally means to check our scriptural paraphrases and translations against other authoritative sources dealing with the same content. I suggest the following four:

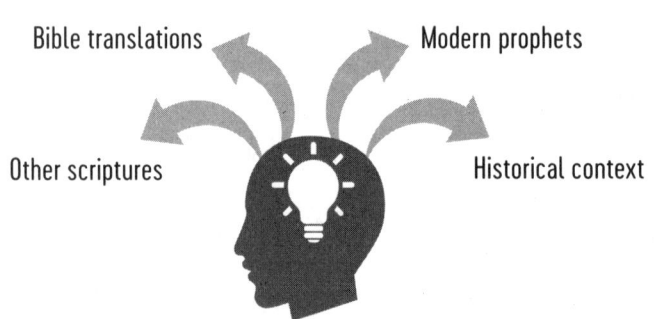

Other scriptures. One of the best ways to render a verse is to see what other scriptures say about the verse. "Let scripture interpret scripture," Elder B. H. Roberts once said.[27] Many Old Testament teachings are interpreted in the New Testament, Book of Mormon, and Doctrine and Covenants. Read how Jesus renders Old Testament passages in the New Testament. Listen to how Nephi interprets Isaiah in the Book of Mormon or how Joseph Smith does in the Doctrine and Covenants. Numerous New Testament teachings and parables are given modern interpretation in the Doctrine and

Covenants, such as the parable of the wheat and tares (see D&C 86) or the ten virgins (see D&C 45:56–57). Look for what scriptural scholars call "intertextuality," the similar usage of phrases from one author incorporated by another. The Book of Mormon is loaded with biblical intertextuality;[28] the Doctrine and Covenants also.[29] The more you study scripture carefully, the more you will begin to recognize expressions being repeated by scriptural writers. Intertextuality can shed new light on interpretations of the scriptural phrase and uncover potential meaning.

Other biblical translations. As Latter-day Saints, we need to collectively warm up to other translations of the Bible. If you don't believe me, just ask if you felt your King James fists fly up when reading that previous sentence. The KJV is currently the English standard for the restored Church, perhaps because it is the intertextual language of Restoration scripture. That said, much is to be gained from reading other faithful Bible translations. Brigham Young once suggested that if someone "understood Greek and Hebrew," that person was "under obligation" to render a better translation of the Bible if he or she saw shortcomings in the KJV.[30] At times, King James expressions can be awkward, generally when its translators chose not to use Tyndale's original phraseology. For example, look at Matthew 6:34, about why Jesus said we should take no thought of tomorrow:

KING JAMES	TYNDALE
"Sufficient unto the day is the evil thereof."	"The day present hath ever enough of his own trouble."

To me, Tyndale's translation offers more clarity than the King James Version.

Aside from King James, the two other most popular English Bibles are the New International Version (NIV) and the New Revised Standard Version (NRSV). There are many others, each with its strengths and weaknesses. See, for example, Matthew 6:16–17 rendered in some of these popular Bibles, and note the insight gained from looking at multiple translations:

KING JAMES	NIV	NRSV	NLT
"Moreover when ye fast, be not, as the hypocrites, of a sad countenance: for they disfigure their faces, that they may appear unto men to fast. Verily I say unto you, They have their reward."	"When you fast, do not look somber as the hypocrites do, for they disfigure their faces to show others they are fasting. Truly I tell you, they have received their reward in full."	"And whenever you fast, do not look dismal, like the hypocrites, for they disfigure their faces so as to show others that they are fasting. Truly I tell you, they have received their reward."	"And when you fast, don't make it obvious, as the hypocrites do, for they try to look miserable and disheveled so people will admire them for their fasting. I tell you the truth, that is the only reward they will ever get."

Of course, of all Bible translations to consult as you render biblical verses, the Joseph Smith Translation of the Bible, or the "New Translation," as it is also called, should be Latter-day Saints' top choice. It was done by commandment of the Lord under prophetic authority. As Joseph Smith Translation scholar Robert J. Matthews once said, "Reading the JST is like having Joseph Smith for a study companion."[31]

Modern prophets. When you reword scripture to express your private understanding, check it against how prophets have publicly interpreted those same passages for the Church. Use scriptures.byu.edu, as was described in detail in Chapter 3, to see how prophets have used and referenced verses in general conference settings. For example, look how President Spencer W. Kimball once gave an interpretation of the word "hear" in D&C 29:17 in conference, saying: "The Lord teaches that he cannot forgive people in their sins; he can only save them from their abandoned sins. The Lord clearly says, 'My blood shall not cleanse them if they hear me not.' (D&C 29:17.) *Hear* in this instance means to accept and abide his teachings."[32] Or see how Elder David A. Bednar interprets the "windows of heaven" in Malachi 3:10.[33]

Prophets have not interpreted every verse of scripture and won't definitively declare what each word ultimately means. This is an unrealistic and futile expectation that misses the point of both revelatory scripture and living prophets. One reason is because scripture has multiple correct interpretations depending on context. Although there can be multiple truthful views of a text, prophetic commentary acts as a ballast to our personal scriptural interpretation, balancing where our understanding may be tipping into troubled doctrinal waters. Thus, as President Dallin H. Oaks taught, seekers should "make careful study of the scriptures and of the prophetic teachings concerning them and [then] prayerfully seek personal revelation to know their meaning for themselves."[34]

Historical context. Although scripture can and should be applied in multiple and modern contexts, it is crucial to study scripture in its original historical context and for its original intent. Context changes intended meaning. Using art to illustrate, nearly everyone is familiar with Michelangelo's fifteen-foot masterpiece statue of David. Originally the sculpture was commissioned to be placed among many other biblical heroes up high in a nook in the Cathedral of Florence, sending a message of David classed among the prophets. When the sculpture was finished, however, a committee decided to place the masterpiece statue in the Palazzo della Signoria at the entrance of the town hall in Florence, facing Rome. The statue now took on a *new* meaning, that of a political statement, sending an immediate message of liberty and independence by smaller Florence toward the Goliath of Rome. In 1873 the statue was moved to its current location, where museum-goers admire the beauty of the sculpture's symmetry, artistry, and proportions, but the political message it sent for four hundred years is lost on most.[35] Context changes meaning.

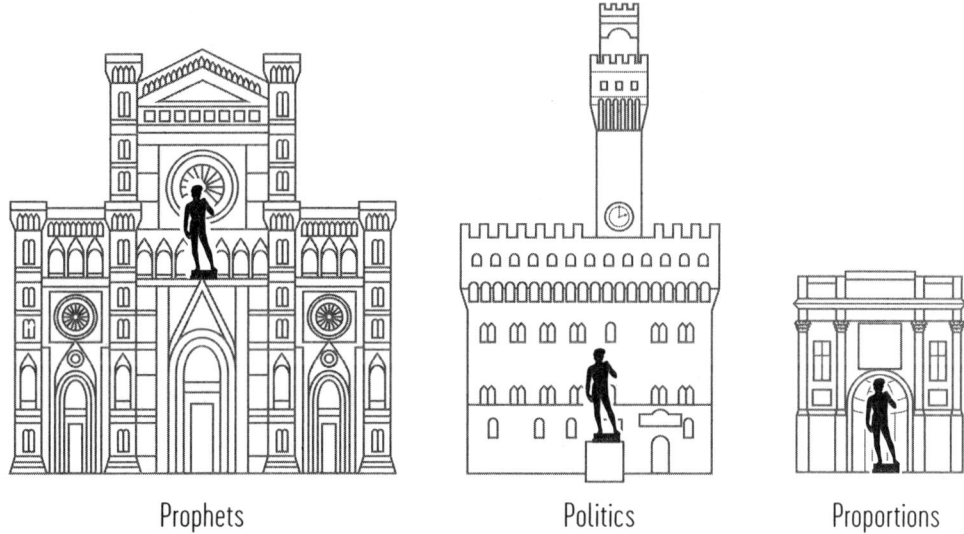

Context Changes Meaning

Prophets — Politics — Proportions

Similarly, if we don't understand the original setting, customs, cultures, issues, and idioms in scripture, we will miss out on correct context and intended inspiration. To better understand correct historical context and intent in both ancient and modern scripture, scholarly commentary can be extremely helpful. Scholars who have dedicated their professional lives to understanding scriptural text provide insights that generalists simply cannot. When we study using scholarly commentary, we can see with their eyes, hear with their ears, and think with their minds. Although not authoritatively binding or always correct, scholarly commentaries can fill in knowledge gaps to help you understand scriptural text. Certainly, Paul understood and interpreted scripture better because of his schooling "at the feet of Gamaliel," a master scholar on "the law of the fathers" (Acts 22:3). President M. Russell Ballard acknowledged the benefit he gains by seeking learning from those "with appropriate academic training, experience, and expertise."[36] To be clear, I do not intend to suggest that the *only* way to interpret scripture is how it was meant originally or contextually as supported by scholars. Scripture is dispensationally pliable and can intentionally shape-shift to fit modern applications. We can and should, however, read in context and learn from scholars to help us better externally substantiate our personal interpretation of scripture.

Conclusion: Seeking in Scripture

As the Lord instructed some early Saints about "that which is written" in scripture, you and I are to "pray always that [the Lord] may unfold the same to [our] understanding" (D&C

32:4). Written revelations are not the revelations themselves, but rather records captured in limiting human language. Although scriptures carry power, paradoxically, to extract the maximum from their revelatory potency, we need to acknowledge their inherent limitations. The purpose of scripture is not to be a perfect record of God's dialect or diction but to act as a personal Urim and Thummim—a launchpad for revelation to connect us to the same divine source that revealed the truths in the first place. To better understand scripture, we must be willing to *interpret* it anew into our understanding. To properly interpret scripture, we can read the text mindfully, listen reverently by the Spirit, restate the words personally, and then substantiate our interpretations externally. You will know when you are interpreting scripture when you find yourself being illuminated and filled with the Spirit of inspiration as you study (see D&C 50:22–24) and coming unto Christ to serve God (see Moroni 7:16–17). I conclude with a question from Brigham Young that summarizes many of the concepts in this chapter for scriptural seekers: "Do you read the scriptures, my brethren and sisters, as though you were writing them a thousand, two thousand, or five thousand years ago? Do you read them as though you stood in the place of the men who wrote them? If you do not feel thus, it is your privilege to do so, that you may be as familiar with the spirit and meaning of the written word of God as you are with your daily walk and conversation."[37]

 Hide or Go Seek

Hide

> I don't read scripture.
> I read scripture but don't really study it.
> I think scripture is inerrant and infallible.
> I don't think I should interpret scripture.
> I think my interpretations of scripture are the only correct ones.

Go Seek

> I view scripture as a launchpad for revelation.
> I view the language of scripture as imperfect and needing grace.
> I read scripture mindfully.
> I seek to listen to the Holy Ghost as I study.
> I restate and rewrite scripture in my own language and understanding.
> I substantiate my scriptural interpretations with other scriptures, alternate Bible translations, modern prophetic interpretations, and historical context and commentary from scholars.

Chapter 5

EMBRACING AMBIGUITY

🔍 **Seeking Sentence: Ambiguity can be one of the best friends of faith.**

Take a look at the following sentence:

"I saw a woman on a mountain with binoculars."

That sentence has at least four possible meanings:

There is a woman on a mountain, and I saw her through my binoculars.

There is a woman on a mountain, and she is holding binoculars.

I am on a mountain with binoculars, and I looked through them and saw a woman.

There is a mountain that has binoculars on it, and a woman is also there.

So, which is it? We don't know. It's *ambiguous*. Ambiguity means that something lacks clarity or has more than one possible interpretation.[1] In writing, it is good to avoid ambiguity. In religion, it's essential to embrace it.

At times we want to avoid doctrinal and historical ambiguity the way good writers avoid it in sentences. We want definitive answers. We want bold statements of "capital-T" Truth. This is the Restoration of all things, after all. This marvelous work began by a boy asking questions and having the heavens opened, and we should expect the same. We are the true Church, and the true Church has answers that others don't! A *Liahona* article talks about two Latter-day Saints who are trusted by friends because "Latter-day Saints will have answers."[2] While indeed we do have doctrinal answers that others don't, if we are not careful, we can unconsciously confuse the restored fullness of the gospel (the exalting covenants of Christ) with a fullness of knowledge. There's a difference.

Perhaps it isn't only a restoration culture that contributes to this idea that answers must be definitively known. After all, the Church and its leaders have repeatedly stressed that there are simply things we don't know or have answers to.[3] Perhaps our incessant desire for the definitive is a result of our internet generation, in which we can ask Alexa anything and Siri for solutions. Google has become our modern-day revelator and smartphones our telestial Urim and Thummim. We hold more knowledge at our fingertips than any previous generation. Modern technology can create false expectations that all answers exist and should be given when we merely ask. We forget that divine answers cannot come when "you have supposed that I would give it unto you, when you took no thought save it was to ask me" (D&C 9:7).

Or maybe it is our scientific, post-enlightenment society with its attitude that all things are possible and any knowledge attainable with enough grit and determination, work and study, research funding and statistical analyses. First-world culture has developed a zealous, almost religious "faith-in-science" attitude to the degree that many are dumbfounded when we hear that something is "unknown" in today's scientific age. Most diseases, however, still lack cures. Chronic pain is still a mystery. The largest feature on our own planet—the ocean—is barely known.[4]

Or, perhaps it is just that we, as humans, are acutely insecure beings, fearful of the unknown. Most of us are uncomfortable with uncertainty. We naturally desire to make sense of the world and cram complex concepts into bifurcated boxes: right/wrong, good/bad, easy/hard, nice/mean, pretty/ugly. Humans like to avoid things that are out of our control, or simply, out of control (read: the neighbor's dogs, earthquakes and tornados, and all teenagers). We use Google Maps for our next vacation route and print off the subway stops—checking them off as we go—to protect ourselves from walking down an unknown street or feeling lost. Combined with Church culture, modern technology, and faith in science, our human desire to "know the road" adds the fourth wheel to the vehicle taking us down "there's got to be an answer" avenue. Who knows all the reasons we inherently want answers and are often uncomfortable when there doesn't seem to be anything definitive? It's somewhat—how should I say it?—well, *ambiguous*.

Declarative Definitives

Some of this latter-day need for definitive answers may be the result of the last hundred years of Church doctrinal culture, when there have been strong, authoritative voices making declarative statements. Perhaps two who shaped Church teachings more than any others were President Joseph Fielding Smith and Elder Bruce R. McConkie. Assistant Church historian

Reid Neilson wrote that Joseph Fielding Smith's "direct and authoritative tone provided an interpretation of Mormon history and doctrine for a Church without a formal creed but in search of definitive answers to ambiguities in the restored gospel. . . . Smith ensured the vast stream of Mormon doctrine and practice flowed steadily toward conservatism."[5] If Joseph Fielding Smith moved Church doctrine toward conservatism, Bruce R. McConkie's brilliant and bold spirit pushed its teachings toward being declarative. His powerful, cut-and-dry, matter-of-fact, all-or-nothing, assertive tone resonated with generations of Saints. McConkie's *Mormon Doctrine* remains one of the best-selling Church books of all time, as ubiquitous in most Latter-day Saint households from the 1950s to the turn of the century as Del Parson's *Christ in Red Robe* painting hanging above a flowered-patterned sofa in church foyers.

An outgrowth from that time was a bent toward declarative answers. A related word for declarative is "dogmatic," or assertive and unyielding. Being dogmatic means that you are inclined to lay down claims as incontrovertibly true,[6] although there may be possible alternatives. In our open-minded modern cultural climate, being labeled as dogmatic is inherently pejorative. What one person negatively labels as closed-minded dogma, however, another person can laud as conviction, unwillingness to compromise standards, and loyalty to truth. Dogma is an easy accusation, but often those who hurl it as an epithet are equally dogmatic in their own views.

Dogmatism is primarily problematic when we are boldly declarative over things that are tenuous, such as the question of whether there is progression in the next life from kingdom to kingdom, as discussed in Chapter 2. That doctrine, it seems, is open for alternatives. Its possibilities are ambiguous. As seekers, we need to allow ourselves the opportunity to explore uncharted doctrinal spaces that haven't been accepted as the united prophetic voice or as definitive revelation. Being declarative on an ambiguous point closes off potential revelatory possibilities, can unnecessarily make believers feel unfaithful toward the Brethren, and can be pointlessly contentious and divisive, something that Jesus decried (see 3 Nephi 11:29).

Intolerance of Ambiguity

Elder Paul V. Johnson of the Seventy taught: "Many of us have a difficult time dealing with ambiguity, especially in issues concerning the Church. In fact, we may be drawn to use quotes in our teaching that are definitive because they seem to dispel the ambiguity. But some quotes are definitive on issues where there is no official answer. People who are more tentative on a subject that hasn't been revealed or resolved don't get quoted as much but may be more in line with where our current knowledge is."[7]

We tend to avoid ambiguity because it exposes insecurities. Like unstable ground underneath an uncertain hiker, spiritual ambiguities can cause us to desperately grab hold of weak conclusions—doctrinal or historical claims that have no roots and no ability to hold the weight of time and truth. Riveted to weak conclusions that will eventually uproot or snap, our ambiguous insecurities cause us to be tense and fearful, to cease moving forward, and to eventually stumble or fall. Like a desperate single man or woman desiring the security of marriage, our need for the declarative can cause us to bind ourselves to the first confident doctrinal suitor who comes our way, no matter how well (or ill) fit. Our inability to be comfortable with uncertainty causes us to lose the patience needed to wait and see if a better answer may exist—which it often does—or to be available when it inevitably presents itself by revelation.

Some psychologists study people's tendency for the definitive and their discomfort with ambiguity. Around 1950, a researcher named Else Frenkel-Brunswik coined the phrase "intolerance of ambiguity."[8] She claimed that "those who are intolerant of ambiguity are described as having a tendency to resort to black-and-white solutions, and characterized by rapid and overconfident judgment, often at the neglect of reality."[9] Other researchers soon followed, finding that those with low tolerance for ambiguity tend to solve problems without adequate information and were prone to authoritarian syndrome.[10] Later researchers sought to develop valid metrics to quantify and measure this phenomenon.[11] Participants were given a survey[12] to answer about themselves with True/False, such as, "A problem has little attraction for me if I don't think it has a solution," "There's a right way and a wrong way to do almost everything," "I would rather bet 1 to 6 on a long shot than 3 to 1 on a probable winner," or my favorite, "The best part of working a jigsaw puzzle is putting in that last piece."[13] Is that true for you? Or do you more value the process? It may depend on your tolerance for ambiguity.

Sometimes we struggle with the ambiguous because it is novel and we fear it, or because it is too complex and therefore we avoid it, or it has no potential solution so we ignore it, or it has conflicting interpretations so we grow frustrated with it.[14] Thus, some Saints are willing to swallow convenient doctrinal pills that allow us merely to sleep well at night. Revelation, however, often requires sleepless nights and jolts from ambiguous dreams (see Genesis 37). It asks for seekers to go forward, not clearly knowing what the Lord intends or plans (see 1 Nephi 4:6). Church members who just want to rest easy are not truth seekers; rather they are comfort seekers. True seekers understand that, of necessity, ambiguity and gray areas exist, and they embrace rather than fear the inherent uncertainties. The possibilities fascinate them rather than threatening the veneer of peace that the overly definitive creates. It is the very acknowledgement of uncertainties that causes true seekers to look at subtleties, new angles, and potential alternatives and to be open to new ideas, often leading to further light and truth. Embracing ambiguity, ironically, can eventually lead to clearer answers in the end than the comfortable, dogmatic declarative. *Ambiguity can be one of the best friends of faith.*

If we are to increase our faith and open doors of possibilities that can lead to clearer truth, we must embrace the unknowns. For example, embracing ambiguity means we acknowledge that we don't exactly know how Joseph Smith translated the book of Abraham. Was it by direct revelation, as John Whitmer recorded in 1835 or Warren Parrish did in 1838? Or did Joseph Smith receive the words by Urim and Thummim, as Wilford Woodruff and Lucy Mack Smith recorded?[15] Or, did the text come by a catalyzed revelation *about* Abraham, like John the Beloved's parchment manuscript in D&C 7? We don't know, and being open to multiple possibilities opens potentially new ways of understanding the revelatory text.

Embracing ambiguity means we are unsure about the exact relationship between freemasonry and the temple endowment. Is the temple endowment a *restoration* of ancient practices later apostatized by masonry, as many early Saints claimed?[16] Or is it an *adoption* of effective elements from the masonic rituals that Joseph Smith applied to teach what God had revealed to him over his prophetic career, as some scholars today suggest?[17] It could be either one, or neither one, or a little of both. Exploring these alternate ideas is both exciting and potentially illuminating.

Embracing ambiguity means it is unclear why Brigham Young restricted black African members of the Church from the priesthood and the temple. Some want to claim with certainty that Brigham Young implemented the priesthood and temple restriction on black African Saints because he was bigoted and racist. Others want to defend him and state positively that the restriction came by divine revelation. The unsettling answer is that based on the historical record, neither position seems entirely defensible. To the perspective that Brigham was purely racist, how do we explain him acknowledging in 1847 that there were elders who were black, progressively calling the black elder Q. Walker Lewis "one of our best elders"[18] and saying that in the Church, "We don't care about color"?[19] To those who argue that the restriction was a revelation from God . . . where is the revelation? Even the Church's heading to Official Declaration #2 (ending the priesthood and temple restriction) says, "Church records offer no clear insights into the origins of this practice." It isn't even clear what year the ban began. Embracing ambiguity doesn't mean we avoid searching for answers to questions such as these and others. In contrast, we *do* search and study, but we humbly acknowledge there are some gray areas, some unknowns, some undecideds. Then, embracing some flexibility, we begin to seek more openly. The design company IDEO has a tagline they reinforce with their designers to get more comfortable with ambiguity: "I don't know yet."[20] That line displays humility, action, and confidence all in one.

ANSWER
I Don't Know Yet

back pocket

How to Embrace Ambiguity

What, then, are some specific skills and ways of thinking to help us be less overly declarative and better embrace ambiguity? I offer the following three suggestions: be "firm but flexible," "avoid over-claiming," and make "split decisions."

Be Firm but Flexible

Embracing ambiguity doesn't mean you are so open-minded that you allow your brain to fall out, as the colloquial saying goes. There are absolutes that the Church proclaims and God has revealed. The first step to embracing ambiguity, counterintuitively, is clarifying and declaring what is absolutely essential to a person's faith. Perhaps a better way to say it is to establish the "nonnegotiables" of the faith, to borrow a phrase from the evangelical scholar Dennis Okholm.[21] Nonnegotiables are the aspects of the faith that are essential, without which the faith cannot exist. They are the areas where we are firm, so that we can be flexible in others.

"Firm but flexible" seems to be a contradiction, but it isn't. A buoy is anchored down to a spot on the ground but can bob about on the surface as currents change and waves flow. Your ear is fixed to your head but is soft and pliable to accommodate your helmet or earrings. Your car seat is firmly bolted down to your vehicle to hold you in place in a speeding car, yet it can move up and down, forward and backward, and higher and lower. Firm but flexible exists everywhere and can exist spiritually for seekers as well.

Settling on non-negotiables grounds us securely in the core essentials but allows us to be flexible elsewhere on the edges. For example, the bodily Resurrection of Jesus Christ is a non-negotiable for me. It is central to Christianity and to Christ's claim as the divine Messiah. If the tangible, bodily Resurrection of the Savior didn't happen or isn't real, my faith lacks its foundations: "If Christ be not risen, then is our preaching vain, and your faith is also vain," said Paul (1 Corinthians 15:14). The Resurrection is *the* confirming witness of Jesus's divinity, the conquering of sin and death, our hope of eternal life and glory. I am firm and fixed in the bodily Resurrection of Jesus. But now, the flexible parts: *how* Jesus resurrected, the day of the week upon which He did so, whether His body looked the same or different after He rose, whether there were one or two angels at the tomb, or who saw Him risen first (was it Mary Magdalene alone, or multiple women together, as some of the other gospels imply?) are not foundational to me. I am flexible on all those points. They can change and alter, yet my faith is still firmly attached to Christ's divine Resurrection.

Similarly, the Book of Mormon being the word of God is a non-negotiable for me. That book is the witness to the Restoration, the "new covenant" (D&C 84:57), the evidence that indeed "God does inspire men and call them to his holy work in this age" (D&C 20:11). The

Savior Himself testified, "As your Lord and your God liveth," its translation "is true" (D&C 17:6), connecting the book's fundamental position to the Lord's own Resurrection. But where the events of the Book of Mormon took place, if the plates were gold or a metal that had the appearance of gold, who exactly the descendants of the Lamanites are, precisely how the record was translated, whether it contains historical anachronisms, or if Nephi was biased in his views, are pliable for me. Like a buoy in the ocean, I can roll with various waves as further information and understanding come.

Prophetic keys of authority are another non-negotiable for me as a believer in the Restoration. Without priesthood keys, we have no authority, and therefore no true ordinances; and without ordinances, we have no covenants, and without covenants, we have no powers of godliness (see D&C 84:20–22). It all unravels without priesthood keys from John the Baptist, Peter, James, John, Moses, Elias, Elijah, and others. But what exact role the experience in the chamber of Father Whitmer had in priesthood restoration is ambiguous (see D&C 128:20–21). I am okay with that. Can anyone find a source that tells us what priesthood "Raphael" restored to Joseph Smith, or who he is (D&C 128:21)? If the Prophet announced tomorrow or a new document were discovered that said that the angel Raphael restored the keys of healing, so be it. Awesome. If not, my faith goes on. It's negotiable. The ambiguity doesn't undermine my moving forward in the Restoration, fixed to the core concept of priesthood power.

A good way to settle on your non-negotiables is to ask the question, "What if a revelation or definitive information came that changed or got rid of _____? Would my faith still exist?" Paradoxically, this definitive question allows you the freedom to better accept ambiguity.

 ## Seekers wanted!

What are the non-negotiables of your faith? What are the areas where you are firmly set that are central to your beliefs about God, His plan of salvation, or the Restoration? Think about them deeply and write down at least five.

Why are these non-negotiable? Could they change, and your faith remain? If those are the fixed non-negotiables, where may you be freed up to be potentially more flexible in other areas of belief?

Avoid Over-claiming

In 1988, an influential educator named E. D. Hirsch Jr. wrote a book called *Cultural Literacy: What Every American Needs to Know.* The subtitle says it contains "5,000 Essential Names, Phrases, Dates, and Concepts" that every American student should be able to answer to function in a democratic society. You read that right: five thousand. To see how culturally literate you are, here are fifteen items from the Physical Sciences subsection that Hirsch says educated people should know. Take the following survey and rank on a scale of 0 to 6 how familiar you are with the following terms:

> Using the following scale as a guideline, write a number from 0 to 6 beside each item to indicate how familiar you are with it.
>
> | NEVER HEARD OF IT | | | | | | VERY FAMILIAR |
> |---|---|---|---|---|---|---|
> | 0 | 1 | 2 | 3 | 4 | 5 | 6 |
>
> **PHYSICAL SCIENCES**
>
> ____ Manhattan Project   ____ asteroid   ____ nuclear fusion
> ____ cholarine   ____ atomic number   ____ hydroponics
> ____ alloy   ____ plate tectonics   ____ photon
> ____ ultra-lipid   ____ centripetal force ____ plates of parrallax
> ____ nebula   ____ particle accelerator ____ satellite

How do you think you did? Probably not as well as you think, unfortunately. That is because this was a setup. The fifteen items upon which you were tested didn't test your cultural literacy. They tested your tendency to over-claim knowledge. Three of the items on the list are foils—they don't exist. Uh-oh.

Which are they?

Cholarine

Ultra-lipid

Plates of parallax

This survey, based on items from Hirsch's book, measures what researchers call "over-claiming." Over-claiming is when people claim knowledge that they don't have. Why would we do that? Well, frankly, because we want to appear literate. When I wrote that these were items that "educated people should know," something inside of you probably went, "Hey, I'm educated. I'm smart. Let me see: Manhattan Project? Oh, the nuclear bomb! I'll rate myself a 6. Cholarine? Probably a chemistry term, I think. I'll give it a 2." Our desire to be competent causes us to over-claim. Researchers have tied over-claiming results to a personality test measuring narcissism and found, "When trying to give a positive impression, participants showed a substantially higher rate of over-claiming" and "narcissists over-claimed more than did non-narcissists."[22] Our insecurities reveal our ineptitude.

Similarly, many of us in the Church are well educated in the gospel. We are capable and smart people professionally and spiritually. We have served missions, read the Book of Mormon multiple times, and studied the scriptures daily. We have decades of experience in the Church and serving in callings. We've been to seminary and Sunday School. We've read *Jesus the Christ* and browsed the Joseph Smith Papers. We've been endowed in the temple. How could we not know something about the Church? In our desire to appear competent regarding the faith, we can have a tendency to over-claim what we know.

President M. Russell Ballard cautioned: "A recent study revealed that 'the more people think they know about a topic, the more likely they are to allege understanding beyond what they know, even to the point of feigning knowledge of false facts and fabricated information.' Identified as 'over-claiming,' this temptation must be avoided by you [Church members]. It is perfectly all right to say, 'I do not know.' . . . The authors of the 'over-claiming' study noted that 'a tendency to over-claim, especially in self-perceived experts, may actually discourage individuals from educating themselves in precisely those areas in which they consider themselves knowledgeable."[23] Over-claiming our knowledge about Church history and doctrine can lead to serious problems, spreading false explanations that do people harm, particularly when the answer turns out to be unfounded. Likening a medical example, a woman suffering from an unexplainable illness was misdiagnosed with an old, sexist condition of "hysteria." Notice what she said, and connect it to unfounded over-claims we sometimes give in the Church: "Why has this idea [hysteria] had such staying power? . . . Fundamentally, doctors want to help. They want to know the answer. And this category allows doctors to treat what would otherwise be untreatable, to explain illnesses that have no explanation. The problem is that this can cause real harm."[24]

The Book of Mormon prophet Nephi displayed his ability to avoid over-claiming when the angel asked him if he understood the condescension of God. Nephi gave a beautiful answer, displaying his non-negotiables all the while avoiding over-claiming: "And I said unto him: I know that [God] loveth his children; nevertheless, I do not know the meaning of all things" (1 Nephi 11:17). Nephi's ability to avoid claiming knowledge that he didn't have allowed the Spirit of the Lord to open a vision of the Savior's future ministry to help him better grasp the unknown concept of divine condescension. Letting go of the tendency to over-claim helps us to embrace ambiguity and be receptive to new ideas, giving space for sprouting truth to grow.

Make a Split Decision

Another potential way to better embrace ambiguity is to divide what is and is not known about a certain subject. Rarely is something *completely* known, or, conversely, completely unknown. To consciously split the known from the unknown is helpful to create space for ambiguity and possibility. Read through the following four-step flow chart to see how this might be approached:

AMBIGUITY SPLIT DECISION TREE

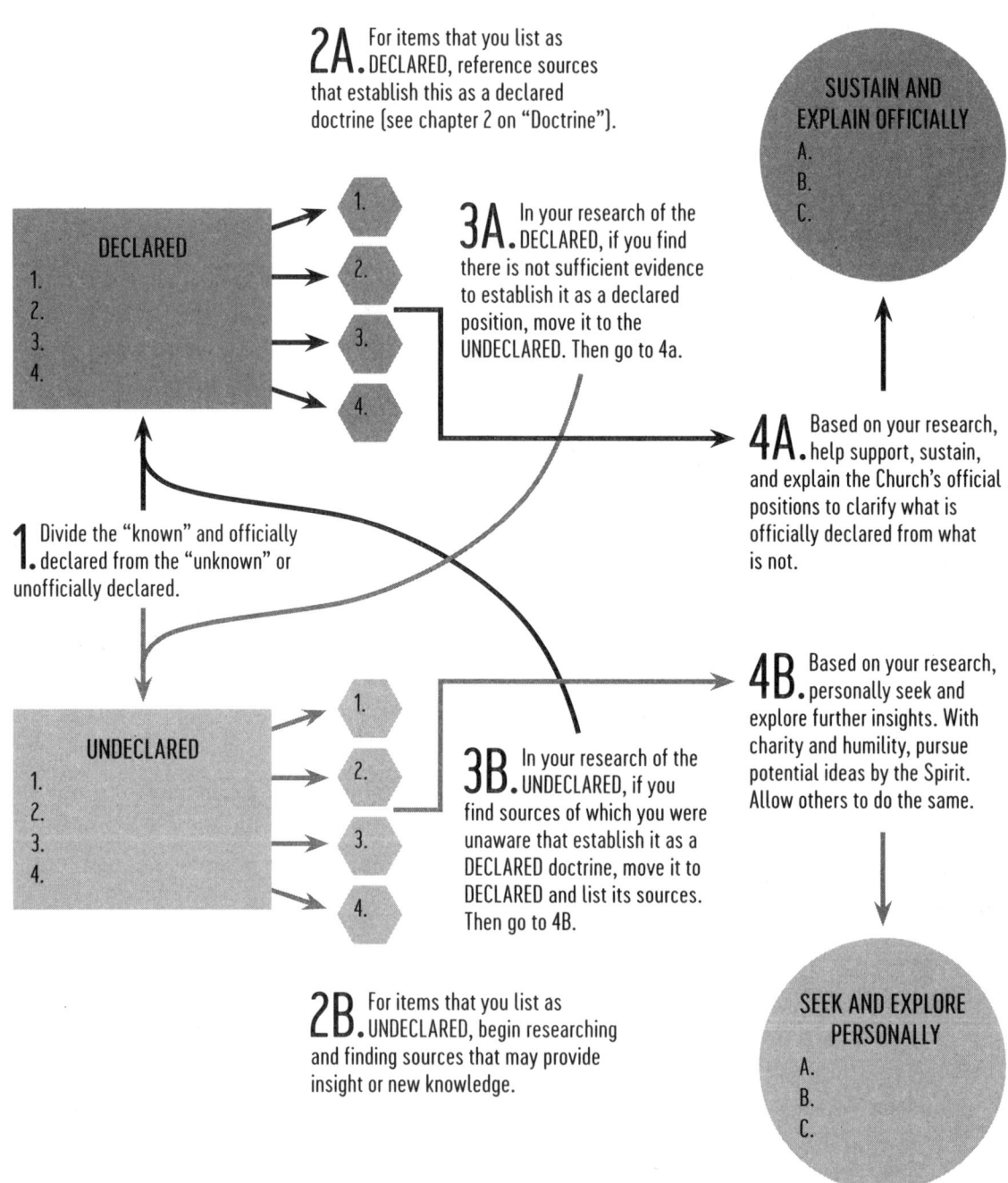

While admittedly formulaic and overtly explicit, this decision tree gives a visual mapping to an internal process—or something similar to it—that faithful seekers could follow. The intended goal is to help learners know what should be *sustained and explained* as part of the Church's teachings, and to give them freedom to *seek and explore* by the Spirit for further knowledge and potential ideas on what isn't clearly declared.

As an example, I've had people ask me about Joseph Smith's statement in the King Follett sermon where he taught that God the Father "was once a man like us—yea, that God himself, the Father of us all, dwelt on an earth, the same as Jesus Christ himself did."[25] This distinctive teaching has a lot of unanswered questions and opens a multitude of potential ideas. I first ask myself what is known and declared on the subject—and where it is declared? It is known/declared that God has a tangible body of flesh and bone (see D&C 130:22). There are united statements from the First Presidency that articulate God was once a man (see 1909 First Presidency statement, reprinted in a 2002 *Ensign*) as well as numerous cumulative statements from Church leaders over the years declaring God was once a man (about twenty times in general conference, although not since 1978). There is a Gospel Topics Essay, "Becoming Like God," that mentions the teaching, as well as it being included in various Church manuals, past and present.

What is undeclared or unknown on the subject? Nothing directly mentions God being a man in scripture; it is only implied or hinted—an inference we might make. In two interviews in 1997 (one with the *San Francisco Chronicle* and one with *TIME* magazine), President Gordon B. Hinckley suggested we didn't know much about the teaching. When he was asked by *TIME* magazine: "About that, God the Father was once a man as we were," President Hinckley stated, "I don't know that we teach it. I don't know that we emphasize it. I haven't heard it discussed for a long time in public discourse."[26] There are many unknowns related to God once being a man: Where did God live as a mortal? How did God live? How did He die? Was He a Savior of His people? Was He sinless? It's ambiguous.

Thus, I conclude that I should SUSTAIN/EXPLAIN:

1. The united voice of the First Presidency/Twelve, cumulative teaching from Church leaders, and Church publications have and continue to support the teaching that God was once a man.
2. The canonized scriptures teach that God has a body of flesh and bones.
3. There is not much that is understood about the nature and details of God's mortal life.

This then leaves me open to seek and explore unanswered questions or potential ideas related to this in my personal study, as most of the details surrounding this distinctive teaching are ambiguous and not clearly defined.

Conclusion: Ambiguity in Religious Life

Although I have shaped the narrative around this chapter toward knowledge-level ambiguity, it is also important for seekers to embrace similar ambiguity when it comes to the divine direction of one's life and purpose. Oh, how we wish God would lay out a specific twenty-point plan for our futures! Oh, that our patriarchal blessings were more like paint-by-numbers than general, spiritual compositional sketches. It seems, however, that often God intends for us to not know the next step. The destination is uncertain. For now, the exact outcome is unclear. Perhaps this is because we can't handle the entirety at once. Maybe we are unprepared and would shirk. Maybe He just wants us to learn to walk by faith, which seems most likely.

Brigham Young offered this great insight into the line-upon-line ambiguity of our lives by discussing Joseph Smith: "The Lord can't reveal to you and I that [which] we can't understand . . . for instance when Joseph first received revelation the Lord could not tell him what he was going to do. He didn't tell him he was going to call him to be a prophet, seer, revelator, high priest, and founder of [the] kingdom of God on earth. Joseph would have said . . . 'just what does that mean? You are talking that I can't understand.' He could merely reveal to him that the Lord was pleased to bless him and forgive his sins and there was a work for him to perform on the earth and that was about all he could reveal. The first time he sent [an] angel to visit him he could then lead his mind a little further. He could reveal to him there [were] certain records deposited in the earth to be brought forth for the benefit of [the] inhabitants of the earth. He could reveal after this that Joseph could get them; then he could reveal he should have power to translate the records from the language and characters in which it was written and give it to the people in the English language, but this was not taught him first. . . . He could then tell him he was to be called a prophet. . . . This is the way the Lord has to instruct all people upon the earth. I make mention of this to show you that . . . the Lord can't teach all things to people at once. He gives a little here [a] little there, revelation upon revelation, on revelation after revelation, a precept today, tomorrow another, next day another. If the people make good use of it and improve upon what the Lord gives them, then he is ready to bestow more."[27]

Elder Dieter F. Uchtdorf used the analogy of nineteenth-century pointillism paintings to illustrate this idea of bit-by-bit direction from God. "Sometimes our lives are like neo-impressionistic art. The dots of color that make up the moments and events of our days can appear unconnected and chaotic at first. We can't see any order to them. We can't imagine that they have a purpose at all." Then, he called for patience in the ambiguity of life: "You may not see how the dots connect now, and you don't need to yet." If we will daily strive to follow the Savior, Elder Uchtdorf promised we will one day look back to "see that the dots really did connect into a beautiful pattern, more sublime than you ever could have imagined. With unspeakable gratitude, you will see that God Himself, in His abounding love, grace, and compassion, was always there watching over you, blessing you, and guiding your steps as you walked toward Him."[28]

Embracing ambiguity requires humility and trust. It requires us to sacrifice the comforts of the assumed. Ambiguity puts down pride and questions over-claims, causing us to settle in on the fundamentals and truly non-negotiables of our faith. It allows us to let go of the false traditions we have assumed and ignorance we have espoused in our desire for certainty. Its discomfort may cause us to lose sleep and occasionally get lost and stumble, but it opens us to new ways of thinking and being, coming out on the other side clearer and more confident in truth. Embracing ambiguity carries us forward in faith, hope, and charity. It fosters an eye single to God's glory with temperance, patience, brotherly kindness, humility, and diligence (see D&C 4:5–6). Perhaps we should add embracing ambiguity to the list of these heavenly virtues?

 Hide or Go Seek

Hide

> I am uncomfortable with uncertainty.
> I latch on to overly definitive and declarative statements.
> I am dogmatic and unwilling to consider viable alternatives.

Go Seek

> I avoid over-claiming and instead say, "I don't know, yet."
> I have clearly identified the "non-negotiables" of my faith.
> I make "split decisions" on what to sustain and explain officially and where to seek and explore personally.
> I act in faith to let the Lord lead me step by step, even if the outcome is uncertain.

Chapter 6

DISCERNING TRUTH FROM ERROR

 Seeking Sentence: The essence of being deceived is being convinced you're not.

"Professor Sweat, can I talk to you as you walk back to your office?" a young man kindly asked as our class lecture wrapped to a close. Sure thing. What did he want to talk about?

"I think I married the wrong woman," he pointedly told me.

I decided at that moment we should take the long way around campus back to my office.

As we walked I asked him why, after being married only a year or so, he had come to that startling conclusion. Was his wife unfaithful? I asked. No, no, no, he answered, waving his hands. Was she verbally or emotionally abusive? She was sweet and kind. Has she lost her faith in God or left her covenants? She was a deeply active believer, was his reply. Is your relationship strained in some way then? They got along really well. Needless to say, I was perplexed.

"Why do you feel you married the wrong woman, then?" I asked. His answer stunned me.

"Because I still feel attraction toward another girl I dated, and I wonder if that is the Holy Ghost telling me that I should have married her instead of my wife. Why else would I still feel this way?"

I share this real-life situation at the front of this chapter because—although extreme—it illustrates a potential difficulty for seekers in their skill to discern truth from error by the Holy Spirit.

We are commanded in our baptismal confirmation to "receive the Holy Ghost." To better understand the skills related to receiving the Spirit in this chapter, I will first briefly go over our theology on that statement. Although this may be a review for some, it provides a clear foundation to better inform the latter part of the chapter, which seeks to clarify questions about avoiding deception while seeking to receive and listen to the Spirit.

Theology on the Holy Ghost

As a noncorporal member of the Godhead, the Holy Ghost and His influence can dwell within us (see D&C 130:22–23). The Spirit is like the wind: we cannot tell from whence

He comes nor where He goes, but we can see His divine effects upon a people's lives, causing them to be born again unto God (see John 3:3–8). The primary role of the Holy Ghost is to deliver the effects of the Atonement of Jesus Christ into our lives.[1] In fulfilling His role as the agent of Christ's Atonement, the Holy Ghost teaches, testifies, reveals, guides, enlightens, comforts, and sanctifies individuals in the truth. As the source of miracles, the Spirit may reveal Himself through visions, dreams, audible voices, or other miraculous phenomena (see Chapter 7, "Obtaining Spiritual Gifts"). Most often, however, the Holy Ghost reveals Himself through divine thoughts and feelings.

The Mind

The scriptures tell us that the Holy Ghost speaks to our mind and to our heart (see D&C 8:2–3). Spiritual influence through the Holy Ghost can come to a person's mind in multiple forms. One way that the Holy Ghost influences our minds is through providing enlightenment—or clarified understanding—of ideas and concepts related to truth. *Preach My Gospel* states that "the Holy Ghost will open your mind and heart to greater light and understanding" and instructs individuals seeking spiritual influence to "pay careful attention to ideas that come to your mind."[2] Mental influence through the Holy Ghost also comes by helping individuals remember important spiritual truths that have been previously learned: "But the Comforter, [which is] the Holy Ghost, whom the Father will send in my name, he shall teach you all things, and bring all things to your remembrance, whatsoever I have said unto you" (John 14:26). Spiritual influence to the mind can also come in the form of "instruction of [the] Spirit" (D&C 6:14). These instructions are messages akin to, "Go here," "Don't go there," "Say this," "Don't say that," "Do this," "Don't do that." Mental directives from the Holy Ghost are exemplified in Nephi being impelled or "constrained by the Spirit" to do something (1 Nephi 4:10) or Ether being "restrained because of the Spirit of the Lord" to not do something (Ether 12:2).

Additionally, the Holy Ghost can help us mentally discern between right and wrong, truth and error, and good and evil, thus helping us to judge righteously in moments of decision (see Moroni 7:16; D&C 11:12). To summarize, cognitive spiritual influence by the Holy Ghost can come in the form of enlightened thoughts and ideas, clarified understanding, remembrance of spiritual truths, directive action, and ability to discern clearly between truth and error.

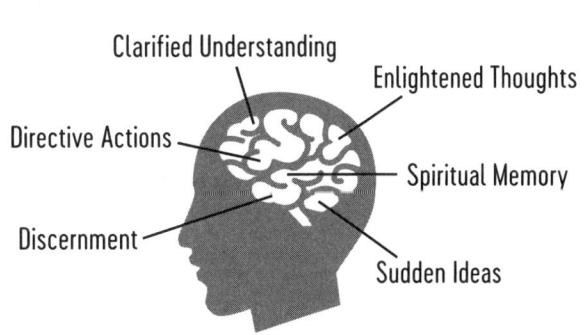

The Heart

Latter-day Saint theology also teaches that spiritual influence comes to the heart through a person's feelings. The Doctrine and Covenants describes some of these feelings by saying that the Holy Ghost "will cause that your bosom shall burn within you; therefore, you shall feel that it is right" (D&C 9:8). *True to the Faith* describes this feeling of a burning in the bosom as "a feeling of comfort and serenity."[3] In general, feelings that edify and uplift—such as hope, optimism, gratitude, and others—are usually associated with the spiritual influence of the Holy Ghost (see D&C 50:23). One of the repeated titles of the Holy Ghost in scripture is that of "the comforter,"[4] denoting the Holy Ghost's role in bringing peaceful, uplifting, comforting feelings to us. However, the Holy Ghost can also give feelings of warning or a "stupor of thought" (D&C 6:23). The affective component of the influence of the Holy Ghost also encompass such feelings as courage, boldness, and confidence (see 1 Nephi 10:22; Moroni 8:16; D&C 121:45–46) to act on divine direction or inspiration. Thus, to summarize, affective spiritual influence through the Holy Ghost can come to an individual through uplifting feelings such as love, hope, gratitude, joy, peace, confidence, courage, and comfort.

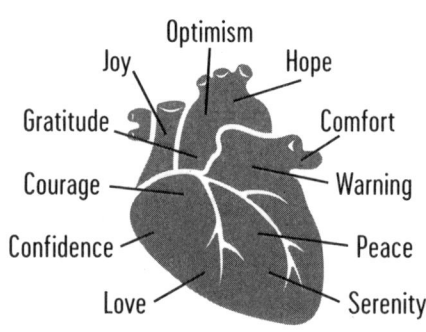

When we receive the Holy Ghost, He seems to work *jointly* upon our mind and heart. "I will tell you in your mind *and* in your heart, by the Holy Ghost" (D&C 8:2; emphasis added). Elder Richard G. Scott taught, "An impression to the heart, if followed, is fortified by a more specific instruction to the mind."[5] Notice the following key from Joseph Smith that provides insight: "I now resume the subject of the baptism for the dead, as that subject seems to occupy my mind, and press itself upon my feelings the strongest" (D&C 128:1). Joint thoughts and feelings that strongly and repeatedly impress us—ones we can't seem to shake or ignore—are often the Spirit working upon us.

The Fruits of the Holy Ghost

Divine thoughts and feelings from the Holy Ghost produce righteousness. Paul calls these the "fruits of the Spirit" in Galatians 5:22, and they include "love, joy, peace, longsuffering, gentleness, goodness, faith, meekness, temperance." These aren't mere emotional feelings; these are fruits, outcomes, or results, stamped and embedded upon our *character*. The thoughts and feelings from the Spirit are like celestial sun and water that produce the fruits of godliness, dispositions that "leadeth to do good—yea, to do justly, to walk humbly, to judge righteously" and which "fill your soul with joy" (D&C 11:12–13).

Thus, truth revealed from God through the Holy Ghost rests upon a tripod, connecting the intellect (mind), the affect (feelings), and the effect (righteous results).

This Tripod of Truth is an important concept to balance true revelatory influence from the Spirit. I once had a preacher from another faith tell me that our Latter-day Saint missionaries were deceptive because they told people to pray about the Book of Mormon and to pay attention to their feelings. "Feelings can be deceptive," he told me. I agreed, which seemed to surprise him. I then referenced Alma 32 about planting a seed. Indeed, a good seed from God causes positive feelings to "swell within your breasts" (the heart), but a true seed is also evident because it "enlighten[s] my understanding" (mind) and "beginneth to enlarge my soul" (fruits) (Alma 32:28). Uplifting feelings, yes, but supported also with inspired thoughts and righteous fruits are what should guide seekers of truth. The preacher seemed more satisfied with that answer because, indeed, sometimes feelings can be deceptive and thoughts can be confusing if we rely on either alone.

This is the point where I want to diverge from more typical Church discussions on the Holy Ghost. How exactly the Spirit works on your mind and heart is somewhat irrelevant and can actually be confusing for some. I've heard it said, "We all feel the Spirit differently." Not only is that generic statement not overly helpful, but it also places the emphasis on the *process* instead of the *product*. This can lead to problems. It's like focusing on how your taste buds work or your stomach digests food. The better question is, "Does it make me healthy?" We could mitigate some of our confusion about whether thoughts and feelings are or aren't from God by simply asking ourselves, "What does this *produce*?"

The Book of Mormon and Doctrine and Covenants both teach us the way to judge, focusing on the fruits: if something uplifts you by inviting and enticing you to love God and to serve Him and keep His commandments, it is from God (see Moroni 7:16–17; D&C 50:22–23), no matter how it comes. It may come from a teacher. It may come from a parent. It may come from a movie or a song or a piece of art or music. It may be a thought or a feeling. If it leads you to do good and love and serve God and keep His commandments, it's from God. It's that simple. Thus, as Elder David A. Bednar said regarding this question, "I think we overcomplicate this. I think we over analyze it. . . . If you have a thought to do something good, it's from the Holy Ghost. . . . Is that the Holy Ghost or is that you? What difference does that make? . . . If it invites and entices to do good, it comes from Christ, and we ought to do it."[6]

Spiritual Deception

Unfortunately, some in the modern Church do focus on the spiritual method instead of the outcome. Fixating on their thoughts and feelings, they assume that if they think or feel strongly about something, then that must be God guiding them by the Spirit. Balancing unsteadily on one leg of the Tripod of Truth, they often lean entirely on emotion. "I *felt* the Spirit" is a very common Church phrase; "I *thought* the Spirit" is not. We are sometimes told in Church classes and messages to "pay attention to how you feel" about things.[7] If it feels right, it is. This is good and wise counsel, but taken on its own it can be foolishness. Our feelings can utterly confuse us. Our emotions can betray us. Our passions can torpedo us. *Not all Spirit is emotion, and not all emotion is the Spirit.* Positive feelings aren't a default from God, nor are negative feelings always a sign of error. Some things that are wrong, like immorality or separating yourself from the Church and its covenants, can feel good and liberating. Some things that are true and good, like the temple endowment ceremony, may feel strange to some at first because it is unknown, foreign, or confusing. Some feelings of discomfort can be from God because they can lead people to repentance and growth and change. Sometimes people have an adverse emotional reaction to something that is true simply because it contradicts their assumptions, culture, or traditions.

Sometimes we lay down a spiritual trump card in the Church by leading with, "*I feel strongly* that . . ." Feelings, however, are the result of a concoction of human phenomena: insecurities, anxieties, fears, relationships, tradition, pride, ego, hormones, nutrition, sleep, health, time of day. We sometimes interpret all feelings as being divine when the reality may just be the result of low blood sugar. *I feel strongly that I may just need to eat lunch and take a nap.* In a fascinating study, the National Academy of Sciences followed eight Israeli judges for ten months as they deliberated on over one thousand petitions before a parole board to have sentencing minimized or dropped. Researchers found that at the start of the day, the judges approved about two-thirds of the cases. As the hours passed, the judges grew harsher, approving almost no cases by lunchtime. After they had lunch, however, they became more lenient and generous again. The cycle repeated itself in the afternoon, becoming harsher just before dinner.[8] Blind, impartial justice based on reason and intuition? No, they were just hungry.

In the early Church, Saints were prone to think that any unexplainable manifestations were from God. When some were overcome at a church meeting and fell on the floor comatose or suddenly howled at the moon or chased invisible objects, as some Saints did in Kirtland, they supposed that was God working within them. Joseph Smith once lamented that a certain Mr. Irving was guilty of "falling into the common error of considering all supernatural manifestations to be of God."[9] Today, some seekers fall into the common error of thinking that all strong emotional feelings are of God. "I get concerned," President Howard W. Hunter once said, "when it appears that strong emotion . . . [is] equated with the Spirit."[10] Similar deception occurs cognitively. Saints come to a mental conclusion on a point and blindly ignore their feelings or the fruits of those positions. We can play mental gymnastics, practice self-deception, rationalize, justify, rewrite history, and ignore contrary positions and evidence. In relying only on either our thoughts or our feelings, we can easily be deceived. Notice what the Prophet Joseph Smith said threatens seekers: "Nothing is a greater injury to the children of men than to be under the influence of a false spirit, when they think they have the Spirit of God."[11] When they *think* they have the Spirit, but don't.

Learning how to avoid deception is necessary for seekers because in searching we may get lost; in discovering we may get disoriented; in receiving the Spirit we may receive false spirits. This was a common theme in the early Church as Saints incessantly battled false doctrines, cultural values, competing agendas, and human shortcomings to try to stay on the right track, particularly in the formative years of 1830 and 1831. In less than one calendar year, the Lord gave multiple principles related to spiritual deception found today in Doctrine and Covenants sections 28, 43, 45, 46, 49, 50, and 52.

For the remainder of this chapter we will look, in historical sequence, at three events from Church history that led to some Saints being spiritually deceived: Oliver Cowdery's command, Hiram Page's stone, and the Kirtland confusion. Each story provides a general litmus test for detecting truth from error in personal revelation. Those three tests are the *Stewardship Test,* the *Brethren Test,* and the *Edification Test.*

Oliver Cowdery and the Stewardship Test

Oliver Cowdery was in a tough position in the summer of 1830. Told he had the gift of revelation (see D&C 8:2–4), he had been sustained as the second leading elder of the Church and directed by God to "admonish [Joseph Smith] in his faults" (D&C 6:19). As a revelatory second elder, in the late summer of 1830 he believed he saw a fault in something the young prophet Joseph had done.

Oliver Cowdery had been given the task to compile the Church's articles for its official organization. In D&C 18 he was told to do so by relying upon what is found in the newly translated Book of Mormon. Oliver diligently scoured the Book of Mormon for passages related to how the Church of Christ should be organized and administered so that he could compile the Church's "articles" for government and organization. He had done well, and the document served its purpose for about a year up until the Church was organized in April 1830.

A few days after the Church's organization, by the "spirit of prophecy and revelation" (D&C 20 section heading) Joseph Smith expanded and clarified passages in the Church's articles. One such passage was the requirement for baptism, which originally read in Oliver's draft, "Whosoever repenteth & humbleth himself before me & desireth to be baptized in my name shall ye baptize them."[12] By revelation the Prophet Joseph added to this passage that people being baptized must also "manifest by their works that they have received of the Spirit of Christ unto a remission of their sins" before they can receive the ordinance (D&C 20:37).

Not long afterward, Joseph received a surprising and disturbing letter from his second elder and scribe. Joseph remembered, "I received a letter from Oliver Cowdery, the contents of which gave me both sorrow and uneasiness. . . . He wrote to inform me that he had discovered an error in one of the commandments . . . 'and truly manifest by their works that they have received of the Spirit of Christ unto a remission of their sins.' The above quotation, he said, was erroneous, and added: 'I command you in the name of God to erase those words, that no priestcraft be amongst us!' I immediately wrote to him in reply, in which I asked him by what authority he took upon him to command me to alter or erase, to add to or diminish from, a revelation or commandment from Almighty God."[13]

Perhaps Oliver thought he was doing his job in admonishing Joseph. In that vein, Oliver also spent time convincing others (as many often do) that he was right and Joseph was wrong, including the Whitmer family. At the Church's September 1830 conference at the Whitmer home, the issue was addressed in a revelation. The Lord said: "Behold, I say unto thee, Oliver . . . no one shall be appointed to receive commandments and revelations in this church excepting my servant Joseph Smith, Jun., for he receiveth them even as Moses. And thou shalt be obedient unto the things which I shall give unto him, even as Aaron" (D&C 28:1–3).

The Lord was reiterating Oliver's subordinate position to Joseph, like Aaron's to Moses. Oliver was able to speak things by way of admonition or advice, however, "Thou shalt not write by way of commandment, but by wisdom." And then, the grand principle in the next verse, "*Thou shalt not command him who is at thy head,* and at the head of the church" (D&C 28:5–6; emphasis added).

This Church history story gives us the first principle to help avoid personal revelatory deception, which I call the Stewardship Test. The *Stewardship Test* is that God will not give you revelation *commanding someone outside your defined realm of responsibility.*[14]

Joseph Smith wrote to some confused elders in 1833: "I will inform you that it is contrary to the economy of God for any member of the Church or any one to receive instruction for those in authority higher than themselves, therefore you will see the impropriety of giving heed to them."[15] The ready application of the Stewardship Test is easily seen and understood in Church hierarchy, where we understand that a missionary can't get a true revelation to command his or her mission president, a Young Men president can't get a revelation commanding the Relief Society president, nor can Sister Johnson get a revelation commanding the deacons quorum president how to do fast offerings.

The Stewardship Test also applies to non-Church settings. You and I may get our own ideas—even inspired counsel—about things that others should do, but (outside of keeping general commandments) if we have no stewardship over the matter, we shouldn't confuse it as a *must-do* for that person. To be clear, the issue here is authoritatively *commanding* someone. Using Oliver Cowdery's example, we can *admonish*, we can *advise*, we can *counsel*, we can *suggest*, we can even *strongly recommend*. But we should not command where there is no stewardship. We cannot say, "I've prayed about this and God told me that you must ____, and if you don't you're in the wrong." No, *that's* in the wrong.

This also holds true for parents and children. It is common in the Church to discuss how as parents we are stewards over our children and can receive revelation for them. But what does that even mean? Can I, as a father, receive revelation directing my eight-year-old what he must or must not do? I think so. My sixteen-year-old? I hope so, as teenagers' prefrontal cortex hasn't even fully formed. But what about my twenty-one-year-old? (Odds are if you are a parent, you're saying, "Yes!," and if you're the twenty-one-year-old, you're saying, "No!") However, the question isn't whether you are a parent or a child, but *what stewardship do you oversee? What stewardship responsibilities have you relinquished, or what stewardship responsibilities have you received?* For example, can a child receive a revelation commanding a parent what he or she must do? Wait before you answer. What about a grown daughter who now cares for her aged mother with Alzheimer's? Stewardship affects who gets the real revelation.

Hiram Page and the Brethren Test

In September 1830, the five-month-old, newly formed Church of Christ faced its first real leadership crisis. Hiram Page, a son-in-law to the Whitmers and one of the eight witnesses of the Book of Mormon plates, had found a seer stone and began using it. Joseph remembered:

"Brother Hiram Page had got in his possession, a certain stone, by which he had obtained to certain revelations, concerning the upbuilding of Zion, the order of the Church &c &c, all of which were entirely at variance with the order of Gods house, as laid down in the new Testament, as well as in our late revelations. As a conference meeting had been appointed for the first day of September, I thought it wisdom not to do much more than to converse with the brethren on the subject, untill the conference should meet. Finding however that many (especially the Whitmer family and Oliver Cowdery) were believing much in the things set forth by this stone, we thought best to enquire of the Lord concerning so important a matter."[16]

Although the question about the order of revelation first arose in September 1830, similar issues related to it continue today. What happens when our thoughts and feelings don't align with what is being taught by the prophets and seers? What about when our feelings cause us to feel unsettled about a Church teaching or directive? What about when our mind just doesn't agree with a doctrine? Today most Saints don't seek truth through seer stones but through their senses. Our revelations aren't written on scrolls of paper but on scrolling screens, posted and tweeted and blogged, not just sent to the Whitmers and Oliver Cowdery but to thousands across the web. The Hiram Page crisis lives on today.

Joseph said that just before the conference he received a revelation addressing the crisis, found today in D&C 28. In it the Lord says that "those things [Hiram Page] hath written from that stone are not of me and that Satan deceiveth him" (D&C 28:11). Hiram Page was a faithful man. He was a smart man. He was a seeking man. And he was a deceived man. How do we ensure we are not modern-day Hiram Pages? The Lord provides a second test, which I call the Brethren Test.

The *Brethren Test* is that you will not receive direction from the Spirit to *act contrary or in opposition to accepted Church covenants, revelations, or teachings from the united voice of the current First Presidency and Quorum of the Twelve Apostles.*

The Lord said about Hiram Page's revelations: "These things have not been appointed unto [Hiram Page]," and then He taught the principle, "Neither shall anything be appointed unto any of this church contrary to the church covenants. For all things must be done in order" (D&C 28:12–13). In context, the Church's "covenants" are its revelations and articles. Thus, this verse suggests we will not receive things from God to act in opposition to or rebellion against the Church's accepted revelations and covenants.

An official First Presidency statement in 1913 taught, "From the days of Hiram Page . . . there have been manifestations from delusive spirits to members of the Church. . . . When visions, dreams, tongues, prophecy, impressions or any extraordinary gift or inspiration, convey something *out of harmony with the accepted revelations of the Church or contrary to the decisions of its constituted authorities,* Latter-day Saints may know that it is not of God, no matter how plausible it may appear."[17]

This means we will not receive a confirmation from the Holy Ghost to break covenants and to commit adultery. We will not receive a revelation telling us to stop obeying the Word of Wisdom. The Lord won't direct us to forgo sacrament meetings so we can better commune with Him in nature in our own way. He won't tell us to remove the temple garment in ways that oppose our covenant to do so. All of these are contrary to accepted Church teachings, revelations, and covenants. Although these examples may sound like unrealistic hyperbole, in fact each comes from real-life discussions I have had with various members (young and old) over the years as I have taught religion or served in the Church. In each case, the person was confident he or she was following the right inner voice—what they all thought was the Spirit of God. Returning to the young man at the beginning of the chapter who wondered if God was telling him to leave his wife because he had feelings for another women, I asked him, "Would God give you a revelation to break a faithful temple covenant?" He wasn't certain. I told him I was certain the Lord would not. Hiram Page lives on.

The Kirtland Confusion and the Edification Test

In the fall of 1830, four missionaries from the Church stopped near Kirtland, Ohio, on their way to their mission to the western edge of America in Missouri. Contacting friends, they preached to the people in Northeast Ohio, and the response was electric. "In two or three weeks from our arrival in the neighborhood," Parley Pratt reported, "we had baptized one hundred and twenty-seven souls."[18] Within a month's time there were suddenly more members of the Church in Ohio than in all of New York. The missionaries soon left to continue westward on their missions, however, leaving the newly converted Saints in Ohio with minimal leadership and oversight. Full of passion for their newfound faith, the Ohio Saints experienced spiritual phenomena in their meetings that were common to nineteenth-century, Second Awakening frontier Americans—fainting spells, speaking gibberish, chasing inanimate objects, and so on. John Whitmer remembered, "Some had visions and could not tell what they saw, Some would fancy to themselves that they had the sword of Laban, and would wield it as expert as a light dragoon, some would act like an Indian in the act of scalping, some would slide or scoot [on] the floor, with the rapidity of a serpent, which the[y] termed sailing in the boat to the Lamanites, preaching the gospel. And many other vain and foolish manoeuvers that are unseeming, and unprofitable to mention. Thus the devil blinded the eyes of some good and honest disciples."[19]

In February 1831, the Prophet Joseph Smith arrived to live in Ohio and went to work helping to straighten out the Kirtland confusion. He shortly received a monumental revelation addressing the situation, found in D&C 50. The Lord said, "Verily I say unto you, that there are many spirits which are false spirits . . . And also Satan hath sought to deceive you, that he might overthrow you" (D&C 50:2 3). The Lord then laid out some logic: if you are experiencing spiritual phenomena that doesn't impart "the Spirit of truth . . . it is not of God" (vs. 19–20). Also, if what you are experiencing doesn't edify, or lead you to draw closer to God, "that which doth not edify is not of God" (v. 23). If a spiritual phenomenon is from God, it will bring you "light" or truth that grows "brighter and brighter" (v. 24). "I say it that you may know the truth, that you may chase darkness from among you" (v. 25).

These verses give the third spiritual test, what I refer to as the Edification Test. The *Edification Test* is that spiritual phenomena will *lead us to understand truth and light, bring us closer to God to comprehend Him, and lead us to make and keep sacred covenants.*

President Joseph Fielding Smith taught: "There is no saying of greater truth than 'that which doth not edify is not of God.' And that which is not of God is darkness, it matters not whether it comes in the guise of religion, ethics, philosophy or revelation. No revelation from God will fail to edify."[20] In an editorial in the *Times and Seasons* attributed to Joseph Smith, he wrote on this subject: "One great evil is that men are ignorant of the nature of spirits . . . and imagine that when there is any thing like power, revelation, or vision manifested that it must be of God . . . [people] frequently possess a spirit that will cause them to lay down, and during its operation animation is frequently entirely suspended; they consider it to be the power of God, and a glorious manifestation from God,—a manifestation of what?—is there any intelligence communicated? are the curtains of heaven withdrawn, or the purposes of God developed? have they seen and conversed with an angel; or have the glories of futurity burst upon their view? No! . . . surely such a heterogenious mass of confusion never can enter into the kingdom of Heaven." He then lamented the problem was that they "have not a key to unlock, no rule wherewith to measure, and no criterion whereby they can test it."[21]

If my thoughts and feelings produce anger, pride, jealousy, mistrust, unrighteous judgment, selfishness, immorality, or the desire to break sacred covenants, then they are not of God, as those things do not edify. On the other hand, do my thoughts and feelings lead me to be more charitable, kind, forgiving, loving, obedient, patient, submissive, and humble—to put off the natural man? That's the Lord's Spirit. As discussed in more detail in Chapter 7, a central question each of us should ask is whether the influence that is operating on our minds and hearts leads us to have faith, hope, and charity, or whether it leads us to be full of their opposites: fear, doubt, and pride.

 Seekers wanted!

Balancing Christlike Characteristics and Commandments

Take a minute and write down all the Christlike attributes you can think of. Now, make a second list of commandments and covenants you know He wants you to keep.

Sometimes, we fail the Brethren Test and the Edification Test to try and emphasize Christlike attributes over commandments, or vice-versa. As prophets have taught, we cannot hold up certain Christlike attributes in competition with the very truths that Christ Himself has commanded.²² We cannot sacrifice chastity on the altar of love. We must not worship tolerance by murdering truth. On the other hand, obedience can't lord over nonjudgment. Covenants can't outweigh viewing each other equally. We must not let the one displace the other. Commandments and Christlike characteristics must balance in harmony. The Savior was friends with publicans and sinners, but He did not let His compassion trample on His commandments, which He constantly invited all to keep. How can you seek to do the same?

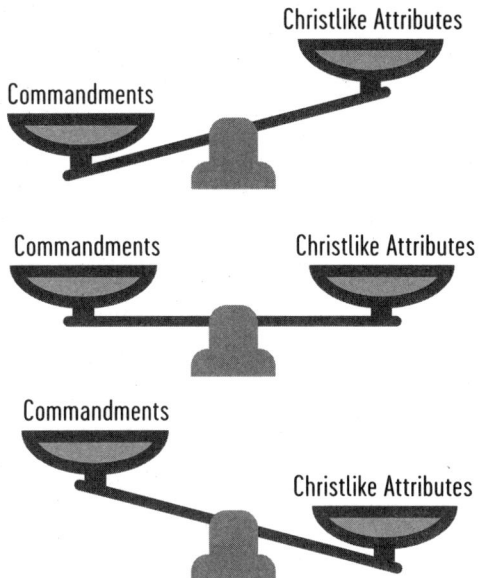

Conclusion: Spiritual Truth or Sociogenic Error

In 1999, a few school kids in Belgium suddenly started complaining about not feeling well, having headaches and nausea. They were quickly taken to the hospital. Doctors and educators couldn't figure out why there had been an outbreak of sickness among the students. The only commonality was that each of the school kids experiencing symptoms had drunk from the same Coca-Cola bottles. Schoolteachers went into other classes asking if any other kids had drunk Coke and weren't feeling well. More kids from the school came forward and went to the hospital, twenty-six in all. The Coca-Cola incident was reported on the Belgium evening news, and after the story spread, more kids were identified with similar symptoms from four more schools. One hundred students in all reported illness. Coca-Cola quickly pulled all their products from Belgium's shelves to figure out the problem, thirty million cans and bottles in all, the largest recall in all of Coke's history.

What caused the outbreak? It wasn't Coca-Cola. It was nothing more than a case of "mass sociogenic illness." One kid started to not feel well, and when he didn't, it caused others to think they didn't feel well. Having gone to school and consumed Coke, kids' minds started playing tricks on them. It was a mental and emotional overreaction.²³

As seekers, we know that the influence of God's Spirit is real. We have felt it, been enlightened by it, and experienced its effects. As we have sought to receive the Spirit through our mind and heart, personal revelations have been received, divine directions given, heavenly answers afforded, celestial comfort and joy imparted. We know and understand these cognitive and affective influences of the Spirit including clarity, joy, peace, understanding, hope, faith, charity, and enlightenment. If we are not on guard, however, like the kids in the Belgium Coke incident, latter-day seekers can also suffer from a type of spiritual mass hysteria, thinking we are experiencing the Holy Ghost when in reality what is happening is purely emotional and/or mental.

"Satan is abroad in the land, and he goeth forth deceiving the nations" (D&C 52:14). The Lord warned in the last days that "the very elect, who are the elect according to the covenant" may be deceived (Joseph Smith—Matthew 1:22). Drinking from certain Church culture can lead us to erroneously think that all emotion is the Spirit, all our thoughts inspired, all positive emotion good and negative emotion bad. Overlooking the most crucial leg of the Tripod of Truth—what the thoughts and feelings *produce in our lives*—we may find ourselves spiritually sick, wondering whether we should break covenants and leave a perfectly great spouse due to what's happening in our mind and heart. We begin to justify our positions, find fault with Church leaders, and distance ourselves from the gospel covenant, thinking something external is the culprit when something is wrong within us. We enter the ground Joseph Smith taught is the most dangerous to seekers: *to think we have the Spirit of God when it is a false spirit.*

To help counteract and detect spiritual deception, I have proposed three litmus tests to help discern truth from error: the Stewardship Test, the Brethren Test, and the Edification Test. These three tests are not all-encompassing. Surely, there are others. Nor are these tests meant to be constraining or controlling on the flood of personal revelation. They are meant to act as checks and balances to what can—like power—be taken to revelatory excess. Spiritual deception abounds in the latter days as much as in any other day. Thousands of Saints the world over—past, present, and future—become erroneously convinced that a passion or conclusion they have is God leading them right, even when those positions lead them right away from the covenant path. Fixated on the methods, they overlook the outcomes.

Of all the skills that can be better refined that are discussed in this book—evaluating doctrine, interpreting scripture, embracing ambiguity, etc.—being able to discern truth from error through receiving the Holy Ghost may be the most essential. According to former General Relief Society President Julie B. Beck, "The ability to qualify for, receive, and act on personal revelation is the single most important skill that can be acquired in this life."[24] Why? Because receiving the Holy Ghost is the key to receiving Truth, receiving God, receiving the Savior and the powers of His Atonement, and thus receiving heaven. "They that are wise and have received the truth, and have *taken the Holy Spirit for their guide, and have not been deceived*—verily I say unto you, they shall not be hewn down and cast into the fire, but shall abide the day" (D&C 45:57; emphasis added).

 ## Hide or Go Seek

Hide

I don't focus on the Tripod of Truth, leaning only on one or two legs.
I think all strong emotions are the Spirit.
I focus on the process instead of the product.

Go Seek

I lean on all three legs of truth—the mind, the heart, and the fruits.
I seek revelation within my stewardship.
I seek revelation in accordance with accepted teachings from the united voice of the current General Authorities.
I seek revelation that leads to increased light and truth and making and keeping sacred covenants.

PART 3

Seeking Holiness

Although we seek learning by study and faith, the goal of mortality is not to know something, but to become something.[1] *As the Lord said in the Sermon on the Mount, "Seek ye first the kingdom of God, and his righteousness; and all these things shall be added unto you" (Matthew 6:33). For the original School of the Prophets, seeking knowledge and truth was a means to a higher end. "Sanctify yourself" the Lord told these early seekers, "that your minds become single to God" (D&C 88:68). Part 3 looks at three ways to seek to have our minds single to God's kingdom and help us become more holy through gaining perspectives and skills related to receiving spiritual gifts, sustaining living prophets, and inviting the presence of God through keeping celestial covenants.*

Chapter 7

OBTAINING SPIRITUAL GIFTS

 Seeking Sentence: We find what we seek.

In the cold January of 1984, Elder Bruce R. McConkie stood in front of a crowd at a Brigham Young University devotional and spoke of fire. Not the fire of discipleship, but the flames of doctrinal heresies, "sweeping like a prairie fire" over apostate Christianity. The first heretical fire was the creedal doctrine of the Trinity, which changed "the nature and kind of being that God is" from an embodied, exalted man into an unknown, three-in-one, mysterious essence. The second great heretical fire, developed centuries later by the Reformers, was "the doctrine that we are saved by grace alone, without works."[1] The first fire created false ideas about God. The second fire attacked the Savior's Atonement. What of the third great doctrinal fire? Although its embers sparked all around him, Elder McConkie was silent. He didn't address the third flame.

What could it be? The third great fire may be the *age of reason*—the rise of strict scientific rationalism, when everything must be logical, reasonable, provable, explainable, and empirically verifiable. If the first fire attacked the nature of God, and the second fire attacked the Atonement of Christ, the third fire of reason seeks to reduce to ashes the remaining member of the Godhead—the Holy Ghost. This last fire says that in the light of logic we must throw off spiritual gifts such as visions, miracles, angels, spirits from beyond the veil, revelations, divine healings, and all things not naturally or scientifically explainable. Those who claim that these things exist, well, are merely ignorant or superstitious. In modern secular society, "Questions are not concerned with *what* people believe as much as with what is believ*able*. . . . The magical 'spiritual' world is dissolved and we are left with the machinations of matter," as one author on spirituality and secularism put it.[2] The Spirit of God like a fire is burnt.

I do not mean this description of the age of reason to be pejorative to rationality. Logical inquiry and evidence-based findings are the basis of all good science and research, and their fruits have immeasurably blessed contemporary society. The problem arises when we see the scientific method as the *only* way for understanding the mortal experience. "The methods of

FIRST FIRE — Change the Nature of God to the Trinity

SECOND FIRE — Simplify the Atonement to grace without works

THIRD FIRE — Reduce Spiritual Gifts to the age of reason

science lead us to what we call scientific truth. But 'scientific truth' is not the whole of life," said President Dallin H. Oaks. "Those who do not learn 'by study and *also* by faith' (Doctrine and Covenants 88:118) limit their understanding of truth to what they can verify by scientific means. That puts artificial limits on their pursuit of truth."[3]

As most seekers are rationally minded, this chapter serves both as a warning and an invitation. The warning is to not let the rational define our religion. I once spoke about Jesus in my home ward, and afterward, a man approached me in the hallway. He told me that what I had said was true, and he knew so because he had once been visited by Jesus and had spoken to Him. What is your knee-jerk reaction to reading that last sentence? I know what mine was. How would you react if, say, one of the priest-age boys in your home ward privately told you that God and angels had visited him and given him a sacred mission? Would we say, "That's really weird. That's not rational. That's not logical. That sounds *crazy*." The *warning* for seekers is to be careful lest we become the modern Methodist minister (see Joseph Smith—History 1:21). Beware the third fire.

The *invitation* of this chapter is to, on the other hand, "seek ye earnestly the best" spiritual gifts, as we've been exhorted (D&C 46:8). No, I mean it—to *really* seek them. When is the last time you prayed for a specific spiritual gift, especially the "best" ones, like faith, hope, and charity? Spiritual gifts are given to benefit Church members in their times of need: A confusing situation has arisen where what's right and what's wrong seems unclear? Then seek the gift of discernment. A parent doesn't know how to best help a struggling child? Seek the gift of wisdom. A young couple is about to make a difficult life choice and needs a glimpse into the future to guide them? Seek the gift of prophecy. A family member is sick or in pain? Seek the gift of healing. A missionary is heading to a foreign land? Seek the gift of tongues. A parent dies and yet you still need his or her guidance in your life? Seek the ministering of angels. You have been assigned as the early morning seminary teacher? Seek the gift to teach. An impossible situation needs to be reconciled? Seek the gift of miracles. These gifts are not measurable and even perhaps not rational, but they are real, and God really does send them to His children who seek them.

What follows in this chapter is a brief analysis of the spiritual gifts for which we should seek, what they may mean, how to appropriately seek them, and a more in-depth discussion on the "best" spiritual gifts which all seekers must obtain: the divine spiritual gifts of faith, hope, and charity.

We Find What We Seek

A few years ago, I read a fascinating study done by the Pew Research Center on religion in public life. They surveyed roughly 35,000 Americans and asked them multiple religious questions, one of which was, "Have you ever experienced or witnessed a divine healing?" One-third said yes. The top three denominations to report having experienced or witnessed a divine healing, in order, were: 1) Mormon (69%), 2) historically black churches (54%), and 3) evangelical churches (50%). By far, the lowest of the listed religions was Jehovah's Witnesses, at 7%. They were tied with agnostics at 7%, listed above only atheists at 2%.[4] Why do Jehovah's Witnesses only minimally experience divine healings compared to those of many other faiths? The answer seems to be that *we find that which we seek*. The Jehovah's Witness *Watchtower* says, "Jehovah's Witnesses have never practiced faith healing. . . . [Jehovah's Witnesses] believe that true Christians are identified, not by faith healing, but by something of far greater importance."[5]

For members of The Church of Jesus Christ of Latter-day Saints, divine faith healings are sought for and, thus, more common. According to Pew, walk into an average Latter-day Saint congregation on Sunday and two-thirds of the attendees will confirm a divine healing in their lives. In the Church, we are taught about healings. We are told to seek healings. We are told to believe in healings. But what about other spiritual gifts? Aren't we also told that speaking in tongues is a spiritual gift (see D&C 46:24)? Yet in the same Pew research study, when asked about tongues, guess which religion came out among the *lowest* in experiencing tongues? Of the members of The Church of Jesus Christ of Latter-day Saints, 86% said they had "never" experienced speaking in tongues. The only religion who reported a higher "never" number? Jehovah's Witnesses, at 88%. However, 31% of Pentecostals said they speak in tongues weekly, 11% monthly, and only 43% said "never." Why? Because "a major focus of Pentecostal churches is Holy Spirit baptism as evidenced by speaking in tongues."[6] Why do very few Latter-day Saints report the gift of tongues today? It is a very interesting question to consider.[7] Whatever the reason, the answer should *not* be that we don't seek for the gift. We must not, with any spiritual gift, "live far beneath our privileges" through unbelief, as Elder Joseph B. Wirthlin taught.[8] We cannot have "lost horizons" regarding spiritual manifestations such as visions, as President James E. Faust warned.[9]

Scriptural Lists of Spiritual Gifts

There are three main scriptural chapters that list spiritual gifts: Moroni 10, 1 Corinthians 12, and Doctrine and Covenants 46. These three chapters each list nine specific spiritual gifts, although their lists vary slightly in description, as can be seen in the following table:

Moroni 10	1 Corinthians 12	Doctrine and Covenants 46
1 teach the word of wisdom	the word of wisdom	the word of wisdom
2 teach the word of knowledge	the word of knowledge	the word of knowledge, that all may be taught
3 exceedingly great faith	faith	faith to be healed
4 the gifts of healing	gifts of healing	faith to heal
5 work mighty miracles	working of miracles	working of miracles
6 prophesy concerning all things	prophesy	prophesy
7 beholding of angels and ministering spirits	discerning of spirits	discerning of spirits
8 all kinds of tongues	divers kinds of tongues	speak with tongues
9 the interpretation of languages and tongues	interpretation of tongues	interpretation of tongues

Moroni's list is most unique related to these nine gifts, whereas Paul and D&C 46 are more closely related. Interestingly, D&C 46 precedes the nine gifts with two other gifts, to total eleven, which the other two chapters do not mention. "To some it is given by the Holy Ghost to know that Jesus Christ is the Son of God, and that he was crucified for the sins of the world" (v. 13). And also, "To others it is given to believe on their words, that they also might have eternal life if they continue faithful" (v. 14). All three chapters also have variations on the same idea that all these gifts come from God and that there are "differences of administration" and "diversities of operations" related to how these gifts can manifest themselves (see D&C 46:16; 1 Corinthians 12:5–6; Moroni 10:8).

The following is a brief translation of the spiritual gifts listed in D&C 46, 1 Corinthians 12, and Moroni 10. This list is not definitive in scope but strives to clarify what is meant by each spiritual gift to assist seekers in why and when the gift may be necessary. Thus, the language is purposefully broad to be inclusive of various potential applications.

The Word of Wisdom: the spiritual gift to correctly apply knowledge; understanding the proper course of action to take.

The Word of Knowledge: the spiritual gift to study, learn, understand, and retain truth.

Exceedingly Great Faith/to Be Healed: the spiritual gift to deeply trust in the Lord, even in the most trying circumstances, resulting in spiritual, emotional, and physical healing.

Faith to Heal: the spiritual gift to be a conduit to pass on the healing effects of the Holy Ghost to others in spiritual, emotional, and physical pain.

Working of Miracles: the spiritual gift to cause the heavens to hearken to your voice, bringing the seemingly impossible into effect.

The Gift of Prophecy: the spiritual gift to see into the future, understanding what is yet to come.

Beholding of Angels/Discerning of Spirits: the spiritual gift to part the veil, commune with the divine, and discern what is and is not of God.

Speak with Tongues: the spiritual gift to speak in a celestial language to express heavenly concepts, or to clearly communicate gospel truths in a way that is understandable to those who do not speak the way you do.

The Interpretation of Tongues: the spiritual gift to translate, understand, and correctly interpret what has been spoken by others under the influence of the Spirit.

Your Spiritual Gifts

The scriptures promise us repeatedly that we each have been given and can enjoy one of these spiritual gifts (see D&C 46:11; 1 Corinthians 12:7). Many people have multiple gifts given (see Moroni 10:17). Some have *all* these spiritual gifts (see D&C 46:29). Aside from the ones identified in these scriptural lists, clearly there are other spiritual gifts for which to seek.[10] In Mark 16:17–18, Jesus adds a few other gifts, such as casting out devils.

Most spiritual gifts listed in scripture do not center on logical, rational, natural capacities but on *miraculous capacities that come through the Holy Ghost.* The revelation of D&C 46 prefaces the description of many spiritual gifts with the qualifier "given by the Holy Ghost" (see D&C 46:13, 15, 16, 17). As Moroni says of spiritual gifts, "They are given by the *manifestations of the Spirit of God* unto men" (Moroni 10:8; emphasis added). Spiritual gifts are not mere mortal abilities inherited by DNA or enhanced by practice. They are enhanced by spiritual influence and come through the DNA of righteousness. A good litmus test for spiritual gifts, as opposed to mortal talents that come by genetics, is this: *If I lose the influence of the Holy Ghost, do I lose the gift?* This is important to understand, as we can each *seek* the Holy Ghost regardless of our natural capabilities or inherent talents. Through the power of the Holy Ghost, God is willing to give us these and many other miraculous spiritual gifts, "severally, according as he will" (Moroni 10:17), if we will but appropriately seek them.

Five Essentials to Seek Spiritual Gifts

After a detailed list of spiritual gifts in D&C 46:13–25, the revelation concludes with six verses (vs. 28–33) that provide direction on seeking spiritual gifts. I have condensed these into five essentials: seek earnestly, seek humbly, seek selflessly, seek gratefully, and seek righteously. According to the revelation, these are appropriate prerequisites to obtaining spiritual gifts.

Seek earnestly. We are specifically told in D&C 46:8 to "*seek ye earnestly* the best gifts." Paul says to "*covet earnestly* the best gifts" (1 Corinthians 12:31). Moroni tells us to "*lay hold upon every good gift*" (Moroni 10:30). These are proactive, agency-centered injunctions. We would do well to ask ourselves, are we earnestly seeking, coveting, and trying to obtain certain spiritual gifts? When was the last time we prayed specifically for a spiritual gift or desired one because it was needed? If we aren't asking, will we ever receive?

Seek humbly. Section 46 is clear that we should not seek after spiritual gifts for selfish, trivial reasons. We should not seek "for a sign that [we] may consume it upon [our] lusts" (D&C 46:9). We can't say, "I want to see an angel because that would be awesome!" or "I want _____ gift to make me look better or be more influential," as that would be seeking the gift for prideful reasons. Nor can we try to hold God hostage by demanding certain gifts or evidences in exchange for belief. There is a difference between seeking gifts and seeking signs. Seeking spiritual gifts submits to God and is righteous. Seeking signs tries to force God, to satisfy spiritual lust, and is adulterous (see Matthew 12:39). "Yea, signs come by faith, not by the will of men, nor as they please, but by the will of God" (D&C 63:10). Thus, "He that asketh in the Spirit asketh according to the will of God; wherefore it is done even as he asketh." (D&C 46:30).

Seek selflessly. We are commanded to ask for spiritual gifts in the name of Christ. "And again, I say unto you, all things must be done in the name of Christ, whatsoever you do in the Spirit" (D&C 46:31). What this implies is to not only pray in Christ's name but to ask for the gift in order to benefit Christ's work and the Father's glory. We are reminded that "all these gifts come from God, for the benefit of the children of God" (D&C 46:26). Or as verse 12 says, "that all may be profited thereby." Spiritual gifts are meant to serve and help others, like Christ, and are not for vain self-glorification.

Seek gratefully. We are to "give thanks unto God in the Spirit for whatsoever blessing ye are blessed with" (D&C 46:32). An expression of gratitude to God shows that we acknowledge His hand in the giving of every spiritual capacity we may have. If we are blessed with the gift to be healed, or the gift of hope, then like the one leper, let us return and give thanks to God for the gift (see Luke 17:17–19).

Seek righteously. "Ye must practice virtue and holiness before me continually" (D&C 46:33). Virtue and holiness are given to "those who love me and keep all my commandments, and him that seeketh so to do" (D&C 46:9). If we are not seeking holiness and virtue, we will not receive spiritual gifts, and we will lose the ones we have. If the Holy Ghost is with us, He endows us through our faithfulness with certain divine spiritual capacities that, without His influence, we otherwise would not have.

As spiritual gifts are appropriately sought, they become manifest in the lives of people of faith everywhere. They are found in missionaries learning foreign languages rapidly, in audible revelations being spoken to individuals, in people being visited in dreams or visions by deceased family members or others from beyond the veil, in heavenly knowledge and wisdom being imparted, in pain being divinely healed, in prophetic glimpses given of future events, and in other miraculous experiences. These gifts are generously given by God to benefit His children the world over. "Signs follow those that believe," the Lord reminds us, "Yea, signs come by faith, unto mighty works" (D&C 63:9, 11). You are not limited to one spiritual gift. Depending on the situation, varied gifts may be sought for, obtained, and called upon. Like having tools in a spiritual toolbox, you can reach for the appropriate gift to build your house of faith as different needs arise.

 Seekers wanted!

Reflect on the previous paragraphs about spiritual gifts. What spiritual gifts have been manifested in your life? Are there gifts that seem abundant, and others that seem absent? Why may that be? What situations in your life right now call for certain spiritual gifts to help you or others? In your upcoming personal prayers, specifically ask God to bless you with the spiritual gifts that you stand in need of, appropriately seeking them in the five ways listed above.

Faith, Hope, and Charity

Of all the spiritual gifts, the three greatest we should seek "with all the energy of heart" (Moroni 7:48) are the divine spiritual gifts of faith, hope, and charity. "These three" are what ultimately matter most, says Paul (1 Corinthians 13:13). Other spiritual gifts momentarily benefit the Church or God's children but ultimately serve to uphold the three greatest spiritual gifts of faith, hope, and charity. For example, when you experience the gift of prophecy, it confirms God has a plan, imbuing us with trust to act (faith). When you are healed, it gives you a personal assurance of Jesus's power (hope). When you have a revelation, it confirms God's love (charity). The "lesser" spiritual gifts, like tributary rivers, flow into and help fill up the great oceans of faith, hope, and charity.

THE DIVINE SISTERS vs. THE TERRIBLE TRIPLETS

 FAITH vs. FEAR
 HOPE vs. DOUBT
 CHARITY vs. PRIDE

In Protestant Christianity these three gifts are almost always referred to in the feminine, or as female. They are sometimes called the three sisters,[11] which is a great metaphor. My three oldest children are girls. Guess what their names are?

Not Faith, Hope, and Charity (but that's great if you name your kids that). They are Lauren, Reagan, and Jane. My daughters share the same DNA and look similar in some ways, but each is unique and different, offering her own gifts and blessings (and, candidly, occasional frustrations). The sisters of faith, hope, and charity are similar—their gifts overlapping in some areas yet distinct in offering their own individual benefits (without the occasional frustrations).

Before I explain each of these three grand spiritual gifts, I need to mention that the three divine sisters also have some competition, what I call the terrible triplets. These triplets have names too. They are fear, doubt, and pride—deceptive emotions from a negative spirit meant to suffocate the abundant spiritual life that comes from receiving faith, hope, and charity. As I discuss each divine sister in the following paragraphs, I will also contrast the terrible triplet antonym that tries to undermine it.

The Sister of Faith

When we give our basic definition, faith is to believe in something that is true but can't be seen (see Alma 32:21). While that is accurate, it is only *one* aspect of the gift of faith. Faith is multifaceted, with many moving gears working together to move us forward.

The first gear is that of TRUST. Faith is when God says, "Trust me." This is the believing without seeing. This is Noah being told to build an ark when the sky was sunny. This is Esther being told to save the Jews. This is Proverbs 3:5: "Trust in the Lord with all thine heart; and lean not unto thine own understanding."

The second gear of faith is ACTION. Joseph Smith and his early associates said that faith is the "principle of action" in all intelligent things.[12] James 2:20 says faith without works is dead. Thus, faith is also putting things into practice and living the divine teachings. This is Noah and his family grabbing their hammers and building a boat in the sunshine. This is Esther fasting and then approaching the throne of the king.

The last gear is EVIDENCE, or substance. Paul tell us in Hebrews 11:1 that faith is the "substance of things hoped for, the evidence of things not seen." This is Ether 12:6, which teaches us that we receive a witness *after* the trial, or action, of our faith. This is when Noah and his family are saved from the flood. This is when Esther is received by the king and the Jews are saved. Faith is also based on evidence—past experiences when God has confirmed our trust-based action with undeniable demonstrations of His divine hand. True faith isn't blind: it sees clearly through the lens of past experiences.

Thus, a more well-rounded definition of faith is trust-based action, confirmed by spiritual evidence.

These three gears work together to help give us the gift of faith: the gear of trust, the gear of action, and the gear of evidence. You can see how they work together: trust the divine teaching, act on it, and then examine the spiritual evidence. Elder David A. Bednar likened this process to a "helix"[13] or coil that moves a person to higher levels of faith as it is repeated, like a staircase taking you to higher floors.

A brief parenting example may help to illustrate. When I take our little kids swimming, at some point I put them on the edge of the pool and ask them to jump to me. Each of my kids has hesitated at first to do this. I stick out my arms and encourage them, and yet they don't want to jump. They reach their arms out and want me to come closer and close the gap. So, parenting 101, what do you do? You don't close the gap. As a parent, you *want* there to be a gap. Why? Because that requires your kids to trust you. You speak assuring words. You promise them they won't sink. You promise them you'll catch them. And little by little they work up the courage, trust you, act and jump, and you catch them. What do you do next?

This is parenting 225: you high-five them and tell them nice job, and then place them right back on the ledge to do it again. This time, you even scoot back a little. Why? To increase their faith and confidence. And you do this again, and again, until they are jumping without restraint. You can readily see the application of this metaphor.

God always allows a gap—a space that invites us to exercise our faith and have it lovingly confirmed. We want God right near us where we are 100% sure. He reassures us and comforts us, but He often leaves an uncomfortable space. He wants us to learn to trust Him, to act, and then to look at the evidence of His hand. He wants us to increase our faith (see Alma 32:29) to higher levels until we've gained a perfect knowledge of Him. As we gain such confidence in Him through experience and we begin to leap at His commands without question, we receive the spiritual gift of faith. The spiritual gift of faith from the Holy Ghost comes in the gift of knowledge about God's will, the gift of courage to follow it, and the gift of divine confirmation that follows our faith-filled actions.

The Terrible Triplet of Fear

The enemy of the sister of faith is the terrible triplet of fear. Faith says trust, fear says mistrust. Faith says act, fear says you'll fail. My kids don't want to jump to me in the pool because they are afraid—afraid I won't catch them, afraid they'll slip, afraid of sinking to the bottom, or maybe just afraid of getting water up their nose. Fear paralyzes them. Similarly, sometimes we don't act on what God wants us to do in faith because we fear what others will think of us, we fear we will fail, we fear we aren't good enough, we fear how hard it will be, we fear it won't be worth it, or we fear the unknown.

The problem is that fear doesn't know what to do, only what not to do. Fear forms protective, padded walls all around you, defending against all possible failures, and thus all possible success. Fear is the emotion of immobility. Thus, fear is a prison. Fear is damning. Fear is hell. Being a seeker doesn't mean we won't experience fear. But it does mean, to paraphrase C. S. Lewis, you know where to tell your fears to get off.[14] It means you can recognize your fears as an obstacle and courageously choose by the Spirit to let faith overpower your fears.[15] Yes, there are always legitimate things to worry and fret about, but once God has confirmed something by the Spirit and asked you to move forward, cast not away your confidence. When fear tries to overtake you, like Oliver Cowdery, cast your mind back on the time God spoke peace to your soul about what is to be done (see D&C 6:22–23).

Wise seekers should question the emotion of fear, particularly if they confuse it as being a fruit of the Holy Ghost (see Chapter 6, "Discerning Truth from Error"). Paralyzing, stifling fear is not from God. Paul said, "God hath not given us the spirit of fear, but of power, and of love, and of a sound mind" (2 Timothy 1:7). "Perfect love casteth out all fear" (Moroni 8:16). "Look unto me in every thought; doubt not, fear not," says the Lord (D&C 6:36). Therefore, let us not take counsel from fear,[16] but instead pray for the spiritual gift of courage and trust to act confidently in faith.

The Sister of Hope

The gift of hope is the sister of faith. They are nearly twins, at minimum born a year apart. The Book of Mormon teaches, "Wherefore, if a man have faith he must needs have hope" (Moroni 7:42). If I asked you to fill in the blank: "I hope that _____," our answers may vary, from hoping a loved one is safe to hoping we have enough money to pay the bills to hoping the weather is good tomorrow. But having the divine spiritual gift of hope is very different from wishful thinking. Hope is when we are personally confident that God will fulfill His promises to us. Notice how Paul describes it: "Shew the same diligence to the *full assurance* of hope. . . . Who through faith and patience *inherit the promises*" (Hebrews 6:11–12; emphasis added).

Thus, the gift of hope is when you receive a personal assurance of God's promises. I want to emphasize that: a *personal* assurance. One could say in faith, "God forgives people's sins," but hope says, "God will forgive *my* sins." A believer could say, "God has a plan for His children," but the gift of hope whispers, "God has a plan for *me*." Ultimately, the greatest aspect of the gift of hope is the assurance that you will go to the celestial kingdom because of Christ (see 1 Thessalonians 5:8–9; Titus 3:7; Alma 13:29).[17] Mormon calls this spiritual gift of hope "the rest of the Lord" (Moroni 7:3).

"What is it that ye shall hope for?" Mormon asks us. "Behold I say unto you that ye shall have hope through the atonement of Christ" (Moroni 7:41). If hope is having a personal assurance of divine promises, it raises the question: what, then, are the promises of God through Christ? They are numerous, but I've broken down six of the Savior's daily, divine promises into these general categories:[18]

> The promise to cleanse us of sin, make us right with God, and take us to heaven.
> The promise to heal us, both physically and emotionally, internally and externally.
> The promise to one day restore us of wrongs, injustices, and unfairness.
> The promise to identify with us, feel with us, and empathize with our pains, struggles, and infirmities.
> The promise to strengthen us against temptation, to bear our burdens, and to perform works beyond our natural capacities.
> The promise to transform our character, to change our natures into the children of God.

Cleansing
Healing
Restoring
Identifying
Strengthening
Transforming

When we, through faith, receive the gift of hope and know personally that these promises and others are true, and that they are *ours*, then amid the storms of life we aren't battered about. Hope becomes an "anchor of the soul," making us "both sure and steadfast" (Hebrews 6:19; see also Ether 12:4). Hope helps us conquer discouragement. Hope helps our mortal worries to be mitigated or overthrown altogether. Hope helps our souls rest assured. Hope is like having a whole season of a show available to view. I was once watching a series on Netflix and one of the lead characters got shot. *How is that going to work out?* I wondered. Suddenly I realized I could skip ahead. I went back to the main menu and pulled up a future episode to see how it was resolved. Then I settled back to the episode I was had been on, with a perfect brightness of hope, fully confident how it would be resolved.[19] As we experience the Holy Ghost and His spiritual gifts, they confirm to us that God is real and His promises are sure, giving the gift of hope.

The Terrible Triplet of Doubt

Without the gift of hope we become lost in the griefs and problems of mortality. As the Book of Mormon teaches us, "If ye have no hope ye must needs be in despair" (Moroni 10:22). Despair, or doubt, is the terrible triplet that fights against hope and can sweep us swiftly down the river of filthy waters. Four times in scripture Jesus specifically tells us to "doubt not" (Mormon 9:27; D&C 6:36; D&C 8:8; Matthew 21:21). As seekers, to "doubt not" doesn't mean we won't have questions and wonder. Those are natural byproducts of ambiguity and seeing through a glass darkly. We all have, and will yet have, unresolved questions. What the Savior seems to be commanding is to *not doubt His divine promises*. Doubt says, "Jesus won't forgive me. I'll never get certain blessings. What was lost will never be recompensed. God helps others, but He won't help me. I won't go to heaven. All is lost. I should give up." Those voices are not of God, nor are they gifts of His Spirit. That's doubting His sure promises. When Christ has promised something, don't doubt His celestial reserves. You can take His promissory note to the bank of heaven. It will be cashed. Hope in Christ through the gift of the Spirit truly is the anchor of souls.

The Sister of Charity

The greatest of all the gifts of God is called charity. It's the big sister of the three—the one that all the other siblings look up to and that organizes the heavenly family reunions. Paul says if we don't have this gift, we are nothing (see 1 Corinthians 13:2). Mormon tells us it's the greatest of all the gifts of God—so great we should cleave to it and pray with all the energy of heart for it (Moroni 7:48).

Sometimes the definition of the gift of charity is overly simplified as doing service or loving others. Although lovingly feeding the hungry, visiting the sick, and taking care of the poor and needy are necessary Christlike actions and the essence of "pure religion" (James 1:27), they are byproducts of charity, not the divine gift itself.[20] *Charity* is a small English word that encompasses a large heavenly concept. Originally the word was *agapē*, which is Greek for "the fatherly love of God for humans and their reciprocal love for God."[21] Nearly all cases in the English New Testament where the word *charity* is translated, it is *agapē*—the love of God for us, and our love for Him in return. The Book of Mormon uses it the same way: "And again, I remember that thou hast said that thou [Jesus] hast loved the world, even unto the laying down of thy life for the world. . . . And now I know that this love which thou hast had for the children of men is charity" (Ether 12:33–34).

Therefore, the foremost definition of charity is God's love for His children, or the love *of* God. But charity is a twofold, reciprocal gift. The second aspect of the gift of charity is returning that love back toward God, or love *for* God. "We love him, because he first loved us," John taught (1 John 4:19). Thus, charity is a loving relationship with God. Charity is when, as a gift from heaven, God says, "I love you," and out of experiencing that divine love, our natural reply to God is, "I love You too." Each spiritual gift we receive—from healing to revelation to tongues to ministering spirits—confirms to our soul that, indeed, "God loveth his children" (1 Nephi 11:17).

Why is charity the greatest of all the spiritual gifts? I believe it is because it is the greatest in helping us become more like God. Like Lehi, when we partake of the fruit of the love of God, as a spiritual byproduct it causes us to instinctively turn toward others (see 1 Nephi 8:12). Putting it into an equation, the spiritual gift of charity is God's love for us + our love for God = loving others more like God.

God's Love for Us + Our Love for God

Loving Others More like God

Thus, when God says, "I love you" and we experience charity, that gift brings about transforming effects in our character and lives. After the resurrected Savior appeared in the Americas, "the people were all converted unto the Lord, upon all the face of the Land" (4 Nephi 1:2), and "there was no contention in the land, *because of the love of God* which did dwell in the hearts of the people" (4 Nephi 1:15; emphasis added). Charity converted them, and charity changed them. When Mormon spoke of charity in Moroni 7:45, it seems he was not defining charity but describing the transforming effects of the love of God upon us—the converting fruits of what happens to us when we receive the gift. A person who experiences the gift of charity "suffereth long, and is kind, and envieth not, and is not puffed up, seeketh not her own, is not easily provoked, thinketh no evil, and rejoiceth not in iniquity but rejoiceth in the truth, beareth all things, believeth all things, hopeth all things, endureth all things" (Moroni 7:45). Feeling love changes people, and feeling divine love divinely changes people. Like water's effect on rocks in a river, when the heavenly influence of charity continually washes over someone, its celestial current rounds the rough and stony edges, smooths them, and spiritually polishes them.[22]

FAITH
Trust-based action with confirming evidence

HOPE
Personal assurance of divine promises

CHARITY
A loving relationship with God

The Terrible Triplet of Pride

If the tree of life is charity, or the love of God manifest in Jesus, then opposite is the building known as the pride and cares of the world (see 1 Nephi 11:36). Pride is the great stumbling block of Zion[23] and is the terrible triplet set up to undermine charity.[24] Why pride? Because pride suffocates love. We can't love others perfectly, and we can't love God perfectly, when pride enters the room. Pride sets us at odds, or with "enmity," as President Ezra Taft Benson called it, with God and others.[25] My wife and I once got into a small disagreement as we were driving home. It was over something trivial, but instead of being meek and humble and full of love, we both pridefully dug in our heels and defended our positions. As the tension in the car mounted and I fumed, silently looking away from her out the driver's side window, I suddenly heard my four-year-old daughter speak up in a rebuking lisp: "Dad, Dad! Have you forgot? Stheeetth you wife! You love her! You be nithe to her! Stheeth is your wife!"

And I had forgotten. My pride had wedged a barrier between our love. Spiritually, pride can do the same between us and God, blocking the divine gift of His love. I think that is what Alma was getting at when he asked, "If you have felt to sing the song of redeeming love [charity] . . . can ye feel so now?" (Alma 5:26).

I can tell when I am being led by the wrong spirit when the opposite of Moroni 7:45 is manifest in me: *"Pride is impatient, mean, envies others, is full of herself, seeketh her own will, is easily provoked, thinketh evil, and rejoiceth in iniquity, beareth with very little, trusts nothing, is secretly in despair."* Charity is pure. Pride is tainted. Charity is selfless. Pride is selfish. Charity gives. Pride takes. Charity says, "Thy will be done, and the glory be thine forever" (Moses 4:2). Pride says, "My will be done, and the glory be mine forever." Charity is Jesus. Pride is Lucifer.[26]

The Divine Sisters or the Terrible Triplets?

A key question for each seeker is, am I being led by the divine sisters of faith, hope, and charity, or the terrible triplets of fear, doubt, and pride?

Asking this question is a spiritual skill. It demonstrates an essential approach to navigate the competing spiritual rivers of mortality. Countless times I have asked myself this spiritually crucial question and found that I was erringly being led by one or more of the terrible triplets, prompting a need to repent and seek for the opposite divine sister. In occasionally working with others who struggle with their belief in God or the Restoration, I often stop them and ask, "Are your actions or questions being governed by fear or faith? By doubt or hope? By pride or charity?" It is amazing how much clarity that simple line of questioning has brought some of them and me in a variety of circumstances. As Mormon encouraged, we should "pray unto the Father with all the energy of heart" (Moroni 7:48) that we be filled with faith, hope, and above all, charity.

Conclusion: God, and His Gifts, Burn Brightly

On April 8, 1966, *TIME* magazine asked a question in bold red letters: "Is God Dead?" The magazine discussed different theologians' perspectives that, while certainly we haven't killed God, many of His divine purposes have died to us as His children. Through various forces, such as the age of reason, we have crowded God out of the social marketplace. His prior miracles are now just science. James Smith wrote, "Employing a kind of intellectual colonialism, [we] rename entire regions of our experience and annex them to natural science and empirical explanation, flattening the world by disenchantment."[27]

The Book of Mormon knew this would happen. It is significant that of all topics he could have concluded with, Moroni ends the Book of Mormon with a discourse on spiritual gifts for his future readers. He pleads to latter-day seekers, "And again, I exhort you, . . . that ye deny not the gifts of God" (Moroni 10:8). He reminds us that God "is the same yesterday, today, and forever, and that all these gifts of which I have spoken, which are spiritual, never will be done away, even as long as the world shall stand, only according to the unbelief of the children of men. . . . And now I speak unto all the ends of the earth—that if the day cometh that the power and gifts of God shall be done away among you, it shall be because of unbelief. And wo be unto the children of men if this be the case; for there shall be none that doeth good among you, no not one. For if there be one among you that doeth good, he shall work by the power and gifts of God" (Moroni 10:19, 24–25).

The concern is almost palpable, Moroni's emotions etched in gold plates together with his words. It's as if, through the spiritual gift of prophecy, he sees the third fire raging today.

As Latter-day Saints, we must be careful not to add logs to the third fire by disassociating ourselves from believing in and seeking spiritual gifts. We must be in the world, with its age of reason and logic and the benefits that derive therefrom, without being of the world and burning up the divine along the way. We are a people of miracles. We are a people who reject the first fire that changed the nature of God, the second fire that diluted Jesus's Atonement, and any third fire that seeks to deny miracles and spiritual gifts through the Holy Spirit. We can receive revelations, part veils, behold angels, divinely heal and be healed, speak and interpret tongues, see and prophesy of the future, know Jesus is the Christ, receive heavenly wisdom and knowledge, and more, if we will seek them in righteousness. As we receive the gifts of the Spirit, they help lead us to Jesus to receive the great gifts of faith, hope, and charity, rejecting destructive forces of fear, doubt, and pride. God is not dead, and His gifts are alive and burning in the hearts and lives of many, "bestowed upon all who are true followers of [God's] Son, Jesus Christ" (Moroni 7:48).

 Hide or Go Seek

Hide

I don't believe in spiritual gifts.

I am only willing to consider gifts that are logical or rational as defined by my culture.

I cannot have or experience miraculous spiritual gifts like visions or prophecy or healing.

I am inherently skeptical of other people's expressions of spiritual gifts.

I am immobilized by fear, beset by doubt, and full of pride.

Go Seek

I believe in all spiritual gifts, including the miraculous that may defy cultural acceptance.

I seek after necessary spiritual gifts *earnestly, humbly, selflessly, gratefully,* and *righteously.*

I act in faith.

I trust Jesus's divine promises.

With all energy of heart, I seek to obtain the gift of charity.

Chapter 8

SUSTAINING MODERN PROPHETS

 **Seeking Sentence: Sustaining prophets is a holistic continuum, not an all-or-nothing dichotomy.**

On a beautiful spring day in April 2015, the Saturday afternoon session of general conference began predictably: a song by the choir, a prayer, another song. Then President Dieter F. Uchtdorf of the First Presidency stood for the sustaining of Church officers. "Brothers and sisters, it is proposed that we sustain Thomas Spencer Monson as prophet, seer, and revelator and President of The Church of Jesus Christ of Latter-day Saints; Henry Bennion Eyring as First Counselor in the First Presidency; and Dieter Friedrich Uchtdorf as Second Counselor in the First Presidency."

"Those in favor may manifest it." Over 20,000 hands silently went in the air.

"Those opposed, if any, may manifest it."

Suddenly, the innocuous turned interesting. A voice was heard shouting, "Opposed!" followed quickly by a few others who stood and overlapped their voices in dissent, "Opposed!"

President Uchtdorf looked down and audibly noted the dissenting votes. He moved on to the sustaining of the Apostles. The same 20,000 people raised their hands in favor, and the same half-dozen shouted their opposition.[1] Six months later at the October conference, audible dissenting votes against the First Presidency and Apostles were heard again, and yet once more in April 2016.

Some members of the Church didn't quite know how to react to the opposing votes. They shouldn't have dissented. *They should have been removed from the Conference Center. They aren't faithful.* It also seemed like those who opposed didn't quite know how to act appropriately either. The protocol is to raise your hand to personally sustain or dissent, not to stand up and shout.

This public moment from recent Church history can serve as a private metaphor for some seekers. While there may be 20,000 reasons to sustain living prophets, there can be a handful of issues that cause us to question our sustaining enthusiasm, or maybe even want to stand up and shout in disagreement. The most recent generations have watched the Lord's hand inspire President Gordon B. Hinckley toward the global expansion of the Church onto the world's stage, President Thomas S. Monson's prophetic ministry in helping Church members reach out to the poor and needy, and President Russell M. Nelson's decisive actions to push for deeper personal conversion and implement changes toward the ongoing Restoration. *All in favor . . . ?*

However, we've also seen a handful of prophetic and social ideas clash loudly, such as contemporary culture's acceptance of same-sex marriage, the fluid definition of gender, and calls for women's equality through priesthood ordination, to name a few. Some think that prophetic teachings that contradict these positions aren't revelatory, reflect personal or generational biases, or will change in the future. *Any opposed . . . ?*

Even if these tensions settle by time, reason, or revelation, new issues will inevitably arise for future generations. In other words, *the issues aren't necessarily the issue.* There is a consistent gospel "paradox," or tension here, as scholar Terryl Givens has expressed, that always exists between people and prophets. On one hand the Restoration articulates the doctrine of individual agency, and on the other hand it has set up a centralized hierarchy of authority. Like a cross, these two principles intersect directly with one another, yet can go in opposing directions.[2] How do seekers stay true to conscience, yet also true to priesthood authority, if they ever contradict? How do we choose to perfectly sustain imperfect leaders? How do we be dutifully dedicated but not blindly believe? How does one see apparent errors or omissions in the Church and seek to address them, yet not become prophets unto themselves who "seek to counsel in your own ways" (D&C 56:14) and disobediently "seek . . . the image of his own god" (D&C 1:16)? It's been said that perhaps "the greatest test for any generation is how it responds to the voice of the prophets."[3] The purpose of this chapter is to articulate ideas, frameworks, and skills to help us pass that crucial test and more fully sustain God's living prophets, who hold the keys of the kingdom of God that we seek (see Matthew 6:33; D&C 27:13; 65:2).

Understanding "Sustaining"

Understanding the gospel, the scriptures, and the Church often centers on how we understand words. You've seen multiple instances in this book where I pause to seek a better understanding of a word, whether that word is *doctrine* or *charity*. Words make meaning, and therefore a clearer understanding of spiritual words makes clearer spiritual meaning. Using synonyms and antonyms is one way to clarify a concept. Below are some of thesaurus.com's synonyms for *sustain*. Read over them and ask yourself, "What does it look like to sustain living prophets using these words?"

SUSTAIN: *verb* keep up, maintain
Synonyms

assist	approve	convey	prop	validate
bolster	back	endorse	protract	verify
buoy	bankroll	favor	ratify	go for
continue	bear	feed	relieve	keep alive
defend	befriend	foster	supply	keep from falling
help	brace	lug	support	keep going
nurse	buttress	nourish	tote	lend a hand
preserve	carry	nurture	transfer	provide for
save	comfort	pack	transport	stand by
aid	confirm	prolong	uphold	stick up for

Isn't that list interesting? What stands out to you? What words possibly provide better insight into what it looks like to sustain living prophets? Now, do the same with the antonyms. What does it look like to *not* sustain modern prophets using the words below?

Antonyms

harm	contradict	hold	maintain	take
hinder	deny	ignore	neglect	trouble
hurt	deprive	injure	oppose	veto
obstruct	disagree	invalidate	refuse	weaken
stop	disapprove	keep	reject	abstain
abbreviate	discourage	let down	shorten	discontinue
condemn	disprove	let go	starve	halt

While these words are not a perfect fit, they may be helpful to better get our arms around the broader concept of sustaining. For example, you can see sustaining as to "support" the prophets in their divine calling and authority or to not "obstruct" them, but you can also see sustaining as to "endure" something difficult with them—like experiencing or "sustaining" a wound—letting God painfully but patiently work His perfect grace on our collective mortal weakness to heal us over time.

More important than thesaurus.com, however, is the question, "How does the *Church* define sustaining prophets?" Using the search tools taught in Chapter 3, I examined the scriptures and words of Church leaders for statements that help define what spiritually sustaining prophets may look like. In analyzing the cumulative teachings on sustaining, common words and themes emerge. Summarizing these common themes, I propose the following model to help seekers more fully evaluate their personal sustaining of living prophets.

A Sustaining Model

Sustaining prophets is more than merely raising our hand. Cumulative Church teachings indicate that sustaining prophets is a *full-bodied covenant to the Lord*,⁴ requiring not just an uplifted arm but also our minds, eyes, ears, lips, hearts, hands, and feet. It is a comprehensive, holistic sustaining as seen in the following model, explained by the authoritative teachings that support this framework.

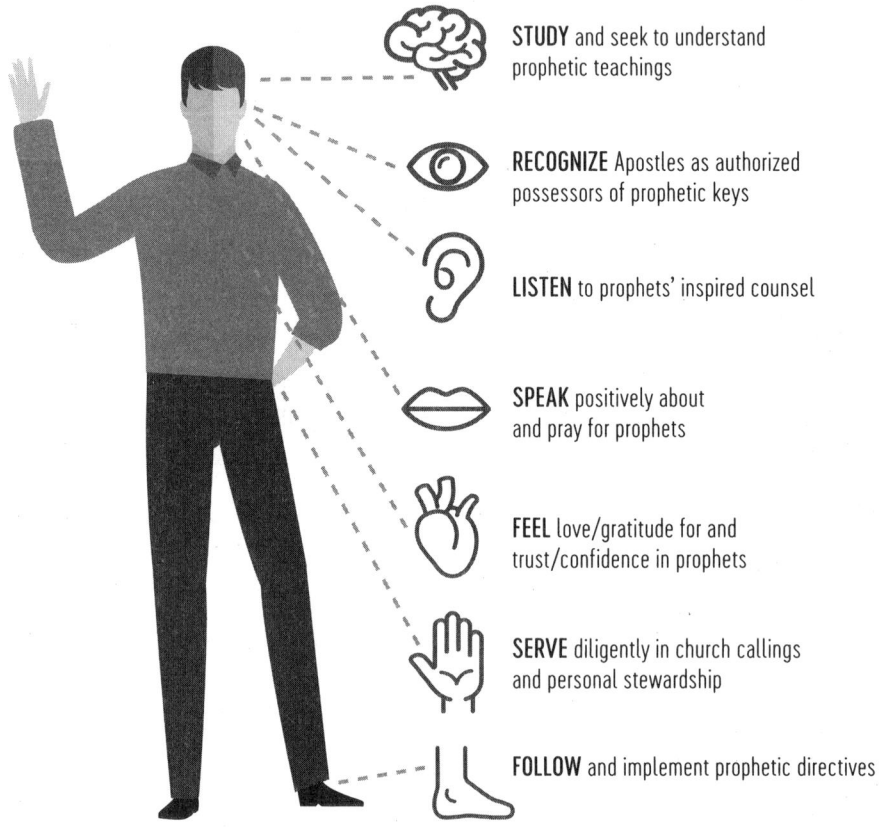

FULLY SUSTAINING MODERN PROPHETS

- **STUDY** and seek to understand prophetic teachings
- **RECOGNIZE** Apostles as authorized possessors of prophetic keys
- **LISTEN** to prophets' inspired counsel
- **SPEAK** positively about and pray for prophets
- **FEEL** love/gratitude for and trust/confidence in prophets
- **SERVE** diligently in church callings and personal stewardship
- **FOLLOW** and implement prophetic directives

Study

Part of sustaining prophets is taking the time to learn and understand what prophets have taught. An article on the Church's website about sustaining tells us to "study the prophetic word."⁵ Elder David B. Haight taught that to uphold them, "We're mindful of what comes from the lips of the prophet."⁶ Sister Carol F. McConkie counseled that we should "read and study sacred prophetic words with faith."⁷ As Joseph Smith wrote in a draft of his history, "We say again, search the revelations of God, study the prophecies, and rejoice that God grants unto the world, seers and prophets."[8] Seekers should ask themselves, do I study the words of modern prophets in general conference talks, listen to their worldwide broadcasts, know the content of the signed letters they send to the Church, and seek to learn their teachings?

Recognize

How we view prophets is also part of sustaining. President Russell M. Nelson taught that to sustain prophets, "We recognize their calling as a prophet to be legitimate and binding upon us."[9] Elder Gary E. Stevenson said we see the prophet "as the only person on earth who possesses and is authorized to exercise all priesthood keys,"[10] summarizing a similar temple recommend question.[11] An essay on sustaining prophets says that to sustain we recognize the Prophet as "the only person on the earth who receives revelation to guide the entire Church."[12] An *Ensign* article on sustaining says "we recognize" that prophets have been "called of God."[13] Speaking to an ailing President Ezra Taft Benson, President Gordon B. Hinckley exemplified how we *view* the prophet to sustain him when he said, "We embrace you as our leader."[14] When we sustain with our eyes, we acknowledge with our uplifted hand their divine call, stewardship, and keys. Seekers should ask themselves, do I view the prophet as the authorized leader of the Church, holding the priesthood keys to give its revelations from the Lord?

Listen

Elder David B. Haight said to sustain prophets means "that we listen"[15] to them. To listen means we give someone our attention.[16] As will be explained later, it doesn't necessarily mean we always agree or see eye to eye, but we don't dismiss their words or treat them lightly. Listening implies that we hear; that we take notice; that we are alert to the voice of the prophets and "give ear to [his] words" (2 Nephi 4:3; 2 Nephi 9:40; Alma 26:1; Alma 38:1). Another word that is often used regarding how we hear the words of the prophets is to give "heed." To give heed means to pay attention to, to notice, to mind, to watch.[17] When Joseph Smith was sustained as the leader of the Church at its organization on April 6, 1830, the Lord said, "Wherefore, meaning the church, thou shalt give heed unto all his words." Thus, D&C 1:14 warns, "The day cometh that they who will not hear the voice of the Lord, neither the voice of his servants, neither give heed to the words of the prophets and apostles, shall be cut off from among the people." Seekers should ask themselves: am I giving prophetic words my attention, taking them seriously, and listening closely?

Speak

One of the simplest ways to sustain prophets is to use our lips to pray for them. "Uphold [the prophet] before me by the prayer of faith," says D&C 43:12. The First Presidency is to be sustained by the "prayer of the church" (D&C 107:22). Wilford Woodruff once said: "I and other men, the apostles, and all who are called to officiate in the name of the Lord need the faith and prayers of the Latter-day Saints."[18] The Church's website suggests to "pray for the Prophet" as the first item in its sustaining list.[19] President George Albert Smith said that not only "we will pray for [the prophet]" to sustain him, but that also we "will defend his good name" with our words.[20] Joseph F. Smith said we should use our speech to "bless [the prophets], and encourage them in the good work in which they are engaged."[21] Seekers should ask themselves, do I pray for the prophet, defend his divine call and reputation, and speak positively about him in public?

 Feel

When President Harold B. Lee was sustained as the new Church President, then-Elder Thomas S. Monson said, "Our upraised hands were an outward expression of our inward feelings. As we raised our hands, we pledged our hearts."[22] President Boyd K. Packer said that "to be able to sustain our living prophet upon the earth today" is "to feel it in your heart and soul."[23] The Church's website says to sustain the Prophet, you "love the Prophet."[24] Our sustaining feelings should not only be loving but should reflect confidence in their divine calling. "Our sustaining is a vote of confidence in the person, because we recognize that he or she has been called of God,"[25] says an *Ensign* article on sustaining. The revelation on priesthood offices in D&C 107:22 uses similar words: "Of the Melchizedek Priesthood, three Presiding High Priests [the First Presidency], chosen by the body, appointed and ordained to that office, and upheld by the confidence . . . of the church." Seekers should ask themselves, do I feel love toward God's prophet and have trust and confidence in the prophetic keys and mantle he holds?

 Serve

Church teachings indicate our uplifted hands are like a volunteer's raised hand, signaling a willingness of someone who is ready to go to work and serve. Using the classic Old Testament story of sustaining, Aaron and Hur literally used their hands to lift Moses's to defeat the army of Amalek (see Exodus 17:11–12). Wilford Woodruff taught that one of the key ways we seek to sustain prophets is by using our hands to lift our share of the work to which we are assigned: "I hope my brethren and sisters will feel in their hearts to sustain the Presidency of this Church by their faith, works, and prayers, and not suffer them to carry all the load, while we hide ourselves in the rear. . . . Let each one bear their share; and if we will correct our own follies, and set in order our own houses, and do that which is right, we shall then do some good, and help to lift the load that rests upon those that lead."[26] Doctrine and Covenants section 21 promises that all those who "labor in my vineyard" will have "a mighty blessing" which will be to "believe on [the prophet's] words, which are given him through me" (D&C 21:9). President Gordon B. Hinckley said the word *sustain* means "to support, to assist"[27] through our efforts. Thus, to sustain with our hands, we put those hands to work to "do everything you can to help them [the prophets]," as Joseph F. Smith taught.[28] Seekers should ask themselves, do I serve dutifully in my calling and stewardship and assist the prophet through faithful labor in the Church and kingdom?

 Follow

The last part of our full-body sustaining has to do with the direction of our lives, the symbolic position of our feet. President Henry B. Eyring said, "To sustain . . . [we] follow His servants,"[29] or, as Elder David B. Haight said, "we follow his direction."[30] President Nelson said following the prophet means to "uphold their prophetic priorities."[31] Elder Ronald A. Rasband taught it is "our willingness to stand with" the prophets.[32] Former Young Women General President Janette Hales Beckham said we sustain when we "abide by the direction and counsel of the prophets."[33] Seekers should ask themselves, do I walk in concert with, stand next to, and strive to abide by prophetic priorities and directives?

A Sustaining Continuum

Some benefits of viewing sustaining in a more holistic way, rather than merely asking if we agree with or do everything prophets teach, is that it helps us see that sustaining modern prophets is *multifaceted*. It requires proactive action, not passive voting. Importantly, using this broader approach, sustaining may look a little different for everyone. One may be strong in one area and weaker in another, yet still a sustaining member. A basketball player who has a good shot, rebounds well, and sets good screens is still a valuable and contributing member of the team, even if her defense isn't the best. There's room for many types of players who are committed to play for the team and are willing to be coached. One may sustain prophets through his dedicated Church service, even if he struggles to study and understand their teachings. Another may seek to sustain through speaking positively about, defending, and praying for prophets, even if she doesn't do too well at implementing the latest Church initiative. Yet another may feel frustration toward certain prophetic personalities or teachings but still deeply believe in and recognize their prophetic mantle. If you're weak in one area, you might be strong in others.

Thus, sustaining prophets may be better considered as a well-rounded *continuum* rather than a more fundamentalist all-or-nothing, yes/no, dichotomous approach. In academic studies, a Likert scale of agreement is often used to evaluate concepts that carry a range or continuum. The same can be applied to the different categories of sustaining. Clearly, this is not a definitive model or complete measure but is merely meant to help roughly gauge areas where you are weak or strong and help identify an overall view of sustaining of prophets.

 **Seekers wanted!**

Carefully review the following questions and mark where you stand in your level of agreement with each question. Total your points below.

Which areas were your strongest? Why? Which areas were your weakest? How can you strengthen them? Overall, what does your full-body sustaining indicate?

	Strongly Agree	Agree	Slightly Agree	Slightly Disagree	Disagree	Strongly Disagree
🧠 **I STUDY** and seek to understand prophetic teachings	5	4	3	2	1	0
👁 **I RECOGNIZE** Apostles as authorized possessors of prophetic keys	5	4	3	2	1	0
👂 **I LISTEN** to prophets' inspired counsel	5	4	3	2	1	0
👄 **I SPEAK** positively about and pray for prophets	5	4	3	2	1	0
❤ **I FEEL** love/gratitude for and trust/confidence in prophets	5	4	3	2	1	0
✋ **I SERVE** diligently in church callings and personal stewardship	5	4	3	2	1	0
🦶 **I FOLLOW** and implement prophetic directives	5	4	3	2	1	0

TOTAL:

| 35 | 28 | 21 | 14 | 7 | 0 |

← Sustaining Living Prophets

Sustaining While Disagreeing

Inevitably, at some point most seekers individually experience the tension of personal agency and prophetic authority crossing against each other: a political stance is stated, a policy implemented, a doctrine articulated. Soon a half-dozen dissenting internal voices vote opposite our 20,000 sustaining reasons. It is, however, a false idea that disagreement is synonymous with disloyalty, or that diverging opinions indicate an adversarial situation. Disagreement is part of every relationship. At times I disagree with my wife, and she with me, and yet we are fully committed to one another in a loving, unified relationship. The Quorum of the Twelve Apostles disagree with each other in their councils, even debate vigorously, yet are still unified as a body as they seek the Lord's will.[34] Commitment is the key, not a lack of disagreement. Unity is based on solidarity, not homogeneity in thought.

The question is not if we may disagree but how we go about handling and approaching the disagreement. As an example, recently my teenage daughter voiced her displeasure with my wife and me over some of our family's smartphone rules. Was it okay for her to let us know that our policies were "lame" and "ruining her social life"? Of course! That's her perspective. That's her opinion. If something is rubbing her wrong or she views it as unfair, as parents we need to hear her reasons why, and in turn she needs to hear and seek to understand ours. The key is *how* we respond, not whether we agree. The disagreement should be expressed respectfully, in the gospel spirit of temperance, love, kindness, humility, and charity (those things that sustain relationships). But what if my daughter decided to organize my other children in a Sweat family smartphone insurrection? What if she decided to aggressively take down our Wi-Fi filters or directly rebel contrary to our counsel and install unapproved apps? What if she voiced her disdain in anger and rage, both privately to us and publicly to her friends, casting dispersions upon the very parents she claims to love? Would that be condoned? The answer is clear.

While respectful disagreement may be acceptable, organized public or rebellious opposition against the Church or its leaders is not.[35] That seems to be where the Church draws a line regarding sustaining living prophets. In 2014, the First Presidency and Twelve said in a statement: "We understand that from time to time Church members will have questions about Church doctrine, history, or practice. Members are always free to ask such questions and earnestly seek greater understanding. We feel special concern, however, for members who distance themselves from Church doctrine or practice and, by advocacy, encourage others to follow them. Simply asking questions has never constituted apostasy. Apostasy is repeatedly acting in clear, open, and deliberate public opposition to the Church or its faithful leaders, or persisting, after receiving counsel, in teaching false doctrine."[36]

Persistently rebelling and publicly opposing is different than personally disagreeing and questioning. One leads to prideful divisiveness, and the other can lead to knowledge and growth. One tears down and divides, the other can edify and unify. We are entitled to our individual opinions, even if our individual opinions differ from the counsel of Church leaders. Elder D. Todd Christofferson clarified that, for example, a Church member may personally support same-sex marriage laws, even on social media, and not be in danger of Church discipline, as it "is not an organized effort to attack our effort, or our functioning as a church."[37] Taking an alternate personal position is different than participating in or seeking to undermine the unauthorized practice.

Like children with parents, we can respectfully say we don't understand things, disagree with things, hope some things change, and propose solutions. An apt example of faithfully disagreeing and proposing solutions to a contemporary concern is Neylan McBaine's book *Women at Church*, which offers multiple ways to potentially mitigate gender differentials while upholding current prophetic teachings on priesthood. What we shouldn't do is cause a civil war or join the rebellion. Remember, President Spencer W. Kimball gave his reasoning for pursuing the revelation that lifted the priesthood and temple restriction on black members of the Church as "witnessing the faithfulness of those from whom the priesthood has been withheld" (Official Declaration #2). Valuing our relationship, we can be in solidarity with and defend the prophetic keys, even if we aren't agreed or can't defend a particular prophetic teaching. To say, "I am not sure I personally agree with or understand that, and this is my view, but I yet sustain him as the Lord's servant" speaks volumes.

Disagreement through Councils

If we occasionally disagree with prophets, however, we must go about it the Lord's way, not contemporary culture's. Some want to adopt a democratic model and stage a protest, form a rally, picket and march, stand up and shout. That's how we get attention in the world and agitate for political change. But Jesus said, "My kingdom is not of this world," and His people should not "fight" for it the way society does (John 18:36).

Returning to the opening story about those who voiced their opposition in general conference, to oppose itself isn't wrong. After all, the Church asks for both approving and disapproving votes as part of standard Church practice (see D&C 124:144). If members give a dissenting vote, they are to meet privately with their assigned priesthood leader to determine "whether the dissenting vote was based on knowledge that person who was presented is guilty of conduct that should disqualify him or her from serving in the position."[38] If this is the case, then opposing is fulfilling a member duty. This, however, does not seem to be why some opposed in April 2015. In meetings with the press and statements on social media after the conference, the opposers said their organization's movement was not against any specific leader, Church teaching, or policy, but rather to open a dialogue for members who may disagree with the Church and provide a clearinghouse where Church members could voice those disagreements.[39] The opposers felt members did not have a satisfactory forum through which "to express feedback, opinions, dissent, or dissatisfaction about the current views, positions and teachings of the LDS Church."[40]

When noting their dissenting votes, ironically, President Uchtdorf directed them to the Lord's established system to express feedback, opinions, dissent, and dissatisfaction when he said, "We invite those who opposed any of the proposals to contact their stake presidents."[41] That was not a curt dismissal of opposing voices. It was a directive about where those voices should turn. The Lord's way of working out issues is through the divine system of councils He has implemented—on a family, quorum, auxiliary, ward, stake, area, and general Church level.[42] In councils, participating members are encouraged to express their views to provide variety and clarity in perspective. In councils, however, we aren't worried just about being heard, but about hearing the voice of the Lord. We aren't concerned about being right but about getting it right. We let all speak, and we listen to each person's sayings in open discussion (see D&C 88:122), seeking to understand and be understood. Here, in councils, is where members should speak, even if their perspectives are not mainstream or disagree with common viewpoints.

The previously unpublished Council of Fifty[43] minutes reveal how the Prophet Joseph Smith handled diverging opinions in Church councils, and in fact *called for and expected it*. Joseph expressed that everyone should "speak their minds . . . and to say what was in their hearts whether good or bad. He did not want to be forever surrounded by a set of 'dough heads.'"[44] In other words, he didn't want a bunch of "yes men." At another Council of Fifty meeting, Joseph said that "the reason why men always failed to establish important measures was, because in their organization they never could agree to disagree long enough to select the pure gold from the dross."[45] *They could not agree to disagree long enough to get to the gold.*

Perhaps we, as a Church, haven't yet implemented and utilized councils and counseling on the level the Lord desires, which may contribute to the frustration of some who feel they aren't heard or don't have a way to express their voice, especially if it is atypical. If that is the case, we as a body must repent and do better. Our ministering discussions, interviews, classes, and councils should be respectfully open to alternate views and even disagreement, remembering that sustaining prophets is a multifaceted continuum, not an all-or-nothing dichotomy. And perhaps we also need to repent in how we express our diverging views, avoiding being defensive, combative, accusatory, angry, divisive, or prideful, not confusing being heard with being agreed with or getting our way. We should all seek to express our views, and let others do the same, "in righteousness, in holiness, and lowliness of heart, meekness and long-suffering, and in faith, and virtue, and knowledge, temperance, patience, godliness, brotherly kindness and charity; Because the promise is, if these things abound in them they shall not be unfruitful in the knowledge of the Lord" (D&C 107:30–31).

Sustaining Mortal Prophets

Equal to clarifying false dichotomies related to disagreement and sustaining is destroying false premises about the infallibility of prophets. Swinging the pendulum far to either side, some want to say that nothing prophets say is true, while others say everything is. Some believe that but little is revelatory; others believe it all is. Like most things, the truth seems more nuanced and somewhere in between. The following principles are important to help seekers to sustain modern, yet *mortal*, prophets.

Prophets Learn Line upon Line

There is a mistaken idea that because prophets are seers, they see all. Remember, however, that although Moses was told there were worlds without number, he was only given an account of this earth (see Moses 1:34–35). His view was limited. Prophets see according to their stewardship and time. Prophets "know in part, and we prophesy in part," according to Paul (1 Corinthians 13:9). For example, even in April 1830, when the Church was officially organized, Joseph Smith did not know about bishops, high priests, patriarchs, or Seventies. Those all came later. The Prophet Joseph slowly learned about the nature of God, a Heavenly Mother, eternal marriage, the divine potential of mankind, and the redemption of the dead, to name a few.[46] As Elder Bruce R. McConkie articulated, "We [prophets] get our truth and our light line upon line and precept upon precept."[47]

Prophets Operate within Culture

We may not want to think that prophets are affected by the cultural times in which they operate, but upon deeper introspection, we want and need them to be. After all, if prophets did not respond to contemporary culture then their words would not reflect the needs of the times. Searching the general conference corpus, you will see, for example, that references to "pornography" jumped dramatically in the 2000s as the internet hit mainstream society but was not much mentioned prior to 1970. Teachings on the Word of Wisdom peaked during prohibition in the 1920s and '30s. Remember, God gives according to the conditions of the children of men (see D&C 46:15). Revelation comes out of contemporary questions, which are often driven by cultural context.[48]

Prophetic Teachings Can Alter

As prophets learn line upon line and respond to culture, teachings of the past may be supplanted by further light and knowledge in the present. For example, Peter preached that Jesus went to the world of spirits to preach the gospel to those in spirit prison (see 1 Peter 3:19). In 1918, Joseph F. Smith revealed that, actually, "The Lord went not in person among the wicked and the disobedient" but "from among the righteous, he organized his forces" to have them carry the gospel message to those in spirit prison (D&C 138:29–30). More recently, the Church has modified positions on some LGBTQ questions. In 1981, the Church taught that homosexual feelings and thoughts, even "without outward sexual behavior," were a sinful violation of chastity.[49] Now the Church differentiates between desires and actions, stating, "Feelings of same-sex attraction are not a sin"[50] and that as long as they keep the law of chastity, gay members of the Church can fully participate in Church callings and ordinances.[51] In the past, Church teachings aligned more closely with past societal views of homosexuality as a learned behavior and mental disorder (classified by the American Psychological Association as such until 1973[52]) caused by sexual perversion.[53] Today, as said by President Dallin H. Oaks, "The Church does not have a position on the causes of any of these susceptibilities or inclinations, including those related to same-gender attraction."[54] While simultaneously reaffirming that the Church's position on marriage between a man and woman is central to God's plan,[55] some of these more modern Church teachings have replaced those from the past.

Prophets Can Make Mistakes

There's a colloquial saying that Catholics claim the Pope is infallible yet in reality believe he is fallible; Latter-day Saints, on the other hand, say the prophet is fallible but in reality expect him to be perfect. However, as Elder Dieter F. Uchtdorf acknowledged, there have been times in the past when "leaders in the Church have simply made mistakes."[56] Joseph Smith lost 116 pages of Book of Mormon scripture to kick off the Restoration (see D&C 3). In the Old Testament, Moses inappropriately smote the rock and took credit for it instead of speaking to the rock and acknowledging God (see Numbers 20). In the New Testament, Peter had to overcome biases toward preaching the gospel to Gentiles (see Acts 10). Elder Neil L. Andersen said, "The leaders of the Church are honest but imperfect men."[57] It is perfectly acceptable, and accurate, to respectfully view modern prophets as authorized key-holders who are yet fallible and imperfect. In fact, to do so helps us place our faith in Christ, not in mortals. But as Elder Jeffrey R. Holland counseled, "Be kind regarding human frailty. . . . Except in the case of His only perfect Begotten Son, imperfect people are all God has ever had to work with. That must be terribly frustrating to Him, but He deals with it. So should we."[58]

Prophets Won't Lead Astray

Remember, although prophets learn line upon line and can make mistakes, the Saints have been repeatedly promised that prophets can never lead the Church "astray."[59] There is a marked difference between prophets making mistakes and leading the Church astray. Drawing again on the family analogy, a helpful way to understand this distinction is to think of parents leading their children. As a dad I make many mistakes (just ask my kids). I have shortcomings and imperfections; I sometimes may say the wrong thing or even the right thing in the wrong way. (Me to my teenager: "You're going out with your hair looking like *that*?" Maybe I could have approached that better.) I, and my wife, make *mistakes*. But what would it look like for us to lead our family *astray*? That is another issue altogether. For parents to lead their family "astray" would be deliberately choosing to take their family off the proper path or knowingly choosing to do their family harm. Although, sadly, some unrighteous parents may rebelliously go against God's will and knowingly do harm, the Lord's prophets will not. In a discourse to the Saints, President Brigham Young asked: "Can a Prophet or an Apostle be mistaken? Do not ask me any such question, for I will acknowledge that all the time, but I do not acknowledge that I designedly lead this people astray one hair's breadth from the truth, and I do not knowingly do a wrong."[60] The promise is not that prophet can't make mistakes, but that the prophet will never be allowed *to purposely lead the Church away from the revealed gospel and priesthood ordinances necessary for salvation and exaltation*. If there are errors in the Church's teachings or practices, the Lord will make course corrections as needed from time to time to keep His authorized ship on course. If the Church begins to drift, which can happen, the Lord will help the captain make adjustments (the proper use of the name of the Church is but one recent corrective[61]). In a revelation to President John Taylor in 1883, the Lord said, "I will reveal unto you, from time to time, through the channels that I have appointed, everything that shall be necessary for the *future development* and *perfection* of my Church, for the *adjustment* and rolling forth of my kingdom."[62]

Prophets Have Safeguards

President Russell M. Nelson once taught that "counterbalances and safeguards abound so that no one [in prophetic leadership] can ever lead the Church astray."[63] One of those safeguards is the united voice of the First Presidency and Twelve. D&C 107:27 is the scriptural foundation for this practice, teaching that unanimous declarations carry power and validity and represent the word of the Lord. As President Gordon B. Hinckley explained: "I can assure all members of this church that in the First Presidency we follow such a procedure [of unanimity in decisions]. . . . Two counselors, working with a president, preserve a wonderful system of checks and balances. They become a safeguard that is seldom, if ever, in error and affords great strength of leadership."[64] President M. Russell Ballard taught, "When the First Presidency and the Quorum of the Twelve speak with a united voice, it is the voice of the Lord for that time."[65] Candidly, in the early Church, this scriptural expectation of unanimity was sometimes not followed as closely as it is today, creating division. The Lord did make allowances for decisions by a majority when unanimity cannot be reached, but it appears less desirable (see D&C 107:28). Modern Church leadership, however, appears to be growing in dedication to the principles of prophetic unanimity. The Church has recently seen prophetic unanimity in operation with changes to the ministering program and the two-hour Sunday meeting schedule. Each announcement was preceded and deliberately underscored with the important qualifier that all members of the First Presidency and Twelve Apostles "are united" in endorsing these changes.[66]

Prophets Are Authorized Agents

Because united prophets cannot lead the Church astray, there is an important principle related to sustaining the words of prophets that I call "the bold doctrine." That phrase comes from D&C 128:9. Referring to the sealing keys that prophets and apostles hold, Joseph Smith wrote: "It may seem to some to be a very bold doctrine that we talk of—a power which records or binds on earth and binds in heaven. . . . Hence, whatsoever those men did in authority, in the name of the Lord, and did it truly and faithfully, and kept a proper and faithful record of the same, it became a law on earth and in heaven, and could not be annulled, according to the decrees of the great Jehovah. This is a faithful saying. Who can hear it?"

The prophet seems to be teaching that whatever the Lord's servants decide 1) in prophetic authority, 2) in the Lord's name, 3) doing it truly and faithfully, and 4) keeping a record of it, *becomes God's acknowledged law on earth and in heaven.* This, indeed, is a "bold doctrine." God's ordained prophets are His "agents," which means people who have authority to act and speak on behalf of someone else. "Wherefore, as *ye are agents,* ye are on the Lord's errand; and *whatever ye do according to the will of the Lord is the Lord's business*" (D&C 64:29; emphasis added). God reveals His will to His authorized servants, but they also act as agents to bring about His will according to their unified decisions, which the Lord honors as His own. Speaking of Joseph Smith, Brigham Young said: "[God] has sent his agent, his minister to act in his name. And if he has got an agent to dictate to us here the organization is here. When a man is clothed with authority to do all business for those who sent him, what he does [is] right, and this is the kind of agent we have got, and God appointed him."[67] This, indeed, is a bold doctrine.

Sustaining Principles

Some seekers struggle to fully sustain modern, yet mortal, prophets precisely *because* of some of the previous examples. They see that the Church has changed positions in the past and they worry that current prophetic words of today may be overturned by later ones of tomorrow. So why should they follow or defend them? Or, members worry that what the prophets teach isn't revelatory and instead merely reflects the reasoning of men, biased by culture. If the past paragraphs' principles were meant to help us more accurately view prophets, the following principles are geared toward ourselves to help aid our sustaining efforts.

Be Meek and Humble

It is requisite for seekers to constantly acknowledge, "I may be wrong," or, "I may not understand all the factors." We all have blind spots. As a matter of fact, try this: Close your left eye and focus your open eye on the cross. Move your head slowly forward or backward, and eventually as you look at the left cross, the dot on the right will disappear.

Why? You have a blind spot (in this case, your nose). Remember, there are always things others see that we don't. Humility calls us to acknowledge that the collective wisdom of fifteen key-holding, called and authorized, deeply experienced and widely traveled, united prophets is most likely better informed than our individual, limited perspective.

Exercise Patience

D&C 21:5 tells us that we are to sustain prophets "in all patience and faith." Prophetic words can, at times, try our tolerance. When this happens, there is a tendency to give up on the prophetic word too quickly before it has time to plant its seed, grow, and bear fruit. We can learn from the example of Brigham Young, who had difficulty with Joseph Smith's revelation on three degrees of heavenly glory (see D&C 76). Brigham said, "When the Vision came first to me, it was directly contrary and opposed to my former education. I said, wait a little. I did not reject it, but I could not understand it."[68] A testimony of its truthfulness eventually came to him as he waited patiently. Don't give up too quickly.

Trust Generously

Scholar Patrick Mason has said that sustaining prophets, even if you disagree, means "giving them the benefit of the doubt, and offering them the same patience, grace, mercy, compassion, longsuffering, loyalty, and forgiveness that we hope they offer us."[69] Any time we approach the words of living prophets, we should do it through a "hermeneutics of trust" rather than a "hermeneutics of doubt," to apply the words of some religious scholars.[70] *Hermeneutics* refers to how we interpret and approach words—in this case, how we interpret prophetic teachings. Like most healthy relationships, trust is a must. Those who view prophets with suspicion and skepticism find it difficult to fully sustain, no matter the teaching. Those who view them with trust often better understand their intent and purposes. What we sow, we reap.

Avoid Evil Speaking

Opposite of using our mouths to pray for, defend, bless, and encourage is to use our mouths to speak evil and voice public criticisms of the prophets. Even if you disagree, you can do so without character assassination. Clearly, speaking evil of others is unchristian: "Cease to speak evil one of another" (D&C 136:23). "Thou shalt not speak evil of thy neighbor" (D&C 42:27). President George Q. Cannon once said, "God has chosen His servants. He claims it as His prerogative to condemn them, if they need condemnation. He has not given it to us individually to censure and condemn them. No man, however strong he may be in the faith, however high in the priesthood, can speak evil of the Lord's anointed and find fault with God's authority on the earth without incurring His displeasure."[71] The Lord warns, "Cursed are all those that shall lift up the heel against mine anointed, saith the Lord, and cry they have sinned when they have not sinned before me, saith the Lord" (D&C 121:16). To speak evil suggests passing unfair dispersions of judgment toward a person and pointing out faults to assail that person's character.[72]

Follow Current Prophetic Law

The Lord does not judge us based on the teachings of past prophets, but current ones. Like civil law, the current spiritual laws of the Church govern our behavior, not previous laws that have been supplanted or future ones that may one day exist. Going 70 miles per hour on the freeway in 1975 earned you a speeding ticket. Today, it earns you a honk for barely keeping up. Similarly, you couldn't rebel against Moses's law to try to get all Israel to hold the high priesthood, as Korah and his followers sadly learned, even though the very thing they asked for later came to pass (see Numbers 16). *We cannot try to get ahead or fall too far behind the voice of the living prophets, and stand approved before God.*

Conclusion: Seeking to Sustain

A few decades ago, a young stake president in Arkansas had a difficult choice to make: do I do what a member of the Seventy is telling me or risk upsetting him by saying I don't agree with what he is proposing? This stake president presided over a geographically expansive stake in Arkansas, roughly 250 square miles. His stake members were primarily poor, first-generation members of the Church. In his words, "Nobody in the stake was unemployed; 100 percent of the members of the stake were underemployed. This member of the Seventy calls and says, 'I'm coming through this area. I'd like to have the members gather on a Wednesday night . . . to teach them.'" The stake president didn't think the Seventy's idea was a good one. He worried about the time commitment, expense, and dangers required of his stake members to travel that far for a meeting—things that maybe the member of the Seventy didn't understand. What should he do? Should he quietly sustain the wishes of the Seventy and hold his peace? The young stake president's name was David A. Bednar.

Elder Bednar said that "with great deference and respect," he told his higher authority Seventy, "It's not a good idea . . ." and gave his rationale, proposing alternate solutions for the stake presidency and high council to meet with the Seventy, but not the whole stake. The Seventy "was not pleased with me," Elder Bednar remembered, but "even though he wasn't happy with it, when he got done listening [the Seventy] said, 'I can see that that's the right thing to do, so we'll adjust the schedule.'" Elder Bednar said, "You want to be strictly obedient, and if he [the Seventy] had said, 'Look, I'm telling you we're going to do it,'" Elder Bednar said he would have responded, "OK, we'll do it."[73]

Although this is a true story between a stake president and a Seventy, it is a great example of how members can seek to sustain modern prophets. In Elder Bednar's example, we can see eyes that recognized authority, ears that were willing to hear, and hands that were ready to serve. We can also see, however, a disagreement. The opposing view was expressed with deference and respect. There was a proposal of alternate solutions. Although, in this case, the authority changed his mind, Elder Bednar was willing to sustain and implement what the authority proposed, even if it went contrary to his ideas—showing feet willing to follow. This is what fully sustaining, even with some crossing tension, looks like.

Let us seek to sustain modern yet mortal prophets. Let us sustain them not only with our uplifted hands but through a holistic, full-bodied commitment that calls upon our minds, eyes, ears, lips, hearts, hands, and feet to uphold them in their prophetic position. Let us sustain even if we may disagree at times by learning how to disagree in solidarity with those whom God has appointed, utilizing councils, without resorting to organized opposition or personal rebellion. Let us sustain prophets by altering unrealistic expectations of them—casting aside a veneer of perfection for a more mature and nuanced understanding of their authorized role as they authoritatively guide the Church and kingdom. We can sustain by being more humble, more patient, more generous, and more graceful. When we seek to sustain prophets in these ways, we can raise our hands personally to heaven, acknowledging to God that—despite some inherent tensions—our personal sustaining is in the affirmative. Although there are some sustaining areas where we are weaker and others where we are stronger, we are "all in," giving "heed unto *all* [the prophet's] words . . . in *all* holiness . . . in *all* patience and faith . . . For by doing these things the gates of hell shall not prevail against you" (D&C 21:4–6; emphasis added).

 **Hide or Go Seek**

Hide

I sustain prophets only by raising my hand.
I think sustaining prophets is all or nothing, yes/no, dichotomous.
I view disagreeing with prophets as disloyalty to prophets.
I publicly oppose and organize against prophets when I think they are wrong.
I think prophets know everything and aren't influenced by culture.
I believe prophets never make any mistakes.

Go Seek

I study and seek to understand prophetic teachings.
I recognize Apostles as possessors of prophetic keys.
I listen to the prophets' inspired counsel.
I speak positively about and pray for the prophets.
I feel love/gratitude for and trust/have confidence in the prophets.
I serve diligently in my Church calling and personal stewardship.
I strive to follow and implement prophetic directives.
I participate in Church councils and encourage others to openly voice their perspectives.

Chapter 9

INVITING THE PRESENCE OF GOD

 Seeking Sentence: We are married unto another.

The holy temple represents the pinnacle of everything holy for which we seek. Every piece of doctrine or history we study, all scriptures we interpret, every spiritual impression and gift we receive, and each item of prophetic counsel we sustain are all subsumed as precursors to a celestial search that culminates in our making and keeping sacred covenants in the temple.[1] The Lord told the early Saints in Zion, "Seek the face of the Lord always" (D&C 101:38) and instructed them to build sacred temples to do so. "My presence shall be there," He told them about these temples, "for I will come into it, and all the pure in heart that shall come into it shall see God" (D&C 97:16). The covenants and ordinances of the holy temple teach us how to seek God's face: "For without [these temple covenants and ordinances], no man can see the face of God" (D&C 84:22). Moses tried to get a group of people ready to "behold the face of God," but because they did not follow the necessary requirements, they "could not endure his presence" (D&C 84:23–24).

As a new Moses (see D&C 28:2; 107:91), Joseph Smith's commission was to raise up a modern-day Israel—a kingdom of priests and priestesses[2]—who knew how to seek the face of the Lord always and experience His holy presence in their daily lives. "Therefore, sanctify yourselves that your minds become single to God," Joseph and his followers were instructed, "and the days will come that you shall see him; for he will unveil his face unto you" (D&C 88:68). It would be in the Lord's "own time" and "own way" that God would manifest His presence to them (whether physically or spiritually), but becoming holy was a requirement, no matter what. To become sanctified, a person must obey God, forsake the ways of the world, and commit to the Lord to "see my face and know that I am" (D&C 93:1; see also D&C 88:121–124). "I want you all to know God, to be familiar with him," the prophet Joseph Smith taught in the last great general conference of his life. "When we know how to come to him, [God] begins to unfold the heavens to us and tell us all about it."[3]

Obedience:
To align your life with God's will

Sacrifice:
To willingly give up what God asks you to let go

Consecration:
To dedicate your time, talents, and means to God

When we know how to come to God. This chapter explores how to come to God and seek His face—in other words, to invite His spiritual presence—through living three central, celestial covenants: obedience, sacrifice, and consecration.[4]

The Law of Obedience

When we hear the word *obedience*, we may be tempted to associate it with a person who doesn't make any mistakes. For mere mortals like you and me, that is a problematic definition. How can we keep the sacred covenant of obedience if we are sometimes, well, human? Perhaps looking at obedience through another lens may prove helpful. The root word for obedience suggests "submission,"[5] not precision. Being "faithful" derives from deep loyalty, not absolute purity.[6] The etymology of "keeping" something (such as commandments) originates from words like "desire," "look out for," and "persist" as much as putting into practice.[7] Thus, I offer an alternate definition for the law of obedience that summarizes submission, loyalty, and persistence: *alignment* with God's will. Surely, doing right and avoiding wrongdoing is one of the ways we show Jesus we love Him (see John 14:15), but the law of obedience isn't the law of perfection or mistake-free living. It is a law for those with flaws.

Consider how this definition of loyal, submissive "alignment" may help incorporate the gospel of repentance into the law of obedience (which seems contradictory if we define obedience as mistake-free living). "Therefore, I command you to repent" (D&C 19:15). "Now, this is the commandment: Repent" (3 Nephi 27:20). "For he gave a command that all men must repent" (2 Nephi 2:21). In Matthew 21, Jesus tells the parable of two children. They both were told to go and do something. The first said, "I won't!" but afterward repented, and went. The second said, "I will!" and went not. "Whither of them twain did the will of his father?" Jesus asked. "The first," was the answer (Matthew 21:31). A repentant son did the will of his father. Repenting is part of the gospel, part of keeping commandments, and part of the law of obedience also. That turns "obedience" on its head slightly, doesn't it? For mere mortals, that's a good turn.

The apparent paradox of "obedient sinners" becomes clearer when we remember obedience is *alignment*. Try this with me at home:

Close one eye and hold up your index finger. Align it with a straight line off in the distance (a corner of a wall, a door frame, a dresser, etc.). Now, with your finger aligned turn your head completely away from your finger (keeping your finger aligned in place) and look over to the complete opposite side of the room, almost turning around.

Now, look back at your finger.

Did you notice that due to turning your head, you became a little (or a lot) out of alignment with the distant vertical line, and you quickly lined your finger back up? That realization that you had turned aside, but then caught yourself and realigned yourself, is repentance.[8] That shows commitment. That shows loyalty. That shows submission. That shows alignment. That shows obedience.

A few years ago, I took my fifteen-year-old daughter out to practice driving for the first time so she could earn her learner's permit. She was all over the place. When we got in the car, her first question was what "PRNDL" meant. She then asked which pedal the brake was and which was the gas. I told her I'd answer her questions, but I first needed to pray. With her first left turn, she turned on to the wrong side of the road, into oncoming traffic. She went too fast on turns and too slow on straightaways. She didn't yield at a roundabout. But she was trying. She was doing. When she was off-base, she corrected herself. She listened to my instructions (between my screams). She didn't do everything perfectly, and I didn't expect her to. But she tried to learn what was right and to do her best at it, fixing it when she didn't. You can connect the analogy.

Repentance takes as long as it takes you to make up your mind to commit to and align your will with God's.[9] If we study scripture we find some people repenting (realigning their will) in mere moments, not months. Alma the Younger, described along with the sons of Mosiah as "the very vilest of sinners" (Mosiah 28:4), "very wicked and idolatrous" (v. 8), and people who sought to "destroy the church of God" (v. 10) repented in "three days" (Alma 36:10), becoming "redeemed of the Lord" and "born of the Spirit" (Mosiah 27:24). Conversion often takes time. Realignment can happen quickly.

One key practice to help seekers seek realignment with God is the daily exercise of sincere prayer. In our morning prayers we express devotion and love and a desire to be faithful, seeking to be led by the Spirit in the day to follow God's will. We then go about our day, striving to be faithful to our covenant commitment, but inevitably we are mortal and fall short. At night we return and report our actions to God. We confess those thoughts, words, and deeds that were out of alignment with His will. We apologize. We ask for forgiveness. We recommit to do good and be good. We again align ourselves with God. In other words, we repent. We follow this process daily, like a spiritual circadian rhythm, committing, living, accounting, repenting, committing, living, accounting, repenting—sometimes through prayers verbalized, sometimes in the quiet recesses of the heart—in a process of continual realignment. On Sunday the Lord offers us a chance to recommit to Him not just in word but in outward covenant deed, witnessing unto the Father in the name of His Son by an ordinance that we persist in being loyal and committed, aligned with heaven's will.

"How great is his joy in the soul that repenteth" (D&C 18:13). Jesus taught: "Joy shall be in heaven over one sinner that repenteth" (Luke 15:7). It matters not if we are eleventh-hour laborers, two-talent workers, or thirty-fold harvesters, so long as we are committed. Loyalty is part of the pattern of heaven. I can't do perfect, but I can do loyal, and so can you. Christ asks for complete commitment to Him, not flawless following of Him. That's why we come unto Christ and are perfected in Him (see Moroni 10:32). We have a Redeemer for a reason. We should drop our perfectionist complex and instead develop a loyalty complex to God. Let us not confuse obedience with perfection. Obedience can be viewed as persistent alignment with God's will. Obedience is seen in covenant commitment. Obedience is manifest in loyalty. We can obey the gospel in weakness.

But is obedience everything? No. The next heavenly covenant to invite the holy presence of God is seeking to live the law of sacrifice.

The Law of Sacrifice

Sacrifice is willingly giving up what God asks us to let go. In the New Testament there is the story of the rich young ruler. Notice the interplay between obedience and sacrifice when the ruler asked Jesus, "What must I do to inherit eternal life?" "Keep the commandments," Jesus told him. "All these I have kept since I was a boy," the young ruler responded. What a remarkable person! "Jesus looked at him and loved him. 'One thing you lack,' he said. 'Go, sell everything you have and give to the poor, and you will have treasure in heaven. Then come, follow me.'" The man couldn't do it, and "he went away sad, because he had great wealth" (Mark 10:17–22, NIV). He was obedient but lacked the ability to sacrifice. I'll return to that story momentarily.

One of the reasons God asks us to sacrifice is to make manifest what we truly love. My wife and I grew up with each other and hit it off after my mission. On our first date we talked, and the subject of love came up (don't ask me how). I had concluded on my mission that the truest definition of love was sacrifice. John 15:13 says, "Greater love hath no man than this, that a man lay down his life for his friends." I asked her how she viewed love: was it a feeling, an emotion, an action, something a person didn't control or that just happened? I'll never forget her response. "I think the best word to describe love is sacrifice," she said. I wanted to ask her to marry me right there on the spot.

God will ask us all to sacrifice because He wants to reveal what's in our hearts. Eve sacrificed paradise for posterity. Abraham's sacrifice was to see if he loved God more than his own boy. Lehi and Sariah sacrificed wealth and comfort for an unknown promised land. The three virgins in the book of Abraham gave up their own lives rather than worshipping false Gods. Jesus sacrificed everything. A young adult I spoke with broke up with her longtime boyfriend when he told her the Church was unimportant to him and he wouldn't marry her in the temple. "An acceptable sacrifice is when we give up something good for something of far greater worth," said Elder Dieter F. Uchtdorf.[10] As we seek to live the law of sacrifice personally, how do we know what God is asking us to let go? Consider the following four ways:

First, we all must sacrifice our natural-man tendencies that are contrary to God's character, such as pride, lust, anger, and the like (see Mosiah 3:19), offering up a broken heart and contrite spirit (see 3 Nephi 9:20). With a submissive spirit and loyal heart (see how obedience prepares us for sacrifice?), we commit to living God's timeless commandments for His children, giving up behaviors such as lying, stealing, and submitting to keeping the Sabbath, paying tithes, doing service, and so on. As we live God's timeless commandments, we next seek to implement timely teachings from modern prophets, such as sacrificing leisure time to worship in the temple more often, abstaining from social media for a time, or studying the Book of Mormon. Last, we sacrifice in ways unique to our own personal promptings from the Spirit. Perhaps these personal sacrifices are prompting us to give up time with friends for more quality time with family, or certain common foods for better health, or maybe certain Sabbath behaviors to hallow the day more fully as God's and not our own. You may wish to consider how God is asking you to sacrifice right now through each of these four categories, because God will ask each of us, in our own way, to let go for Him.

In my own life, my original goals were never to do what I do now for a profession. While I was getting my bachelor's degree, however, God let me know through numerous experiences that He had a different direction for my life than I had planned. It started when I gave a talk in church and a man came up to me and asked what I was going to do for my career. I told him either painting and drawing (my college major) or something in business. He asked me if I had thought about CES.

"What's CES?"

"The Church Educational System," he said.

"Seminary teaching?" I asked incredulously. No, not for me. Later, however, I couldn't shake his suggestion from my mind—the Spirit kept pressing itself upon my feelings and occupying my thoughts with it, to use Joseph Smith's description (see D&C 128:1). I walked to his home and knocked on his door. His wife answered and said, "Ah! He knew you'd come over!" Eventually, I looked into the CES program and went through their training classes, enjoying the experience. They offered me a full-time teaching position shortly after I graduated. At the time, however, I already had a pretty good job. I had worked through college for an up-and-coming communications company, being promoted into a management position by the time I finished my schooling. I had a good salary and stock options, with Excel spreadsheets of how much money I would make as the stock vested over time. But I felt strongly that God wanted me to teach. As flattering as it was to think that God had any plans for me, it was still a hard choice to make. When the representative for CES slid my first contract across the table to sign, my wife literally laughed out loud. It was nearly a 50% pay cut from what I was making at the time. But we felt like I should do it. That was a hard thing as a young, married twenty-four-year-old with a child and wife to care for financially.

After signing the contract, I went back to the office and told one of my coworkers I was going to take this job to teach full-time for the Church. I still remember where we were standing when he said to me, "You are a fool." I wondered if he was right. Maybe I was a fool. I wasn't completely sure I was making the right decision for my career. At that very moment, however, the Spirit brought a scripture to my mind with clarity and power. It wasn't some verse I had memorized, yet I heard it echo in my ears word for word. It said, "Beware of covetousness: for a man's life consisteth not in the abundance of the things which he posesseth" (Luke 12:15). It was almost like God was saying to me, "A person's life is not defined by worldly titles, possessions, or income. Does the world define you, or does my Word? Are you willing to let go of the material to follow the spiritual, rich young ruler?"

Now, don't get me wrong. The issue here is not about wealth or jobs. The issue is about what we love and where our heart is. God needs some Saints with wealth, and He needs other Saints with high-powered corporate jobs. He needs *all* Saints, however, to live the law of sacrifice. That is the requirement to further invite His presence into our lives. That is the requirement to show Him we love Him above all else in this world. That is the requirement that will produce the faith necessary for life and salvation.[11]

Sacrifice may be intimidating, but as many have learned, the irony is that there is no such thing as permanent sacrifice. We are always eventually paid back more than we ever let go by a generous God. Returning to the rich young ruler, after he went away, Peter turned to Jesus and said, "We have left everything to follow you!" Jesus lovingly responded, "No one who has left home or brothers or sisters or mother or father or children or fields for me and the gospel will fail to receive *a hundred times as much in this present age . . . and in the age to come eternal life*" (Mark 10:28–30, NIV). Truly, "sacrifice brings forth the blessings of heaven," as we sing.[12] The greatest reward of sacrifice is more fully experiencing the spiritual presence of God in our lives as we show Him we love Him more than any earthly thing.

When God sees people who are loyally willing to align with His will and to sacrifice as He asks, He can lead their hearts to embrace the highest and holiest of the three divine covenants: consecration.[13]

The Law of Consecration

There seems to be some confusion in the general Church about the law of consecration. A few years ago I did a survey with over 700 of my BYU students. Here was the survey question:

The law of consecration:
a) Is not practiced by the Church today
b) Is not practiced in the Church today but will be brought back in the Millennium
c) Is practiced in part in the Church today through tithes and offerings, but not in full
d) Is practiced in full in the Church today

Which do you think was selected the most often? Half of the students selected "c" and 31% selected "b." Only 17% of them responded that we are living the law of consecration in full today. I don't think the young adult perspective is very different than that of many seasoned adults. A Church leader once gave a temple recommend interview and asked an older man if he kept his temple covenants. "Only the ones God has asked me to keep," the man answered. "Which do you think He hasn't asked you to keep?" the leader responded curiously. Chastity? Obedience? The man responded with saying, "Consecration."

Some of the misunderstanding that surrounds the law of consecration arises by inadvertently mixing three concepts: 1) all things common (sometimes referred to as stewardship of properties), 2) the United Order/firm, and 3) the law of consecration. Those terminologies, although sometimes used interchangeably over the years in various Church teachings, all have unique origins and carry distinct ideas. "All things common" (3 Nephi 26:19; 4 Nephi 1:3; Acts 2:44)—or giving over to the bishop all your property and being deeded back a portion according to your wants and needs (see D&C 51)—is *one application* of consecration. "The United Firm" or "Order of Enoch" (see D&C 78; 82; 104) was a consecration-based business organization of Church leaders in Kirtland and Missouri who, by covenant, united Church businesses (firms). There have been other cooperative movements in the Church over the decades, all with varying ways to apply consecration,[14] but the principles and law have always remained.[15]

Therefore, try not to confuse *applications* of the law of consecration with the divine law itself. We don't sacrifice animals today, but the law of sacrifice has not burnt up. The application of it—how we live the law—has simply altered. To think that we don't live the law of consecration today because we don't meet with the bishop and hand over all our property is like thinking we don't live the law of sacrifice because we don't meet with a priest to hand over a lamb. To quote scholar Steven Harper, "Some Latter-day Saints mistakenly think that [the dissolving of the United Firm or ceasing all things common] ended the law of consecration, but that is akin to saying that if NASA were to stop functioning, the laws of physics would cease to be."[16]

President Gordon B. Hinckley said: "The law of sacrifice and the law of consecration were not done away with and are still in effect."[17] The law of consecration is "a covenant and a deed which cannot be broken" (D&C 42:30). It is a celestial law. It may be *the* celestial law. "The law of consecration," said scholar Hugh Nibley, is "the consummation of the laws of obedience and sacrifice" and "the threshold of the celestial kingdom."[18]

So, what is it, then? The law of consecration is that *as God's agent, you dedicate your time, talents, and means to building up God's kingdom on earth as He directs you.* To consecrate means to dedicate something, or to set it apart as holy.[19] Just like laws of chastity or obedience, we first commit to dedicate and consecrate our lives to God at baptism. Faithful Latter-day Saints renew and deepen their covenant of consecration to God in the holy temple. The Church's booklet *Preparing to Enter the Holy Temple* says that through consecration, "We covenant to give of our resources in time and money and talent—all we are and all we possess—to the interest of the kingdom of God upon the earth."[20]

"The law of consecration," said Elder Bruce R. McConkie, "is that we consecrate our time, our talents, and our money and property to the cause of the Church; such are to be available to the extent they are needed to further the Lord's interests on earth."[21] A good word to help understand consecration is the word *dedicate*. Sacrifice is giving things up. Consecration is dedicating them to God to be available for His use as He directs, but rarely do we let them go. Like we do with consecrated oil, we offer the thing to God for His purposes, but we retain and exercise control over its use as an authorized agent.

Three principles that undergird living the law of consecration in the Doctrine and Covenants are ownership, stewardship, and agency/accountability.[22]

Ownership

The principle of ownership means we understand that God owns everything. If you want to understand what you truly own, ask yourself what you will take with you when you die. Brigham Young once said, "What have we that is really our own to consecrate? Nothing at all."[23] Everything you and I have on this earth is a gift, down to our very breath (see Mosiah 2:21). Doctrine and Covenants 104:14 states, "I, the Lord, stretched out the heavens, and built the earth, my very handiwork; and all things therein are mine." In fact, the Lord wants us to understand this point so much that He says "all things are mine" four times in that same section (see D&C 104:14–14, 55–56). I was once cleaning up our family DVDs because they were irresponsibly scattered everywhere and getting scratched. I was matching up the discs to their cases when I grabbed a case that had a little sticker sent from Disney that said, "This Disney DVD belongs to the Sweat family." I looked at it and said in my mind, "That's false doctrine, Disney! This DVD belongs to . . . God! If this were a true doctrinal sticker, it would say, 'This DVD belongs to God, and the Sweat family are STEWARDS; therefore, Sweat children, be better stewards or there may be weeping, wailing, and gnashing of teeth." The dust of the earth, the elements of its creation, all things upon the face thereof, even our very mortal bodies, are not ours but God's (see 1 Corinthians 6:19–20). Thus, if we are not owners, the next logical principle of consecration is that we are stewards.

Stewardship

The Lord said in D&C 42:32, "Every [person] shall be . . . a steward over [their] own property." Stewardship implies being a temporary overseer of something. Yet it isn't ours. Even though I might say, "This is my home," it isn't really. I am just a steward over it—a temporary controller—paying the mortgage. One day this home and the land it sits on will slip right out of my hands to someone else to become its steward. While it is in my care, however, I oversee it and try to do with it as pleases God. I try to be a good steward and beautify my yard, take care of the walls and carpets and fixtures, and use the space to live and gather family and friends in a way that the Holy Spirit can be present. I retain the home, but I've dedicated it to God in prayer not just to protect it from a potential fire or flood, but more important, for His use and purposes. The same is true of our time, and our talents, and our lives. We temporarily have these bodies, these minds, these opportunities, these callings, these abilities, these temporalities. We seek to consecrate them in a way that pleases God as the giver. "God, what would you have me to do with my_____?" we pray. "Father, I've decided to do _____ with my time. Does that please You?" "Lord, I want to pursue _____ with my abilities. Is that in harmony with Your desires?" These kinds of internal dialogues with Deity indicate the mind of a faithful steward.

Related to stewardship, remember that God tells us to "stand in the place of thy stewardship" (D&C 42:53). He doesn't tell us to stand in the place of our neighbor's. For whatever reason, some people want to tell others what to do with their time, their talents, and their means. Outside of general set Church standards of worthiness, how people exercise their stewardship is individualized. God may be telling you to do something with your time, talents, and means, but He may be giving a different directive to the person sitting next to you on the pew.

God speaks through individual whispers, not bullhorn calls on street corners. Let us stand in our stewardship and avoid stepping on anyone else's toes by inappropriately standing in theirs. God will ask us to account for what we did in our stewardship, not our neighbor's.

Accountability

As stewards, the third principle of consecration is that we are agents who are accountable to the owner. The Lord said, "It is expedient that I, the Lord, should make every [person] accountable, as a steward . . . and to be agents unto themselves" (D&C 104:13–17). An agent is someone who has been authorized to act for God, to represent Him. "Agency" doesn't only mean the ability to choose; it also means the power to represent and act in behalf of others. As consecrated stewards, we are the Lord's agents to bring about His business. One of the great things about consecrated agency is that the Lord doesn't need to tell us everything to do. We know His general will. As parents, it's somewhat frustrating when we must tell our kids every little thing to do for their Saturday chores, holding their hands along the way. They know their assignments. They know how their part of the house should look. They know we shouldn't have to ask, "Why didn't you sweep the kitchen floor?" Nor should they respond, "You never said I had to do that as part of cleaning the kitchen." God says, "It is not meet that I should command in all things; for he that is compelled in all things, the same is a slothful and not a wise servant . . . verily I say, men should be anxiously engaged in a good cause, and do many things of their own free will, and bring to pass much righteousness, for the power is in them, wherein they are agents unto themselves" (D&C 58:26–27). Some of our best consecration is when we use our agency and choose to dedicate our time, talents, and means for good, even if God didn't command or tell us to do it. We are proactively learning to live like God as that happens.

Modern Consecration

We need not wait for any prophetic directive from on high to live this eternal law of consecration. We need only to implement principles of ownership, stewardship, and agency/accountability in ourselves today. You can fully live the law of consecration today by 1) implementing current prophetic directives regarding your time, talents, and means, and 2) asking God in prayer how He would have you use your time, talents, and means and then following personal promptings from the Holy Ghost.

If God whispers to attend college full-time and you do it, that's consecration. If you choose to coach your son's basketball team with your time and talents because you believe it to be consistent with God's priorities for you, then that's consecration. If you get an extra bonus check from work and you feel to share part of it with someone less financially prosperous, that's consecration. If you willingly let the young men and women use your property for youth conference, that's consecration. If you proactively choose to go help a neighbor shovel snow, that's consecration. My wife, thinking of consecration, once said to me, "Everyone has needs and everyone has abundance." When God has thousands of servants who have consecrated their all to Him, what can He bring about? Zion (see epilogue).

 ## Seekers wanted!

Prayerfully reflect on all that God has given you—your life, your abilities, your opportunities, your means, etc. After prayerful reflection, write a brief paragraph in your personal journal under each of the following headings about how you feel you can fully apply and live the law of consecration in your life today.

How can I better consecrate my time?
How can I better consecrate my money and possessions?
How can I better consecrate my talents?
How can I better consecrate myself and my life?

Conclusion: Married to Christ

Seeking to be obedient, seeking to sacrifice, and seeking to be consecrated invite the presence of God and help us "seek [God's] face continually" (1 Chronicles 16:10–11). These holy patterns are like steps to approach the throne of God—first we show our loyalty, next we show our selflessness, and then we show our complete dedication. They show a heart wedded to and one with God.

Indeed, one of the most powerful and frequent metaphors Jesus used to describe His covenant relationship with His followers was marriage (see Luke 5:34; D&C 58:11; Matthew 25:1–13; John 3:28–29). "I am married unto you," He plainly said to the Israelites (Jeremiah 3:14). "Thy Maker is thine husband," Isaiah wrote (Isaiah 54:5). Paul reminded the Romans, "Ye should be married to another, even to him who is raised from the dead" (Romans 7:4). We became metaphorically married to the Messiah when we entered the waters of baptism and made a covenant with Him—a ceremony that greatly parallels a wedding. Usually dressed in white, there were witnesses, vows of faithfulness, a ceremony done by authority, and giving of gifts. We even took upon us a new name. Jesus was and is the Bridegroom, and all of us as His covenant disciples are His bride. Marriage is a powerful metaphor for our covenant relationship with God because we generally understand what a good covenant marriage looks like—and a bad one. Because we all have different personal experiences and backgrounds, the metaphor of marriage may be difficult for some, but whatever our actual marriage status, we can all have an ideal covenant relationship with God if we seek His presence. Obedience, sacrifice, and consecration show us how.

Likening the marriage covenant to obedience, we are deeply committed to God. We are, to quote President Gordon B. Hinckley, "fiercely loyal."[24] We have no other love before Him. We don't let our eye wander at the newest attractive neighboring philosophy and go "whoring after" other gods (Exodus 34:15–16). We desire to be aligned with the Lord and humbly and quickly say sorry when we are out of line. We recommit and pledge ourselves. We participate in the sacrament, an outward manifestation of our inward commitment. Above all, we don't ever give up on this relationship. We "keep" this relationship with persistent love and realignment.

Likening marriage to sacrifice, when we offer our heart to God upon the altar, we say, "I am willing to give up anything that is required for You." It is easy to say I love you, but sacrifice allows us to demonstrate that actual love. We let go of actions that harm our covenant relationship and we forsake attitudes that are abrasive to the Spirit. If our right eye offends God, we cut it out. We bridle our worldly passions. We spend time with God, talk to one another, attend the weekly family get-together on Sunday, and are kind and loving to our in-laws. We give up our individual will to seek a cohesive, unified will.

Likening marriage to consecration, we are completely dedicated to God. We offer up all we have and are to our heavenly spouse. We give our best gifts to Him. We know His mind and know His desires. We have become one with Him. Thus, we begin to represent Him to others, as He is us and we are Him. We have the authority to make decisions for Him— spiritual power of attorney to bring about His desires as we interact in the world in His behalf. What is ours is His, and what is His is ours. We freely share our time, talents, and means, and He freely gives all His divine gifts to us in return as His covenant bride, even all that He has (see D&C 84:38).

As the holy temple teaches, obedience, sacrifice, and consecration are three covenant connections that help us create a deep, close, intimate relationship with God and invite His holy spiritual presence into our lives. Using the Old Testament temple as a metaphor, obedience takes us into the inner court, completing sacrifices take us into the holy place, and dedicated acts of consecration pass us through the veil into the holy of holies, communing with His glory.

President Ezra Taft Benson said: "The celestial kingdom, residence of God, our Eternal Father, is comprised of men and women who have complied with divine law. . . . Celestial laws, embodied in certain ordinances belonging to the Church of Jesus Christ, are complied with by voluntary covenants. The laws are spiritual. Thus, our Father in Heaven has ordained certain holy sanctuaries, called temples, in which these laws may be fully explained, the laws include the law of obedience and sacrifice . . . and the law of consecration."[25]

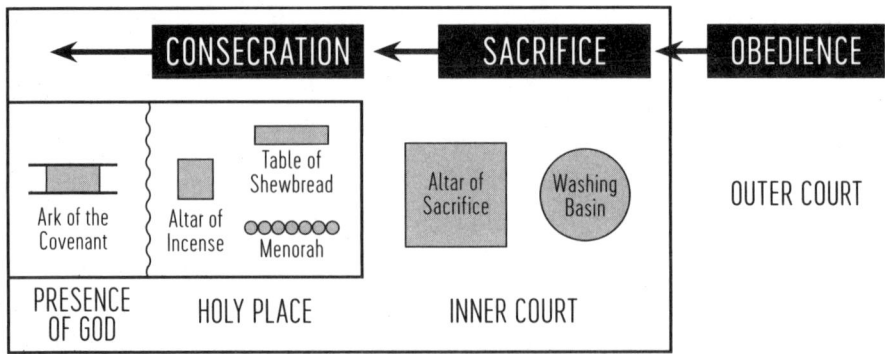

This is how we to come to God. This is what causes the heavens to open and us to be taught from on high, so we can enjoy the spiritual presence of God in our daily lives. Obedience, sacrifice, and consecration are how we "seek the face of the Lord always" (D&C 101:38). Lord, let us seek thee.

 Hide or Go Seek

Hide

    I can't be obedient because I often do things wrong.

    I'm afraid to sacrifice for God because I will lose more than I gain.

    I don't think consecration is required today like it was in the past.

    I can't enjoy the presence of God in my life as others do.

Go Seek

    Obedience is persistent alignment, and I can be loyal to God.

    I am willing to give up whatever God asks me to let go.

    I dedicate my time, talents, and means to do God's will as His agent.

    I expect to have the presence of God in my life as I live sacred covenants.

Epilogue

SEEKING ZION

 **Seeking Sentence: The Restoration of all things is when God's will is done perfectly on earth as it is in heaven.**

We often talk about the Restoration in the past tense—Joseph Smith saw God the Father and His Son, Jesus Christ; he translated the Book of Mormon; the priesthood was restored; and the Church was organized. We should, however, devote just as much time to looking forward in the Restoration as we do in looking back. The ninth article of faith teaches: "We believe all that God has revealed, all that He does now reveal, and we believe that He will yet reveal many great and important things pertaining to the Kingdom of God" (emphasis added).

In other words, THE Restoration of all things hasn't happened yet. It is a future event.

This is a concept that we, as members of the restored Church of Jesus Christ, aren't familiar hearing. There is a major difference, however, between the Restoration of the Church, and "the restoration of all things spoken by the mouth of all the holy prophets since the world began" (D&C 27:6). The Restoration of the Church occurred in April 1830 on a family farm in Fayette, New York, with Joseph Smith and a few dozen of his converts. The Restoration of all things will occur sometime in the future, with Jesus coming in glory out of the sky and the whole world watching. Although it is appropriate to use Peter's discourse in Acts 3 to refer to the beginning of the Restoration in this dispensation, notice Peter's words about when the restoration of "all things" will take place: "Repent ye therefore, and be converted, that your sins may be blotted out, when the times of refreshing shall come from the presence of the Lord; And he shall send Jesus Christ, which before was preached unto you: Whom the heaven must receive until the times of restitution of all things, which God hath spoken by the mouth of all his holy prophets since the world began" (Acts 3:19–21).

The "times of refreshing" that will come "from the presence of the Lord" refers to when Jesus will return to the earth at the Second Coming and the Resurrection and Restoration ensues. The "heavens must receive" Him until He returns in power and great glory. The Restoration of all things is a future event. Thus, Elder Dieter F. Uchtdorf asked: "Are you sleeping through the Restoration? . . . In reality, the Restoration is an ongoing process; we are living in it right now. . . . The exciting developments of today are part of that long-foretold period of preparation that will culminate in the glorious Second Coming of our Savior, Jesus Christ."[1]

Grasping the Restoration of all things as a future event requires understanding Jesus's key role as a restorer. The fundamental premise of restoration is to return things to an unimpaired condition. The basic definition of the word atonement means to reconcile or to restore to harmony;[2] to bring things undone back to at-one; to put things in their rightful state; to return things to an unimpaired condition. The central premise of Jesus's Atonement is to perfectly right all mortal wrongs. This is ultimately what the grace of Jesus does: it restores. As our Savior, He takes things in their fallen condition and perfectly repays, reinstates, renews, refreshes, returns, rectifies, redeems, recompenses, and renews. The divine power that Jesus releases throughout the universe is His power of restoration. The Restoration of all things is when, through the grace and Atonement of Jesus Christ, all the effects of the Fall of Adam and Eve are rectified and made right. The Restoration of all things will culminate with the millennial reign of the Savior, when this earth will be renewed and the knowledge of the Lord will cover the earth. As Biblical scholar N. T. Wright stated, when Jesus returns, He "will perform a great act of new creation through which [the world] will be restored to the way God always intended it to be."[3]

Jesus's sublime prayer, known as the Lord's prayer, includes a prayer for the Restoration of all things. The Lord prayed: "Thy kingdom come. Thy will be done in earth, as it is in heaven" (Matthew 6:10). Those concepts are correlated: God's kingdom is restored to the degree that we help God's will to be done on this earth as it is done perfectly in heaven. This is an exciting concept that suddenly opens us up to become active participants in the ongoing Restoration. It helps us see how we, too, can build the kingdom and establish cities of Zion.

The Ongoing Restoration

In the beginnings of the Restoration, Saints were repeatedly told to "seek to bring forth and establish the cause of Zion" (D&C 6:6; 11:6; 12:6; 14:6) and to "seek the kingdom of God" (D&C 11:23), even to "seek it with all your hearts" (D&C 38:19). Joseph's vision of Zion was a city where the righteous would be gathered together, centered on a temple, where each man and woman were "filled with sacred knowledge, as the waters cover the great deep"; where the people were "of one heart and one mind" and "walk with God like Enoch" because they are "free from sin." Zion is where "honest men" build up "a city of righteousness" so holy that "even upon the bells of the Horses shall be written Holiness to the Lord."[4] When Joseph spoke of seeking Zion, he spoke of creating these holy communities, beginning with one city and then creating another and another, "and so fill up the world in these last days"[5] until, one day, God's will was perfectly done across the earth as it is in heaven.

The vision of Zion is not a past-tense work, martyred with Joseph and buried with nineteenth-century pioneers in black-and-white photographs on American plains. Establishing Zion continues with living Saints in high-def color in cosmopolitan cities today. We have a part in contributing to the Restoration of all things as much as, or perhaps more than, those in Joseph Smith's time. We have more resources, more members, more experience, more temples, more influence, and more reach. Although building literal cities of Zion may not be our task, we are a people who believe in miraculous possibilities to bring about God's will on earth in the communities in which we now live. As Elder Jeffrey R. Holland said, "That miracle is you, the great faithful but often unheralded body of the Church who play your part in the ongoing saga of the Restoration."6 So what role can we play in the ongoing Restoration? I offer three ideas:

THE RESTORATION
God's will on earth
as it is in heaven

Seek active participation in the work of salvation. The purposes of the Church include "helping members live the gospel of Jesus Christ, gathering Israel through missionary work, caring for the poor and needy, and enabling the salvation of the dead by building temples and performing vicarious ordinances."7 We can participate actively in the ongoing Restoration by gathering Israel, serving in callings, teaching Church classes, doing temple work, serving missions, paying our tithes and offerings, teaching the gospel to our families, attending our meetings, and many more righteous efforts.

Seek to bring God's will into your life, family, ward, and community. Seekers can help bring about the Restoration of all things by participating in their families, wards, and communities by living, and helping others to live, in ways consistent with the Lord's will. Anything we do to bring to pass God's will, in any environment, helps us lay a brick to build cities of Zion and the kingdom of God. This could be as small as not taking offense to an ill-advised comment, appropriately reprimanding someone for an off-color comment, or taking dinner to a needy person, or as large as taking in a refugee family. While I have been somewhat critical of certain aspects of modern American culture in previous chapters, many of the things that contemporary Americans are passionate about—such as providing adequate health care, quality education, caring for the environment, or assisting with the international refugee crisis—are the very things the modern Church is also focused on trying to address to bring about God's will. As you use your circle of influence to bring about God's will in your individual arenas, it spreads the tent of Zion for the Restoration of all things.

 Seekers wanted!

The following are a few of the Church's websites that deal with some current social and contemporary issues. How familiar are you with them? Take ten minutes and search one or two of the following Church websites. Explore their content to see how you can contribute to the ongoing Restoration:

I Was a Stranger—An Effort to Help Refugees: https://www.lds.org/refugees
LDS Charities: https://www.ldscharities.org
Helping Those with Disabilities: https://www.lds.org/topics/disability
The Divine Institution of Marriage: https://www.mormonnewsroom.org/article/the-divine-institution-of-marriage
Mormon and Gay: https://mormonandgay.lds.org
Combating Pornography: https://www.overcomingpornography.org
LDS Philanthropies: https://www.ldsphilanthropies.org
Provident Living: https://providentliving.lds.org
Religious Freedom and "Fairness for All": https://www.lds.org/religious-freedom
Environmental Stewardship: https://www.lds.org/topics/environmental-stewardship-and-conservation
Volunteer Time and Talent: https://www.lds.org/topics/serve-and-teach/volunteer-time-and-talent
Family Search: https://www.familysearch.org
Global Education Initiative: https://www.lds.org/church-education?cid=rdb_v_church-education_eng_education
Perpetual Education Fund: https://www.lds.org/topics/pef-self-reliance
Strengthen Families: https://www.lds.org/topics/family
Family Services: https://providentliving.lds.org/lds-family-services
Adoption: https://providentliving.lds.org/lds-family-services/adoption
Employment: https://www.ldsjobs.org
Just Serve: https://www.justserve.org/

Seek to pass the covenant on to your children. Another key to participating in the ongoing Restoration is to understand that ultimately, the Restoration is not "the Church," nor anything organizational. The Restoration is familial. God intends all His children to be "restored" to His presence through the covenants of exaltation, which are centered in eternal families bound up by the holy priesthood. Thus, a major part of your participation in the ongoing Restoration is, through the Church, to receive for yourself and then pass on the covenants of salvation and exaltation to your descendants. In D&C 86 the Lord gave an alternate interpretation of the parable of the wheat and the tares. Instead of the wheat and tares representing individuals, they represented dispensations. The Lord then taught that in this dispensation, "the blade is yet tender" and the kingdom still small, and it needs time to develop. Although the kingdom is small, some have been fortunate enough to have received the restored gospel covenants. Then, the grand lesson: "Therefore your life and the priesthood have remained, and must needs remain through you and your lineage until the restoration of all things spoken by the mouths of all the holy prophets since the world began" (D&C 86:10; emphasis added).

Our key role in the restitution of all things is to pass on the covenants of the Restoration to our lineage—our children—to bind them up into the covenant by the restored sealing power. President Gordon B. Hinckley said, "Never permit yourself to become a weak link in the chain of your generations. It is so important that we pass on without a blemish our inheritance of body and brain and, if you please, faith and virtue untarnished to the generations who will come after us. You young men and you young women, most of you will marry and have children. Your children will have children, as will the children who come after them. Life is a great chain of generations that we in the Church believe must be linked together."[8]

The Lord invites each of us to seek to bring forth and establish Zion, today. We can contribute to the ongoing Restoration by participating in the work of salvation, working in our individual spheres of influence to bring about God's will on this earth, and working within our families by remaining faithful to priesthood covenants and passing those covenant blessings on to our lineage. The Restoration of all things is about restoring the earth, through Christ's atoning grace and power, to its intended and perfected condition. It is about restoring God's ruling will to this earth as it is in heaven, overthrowing evil and anything not in harmony with His ways. It is about restoring our premortal familial relationship with God, our eternal Father and Mother, so we can again enjoy Their presence. It is about restoring our mortal relationships, our earthly ties to spouse, children, parents, siblings, and loved ones that are bound by celestial priesthood powers. In the end, the Restoration of all things is to be restored into our "intended condition" of fulfilled divine potential, on a perfected earth, where gods are enthroned with "kingdoms, principalities, powers, dominions" (D&C 132:19). The Restoration of all things is a future event, but we can seek to assist in helping to bring it to pass today.

 Hide or Go Seek

Hide

I think the Restoration of all things has already happened.
I think the Restoration is about the Church.
I don't think I have an active role in the ongoing Restoration.

Go Seek

I actively seek to build Zion by serving in the Church.
I try to bring about God's will on earth as in heaven in my communities.
I am loyal to my priesthood covenants and seek to pass them on to my posterity.

NOTES

Epigraph
Dieter F. Uchtdorf, "Can You Hear the Music?" BYU Devotional, January 15, 2019, https://speeches.byu.edu/talks/dieter-f-uchtdorf_can-you-hear-the-music/.

Prologue: Seeking God
1. Online Etymology Dictionary, "seek," https://www.etymonline.com/word/seek#etymonline_v_23110.
2. M. Russell Ballard, "The Opportunities and Responsibilities of CES Teachers in the 21st Century," Address delivered to CES Religious Educators, February 26, 2016.
3. Written approval was obtained from Steven Harper to use the same title for this book.
4. Steven Harper, "Seekers Wanted," BYU Women's Conference Address, April 30, 2015. Transcribed by the author.
5. The single most common descriptor associated with "seeker" in general conference talks is the adjective "honest." Search "seeker" on www.lds-general-conference.org, as discussed in Chapter 3.

Part 1: Seeking Knowledge
1. "History, 1838–1856, volume C-1 [2 November 1838–31 July 1842][b]," 904[b], http://www.josephsmithpapers.org/paper-summary/history-1838–1856-volume-c-1–2-november-1838–31-july-1842/86.

Chapter 1: Studying Church History
1. Charles Walker, diary, February 2, 1893, published as A. Karl Larsen and Katharine Miles Larsen, eds., *Diary of Charles Lowell Walker* (Logan, Utah: Utah State University Press, 1980), 755–56.
2. Testimony of Peter Ingersoll in E.D. Howe, *Mormonism Unvailed*, 1834, 235–36.
3. Lucy Smith, Biographical Sketches of Joseph Smith, 1853, 107.
4. See Richard Bushman, *Rough Stone Rolling* (New York: Knopf, 2005), 118.
5. Marlin K. Jensen, "Stand in the Sacred Grove," *Ensign*, December 2014.
6. See Shipps and Welch, *The Journals of William E. McLellin*, 325–27. See also https://history.lds.org/article/doctrine-and-covenants-william-mclellin?lang=eng.
7. "Introduction to Journals: Volume 3," The Joseph Smith Papers, http://www.josephsmithpapers.org/intro/introduction-to-journals-volume-3.

8. Read all of the primary and secondary accounts of the First Vision at http://www.josephsmithpapers.org/site/accounts-of-the-first-vision.
9. https://news.northwestern.edu/stories/2012/09/your-memory-is-like-the-telephone-game; emphasis added.
10. Years after the event, Williams said he was involved in a helicopter that took enemy fire during the war on terrorism in Iraq, which turned out to not be true. It appears he wasn't intentionally deceptive but had confounded and coopted others' memories as his own. See Malcolm Gladwell, "Free Brian Williams," *Revisionist History*, Season 3, Episode 4.
11. https://rsc.byu.edu/archived/volume-12-number-1-2011/seekers-guide-historical-accounts-joseph-smiths-first-vision.
12. Martha Howell & Walter Prevenier, From *Reliable Sources: An Introduction to Historical Methods*, (Ithica, NY: Cornell University Press, 2001), 1.
13. From *Reliable Sources*, 19.
14. Dean C. Jessee, ed., *The Personal Writings of Joseph Smith* (Salt Lake City, Utah: Deseret Book, 1984), xiv, italics in original.
15. Matthieu Santerre, "Can History Be Objective?" https://theartofpolemics.com/2014/09/05/can-history-be-objective/.
16. https://www.lds.org/topics/plural-marriage-in-kirtland-and-nauvoo?lang=eng.
17. http://www.telegraph.co.uk/news/worldnews/northamerica/usa/11223347/Mormon-church-finally-admits-founder-Joseph-Smith-was-polygamist-with-40-wives.html.
18. See James B. Allen, "Eight Contemporary Accounts of the First Vision—What Do We Learn from Them?" *Improvement Era*, 73 (1970): 4–13.
19. See Anthony Sweat, "The role of art in teaching Latter-day Saint history and doctrine," *The Religious Educator*, vol. 16 (2), 41–57.
20. See the preface to the 1830 edition of the Book of Mormon.
21. Jonathan Hadley "Golden Bible," *The Palmyra Freeman*, August 11, 1829. 2.
22. Christian Goodwillie, "Shaker Richard McNemar: The Earliest Book of Mormon Reviewer," *Journal of Mormon History*, vol. 37, no. 2 (Spring 2011), 143.
23. "Last Testimony of Sister Emma," *Saints' Herald* 26 (Oct. 1, 1879), 289–90.
24. *An Address to All Believers in Christ*, 1887, 36.
25. Dean C. Jessee, "Joseph Knight's Recollection of Early Mormon History," *BYU Studies*, Vol. 17, No. 1 (1976), p. 35.
26. *Deseret Evening News*, December 13, 1881.
27. Hedges et al., *The Joseph Smith Papers, Journals*, Volume 2, xxv.
28. *Reliable Sources*, 2

Chapter 2: Evaluating Church Doctrine

1. See George Albert Smith, Conference Report, April 1908; *The Messenger* (Salt Lake City: Aaronic Priesthood Department), August 1961, No. 62; Joseph Fielding Smith, *Answers to Gospel Questions*, Vol. I (Salt Lake City: Deseret Book, 1966), 151.
2. See Spencer W. Kimball, *The Miracle of Forgiveness* (Salt Lake City: Bookcraft, 1969), 243–44.
3. See Joseph Fielding Smith, *Doctrines of Salvation, Vol. 2* (Salt Lake City: Deseret Book, 1958), 31–32.

4. See Brigham Young as cited in Wilford Woodruff Journal, 5 Aug. 1855.
5. See J. Reuben Clark, *Church News*, 23 April 1960, 3.
6. Part of the following content is summarized and amended from two coauthored articles: Sweat, A., MacKay, M., Dirkmaat, G., "Doctrine: Models to evaluate types and sources of Latter-day Saint teachings," *The Religious Educator*, vol. 17 (3), 101–25; Sweat, A., MacKay, M., Dirkmaat, G., "Evaluating Latter-day Saint doctrine" (chapter), in Ostler, C., MacKay, M., Gardner, B,. eds., *Foundations of the Restoration: Fulfillment of the Covenant Purposes* (Provo, Utah: BYU Religious Studies Center/Deseret Book), 23–44.
7. Merriam-Webster's Collegiate Dictionary, 11th ed., s.v. "doctrine."
8. https://www.mormonnewsroom.org/article/approaching-mormon-doctrine.
9. See Dieter F. Uchtdorf, "Christlike Attributes," *Ensign*, November 2005; D. Todd Christofferson, "The Doctrine of Christ," *Ensign*, May 2012; Robert D. Hales, "Come Follow Me by Practicing Christian Love and Service," *Ensign*, November 2016.
10. Strong's Concordance, G1321, rendering "doctrine" as didachē, meaning "1. Teaching" and "2. The act of teaching."
11. Doctrine and Covenants, 1835 ed., http://josephsmithpapers.org/paperSummary/doctrine-and-covenants-1835#!/paperSummary/doctrine-and-covenants-1835&p=13.
12. "Fundamentals of Gospel Teaching and Learning," *Gospel Teaching and Learning: A Handbook for Teachers and Leaders in Seminaries and Institutes of Religion* (Salt Lake City: Intellectual Reserve, 2012), 10–37.
13. David A. Bednar, *Increase in Learning* (Salt Lake City: Deseret Book, 2011), 151. On another occasion, before he was a member of the Quorum of the Twelve Apostles, then BYU–Idaho President David A. Bednar taught, "Doctrine refers to the eternal, unchanging, and simple truths of the gospel of Jesus Christ" ("Teach Them to Understand," Ricks College Campus Education Week devotional, 4 June 1998, 4).
14. Search "Never change" on LDS General Conference Corpus to see some examples, such as J. Golden Kimball, CR 1912; Joseph Fielding Smith, CR 1920; Rudger Clawson, CR 1930.
15. Boyd K. Packer, "Revelation in a Changing World," *Ensign*, November 1989.
16. Boyd K. Packer, "Revelation in a Changing World," *Ensign*, November 1989.
17. See Robert J. McCue, "Did the Word of Wisdom become a commandment in 1851?," *Dialogue*, vol. 14, no. 3, 66–77; see also Steven C. Harper, *The Word of Wisdom* (Orem, Utah), 2007.
18. *Preach My Gospel* (Salt Lake City: Intellectual Reserve, 2004), 204.
19. As cited in Robert L. Millet, "What Is Our Doctrine?," *Religious Educator* 4, no. 3 (2003), 17.
20. *The Joseph Smith Papers*, History, 1838–1856, volume D-1 [1 August 1842–1 July 1843].
21. M. Gerald Bradford and Larry E. Dahl, "Doctrine: Meaning, Source, and History of Doctrine," in *Encyclopedia of Mormonism*, ed. Daniel H. Ludlow (Macmillan: New York, 1992), 1:395.
22. These four categories are based upon those that Robert L. Millet identified. See Robert Millet, "What Is Our Doctrine?," *Religious Educator* 4, no. 3 (2003), 19.
23. B. H. Roberts, sermon of 10 July 1921, delivered in Salt Lake Tabernacle, printed in *Deseret News*, 23 July 1921, 7, as cited in Stephen E. Robinson, *Are Mormons Christians?* (Salt Lake City: Deseret Book, 1991), 15.
24. D. Todd Christofferson, "The Blessings of Scripture," *Ensign*, May 2010.

25. Russell M. Nelson, "Scriptural Witnesses," *Ensign*, November 2007.
26. Gordon B. Hinckley, "What Are People Asking about Us?," *Ensign*, November 1998.
27. LDS Newsroom, "Approaching Mormon Doctrine."
28. Gordon B. Hinckley, "God Is at the Helm," *Ensign*, May 1994.
29. M. Russell Ballard, "Stay in the Boat and Hold On!," *Ensign*, November 2014.
30. D. Todd Christofferson, "The Doctrine of Christ," *Ensign*, April 2012.
31. See M. Russell Ballard, in *Preach My Gospel*: Introduction for Leaders, Missionary Training Satellite Broadcast, 15 October 2004, DVD. See also Benjamin White, "The History of *Preach My Gospel*," *Religious Educator* 14, no. 1 (2013): 129–58.
32. See Russell M. Nelson, opening remarks, in Conference Report, October 2018; see also Russell M. Nelson, "Ministering," *Ensign*, May 2018.
33. LDS Newsroom, "Approaching Mormon Doctrine"; see this exact statement repeated in Elder D. Todd Christofferson, "The Doctrine of Christ," *Ensign*, April 2012.
34. Neil L. Andersen, "Trial of Your Faith," *Ensign*, November 2012.
35. Dean L. Larsen, "I Have a Question," *Ensign*, August 1977.
36. See *Journal of Discourses*, 2:81–82.
37. See *Journal of Discourses*, 2:90.
38. Orson Pratt, *The Seer*, October 1853 (republished electronically by Seagull Book & Tape, 1993), 105.
39. Wilford Woodruff, Wilford Woodruff's Journal, 1833–1898 Typescript (Salt Lake City: Signature Books, 1985), 8:187, July 22, 1883.
40. Charles W. Penrose, "Peculiar Questions Briefly Answered," *Improvement Era*, September 1912.
41. Wayne Lynn, "I Have A Question," *Ensign*, June 1997.
42. "LDS do not endorse claims in 'Da Vinci,'" *Deseret News*, 17 May 2006; retrieved from http://www.deseretnews.com/article/635208214/LDS-do-not-endorse-claims-in-Da-Vinci.html.
43. See Gospel Topics Essays, "Mother in Heaven."
44. See Eliza R. Snow, "O My Father," *Hymns of The Church of Jesus Christ of Latter-day Saints* (Salt Lake City: The Church of Jesus Christ of Latter-day Saints, 1985), no. 292.
45. See Jeffrey R. Holland, "Behold Thy Mother," *Ensign*, November 2015.
46. "The Family: A Proclamation to the World," *Ensign* or *Liahona*, November 2010, 129; emphasis added.
47. "The Origin of Man," *Improvement Era*, November 1909, 78.
48. Gospel Topics Essays, "Mother in Heaven."
49. See M. Russell Ballard, *When Thou Art Converted: Continuing Our Search for Happiness* (Salt Lake City: Deseret Book, 2001), 62.
50. Gospel Topics Essays, "Mother in Heaven."

Chapter 3: Researching Church History and Doctrine

1. See Elder Marion G. Romney, in Conference Report, April 1945, 89.
2. http://www.josephsmithpapers.org/articles/about-the-project.
3. See Revelations in Context, "Oliver Cowdery's Gift," https://history.lds.org/article/doctrine-and-covenants-oliver-cowdery?lang=eng.
4. https://www.lds.org/church/news/church-history-library-launches-new-online-catalog?lang=eng.

5. This is my own transcription of the document letter (Church History Library. Anonymous letter, 1877 Apr 30, New York. Call Number: CR 1234 1. Found In: Brigham Young Incoming Correspondence, 1839–1877, box 37 fd. 05).
6. https://rsc.byu.edu/mission-statement.
7. https://rsc.byu.edu/tre.
8. M. Russell Ballard, "The Opportunities and Responsibilities of CES Teachers in the 21st Century," Address to CES Religious Educators, February 26, 2016, https://www.lds.org/broadcasts/article/evening-with-a-general-authority/2016/02/the-opportunities-and-responsibilities-of-ces-teachers-in-the-21st-century?lang=eng.
9. Inside cover, *BYU Studies Quarterly*, vol. 57, no.1, 2018.

Part 2: Seeking Truth

1. Chieko N. Okazaki, "Rowing Your Boat," *Ensign*, November 1994.
2. See David A. Bednar, "Seek Learning by Faith," *Ensign*, September 2007.

Chapter 4: Interpreting Scripture

1. See Dallin H. Oaks, "Scripture Reading and Revelation," *Ensign*, January 1995.
2. "History, circa Summer 1832," p. 3, The Joseph Smith Papers, http://www.josephsmithpapers.org/paper-summary/history-circa-summer-1832/3.
3. "Letterbook 1," p. 4, The Joseph Smith Papers, http://www.josephsmithpapers.org/paper-summary/letterbook-1/16.
4. See, for example, Joseph Smith's 1832 written expressions of the "sample of pure language," in "Sample of Pure Language, between circa 4 and circa 20 March 1832," 144, The Joseph Smith Papers, http://www.josephsmithpapers.org/paper-summary/sample-of-pure-language-between-circa-4-and-circa-20-march-1832/1.
5. Steven C. Harper, "'That They Might Come to Understanding': Revelation as Process," in *You Shall Have My Word: Exploring the Text of the Doctrine and Covenants*, Scott C. Esplin, Richard O. Cowan, and Rachel Cope, eds. (Provo, Utah: Religious Studies Center; Salt Lake City: Deseret Book, 2012), 19–33.
6. Richard Bushman, *Rough Stone Rolling* (New York: Knopf, 2005), 174.
7. "Articles and Covenants, circa April 1830 [D&C 20]," 4, The Joseph Smith Papers, http://www.josephsmithpapers.org/paper-summary/articles-and-covenants-circa-april-1830-dc-20/1.
8. "Doctrine and Covenants, 1835," 79, The Joseph Smith Papers, http://www.josephsmithpapers.org/paper-summary/doctrine-and-covenants-1835/87.
9. "History, 1838–1856, volume C-1 [2 November 1838–31 July 1842]," 1255, The Joseph Smith Papers, 2018, http://www.josephsmithpapers.org/paper-summary/history-1838–1856-volume-c-1-2-november-1838–31-july-1842/427.
10. See Royal Skousen, "Some Textual Changes for a Scholarly Study of the Book of Mormon," *BYU Studies Quarterly*, Vol. 51, No. 4 (2012), 99, 116.
11. Grant Hardy, *Understanding the Book of Mormon: A Reader's Guide* (Oxford: Oxford University Press, 2010), 15.
12. http://webstersdictionary1828.com/.
13. See Robert J. Matthews, "What Is the Book of Moses?" in *Studies in Scripture, Vol. 2: The Pearl of*

Great Price, Robert L. Millet and Kent P. Jackson, eds. (1985), 37; see also Kent Jackson, "Joseph Smith's New Translation of the Bible," in *Joseph Smith, the Prophet and Seer* (2010), 51–76.

14. "Letter to Church Leaders in Jackson County, Missouri, 2 July 1833," 51, The Joseph Smith Papers, http://www.josephsmithpapers.org/paper-summary/letter-to-church-leaders-in-jackson-county-missouri-2-july-1833/1.
15. *The Joseph Smith Papers, Council of Fifty: Administrative*, vol. 1, 1190.
16. Adam Miller, *Letters to a Young Mormon* (Provo, Utah: Maxwell Institute for Religious Scholarship, 2014), 32–33.
17. See Anne Mangen, Kolbjorn Bronnick, & Bente Rigmor Walgermo, "Reading linear texts on paper versus computer screen: Effects on reading comprehension," *International Journal of Educational Research*, Vol. 58, 2013, 61–68.
18. See Naomi Baron, "Why Digital Reading Is No Substitute for Print," *The New Republic*, July 20, 2016.
19. See Rakefet Ackerman & Morris Goldsmith, "Metacognitive Regulation of Text Learning: On Screen Versus on Paper," *Journal of Experimental Psychology*, 2011, Vol. 17, No. 1, 18–32.
20. See Jeffrey R. Holland, "Students Need Teachers to Guide Them" address to CES Religious Educators, June 20, 1992, 4.
21. See M. Russell Ballard, "Be Strong in the Lord," *Ensign*, July 2004, or Howard W. Hunter, "Reading the Scriptures," *Ensign*, November 1979.
22. Howard W. Hunter, "Reading the Scriptures," *Ensign*, November 1979.
23. Joseph Fielding McConkie, "The 'How' of Scripture Study," *By Study and by Faith: Selections from the Religious Educator*, Richard Neitzel Holzapfel and Kent P. Jackson, eds. (Provo, Utah: Religious Studies Center, Brigham Young University, 2009), 51–67.
24. Robert J. Marzano, "The Art and Science of Teaching / Summarizing to Comprehend," Educational Leadership, March 2010, Vol. 67, no. 6, 83.
25. Dallin H. Oaks, "Scripture Reading and Revelation," *Ensign*, January 1995.
26. Bible.org, https://bible.org/seriespage/1-women-leadership-setting-stage.
27. B. H. Roberts, in Conference Report, 1908.
28. See Nicholas J. Frederick, "Evaluating the Interaction between the New Testament and the Book of Mormon: A Proposed Methodology," *Journal of Book of Mormon Studies*, Vol. 24 (2015): 1–30; see also John Hilton III, "Old Testament Psalms in the Book of Mormon," in *Ascending the Mountain of the Lord: Temple, Praise, and Worship in the Old Testament* (2013 Sperry Symposium), Jeffrey R. Chadwick, Matthew J. Grey, and David Rolph Seely, eds. (Provo, Utah: Religious Studies Center, Brigham Young University; Salt Lake City: Deseret Book, 2013), 291–311.
29. See Lisa Olsen Tait, "Gathering the Lord's Words into One: Biblical Intertextuality in the Doctrine and Covenants," in *You Shall Have My Word: Exploring the Text of the Doctrine and Covenants*, Scott C. Esplin, Richard O. Cowan, and Rachel Cope, eds. (Provo, Utah: Religious Studies Center; Salt Lake City: Deseret Book, 2012), 92–107.
30. Brigham Young, *Journal of Discourses*, 14:226–27.
31. Ray L. Huntington and Brian M. Hauglid, "Robert J. Matthews and His Work with the Joseph Smith Translation," *Religious Educator* 5, no. 2 (2004): 23–47.
32. Spencer W. Kimball, "The Gospel of Repentance," *Ensign*, November 1982, 5.

33. See David A. Bednar, "The Windows of Heaven," *Ensign*, November 2013.
34. Dallin H. Oaks, "Scripture Reading and Revelation," *Ensign*, January 1995.
35. Summarized from Accademia.org, "Michelangelo's David," and Sylvia Prince, "The Politics of David," October 25, 2016.
36. M. Russell Ballard, "The Opportunities and Responsibilities of CES Teachers in the 21st Century," Address to CES Religious Educators, February 26, 2016.
37. *Discourses of Brigham Young*, comp. John A. Widtsoe (Salt Lake City: Deseret Book, 1954), 128.

Chapter 5: Embracing Ambiguity

1. https://literarydevices.net/ambiguity/.
2. See Don Searle, "The Man with Answers," *Liahona*, October 2008.
3. See Richard C. Edgley, "Faith—The Choice Is Yours," *Ensign*, November 2010; Gordon B. Hinckley, "We Walk by Faith," *Ensign*, May 2002; Dieter F. Uchtdorf, "Come, Join with Us," *Ensign*, October 2013; Jeffrey R. Holland, "Lord, I Believe," *Ensign*, May 2013.
4. See Robert Ballard, "The Astonishing Hidden World of the Deep Ocean," 2008 TED Talk, https://www.ted.com/talks/robert_ballard_on_exploring_the_oceans/transcript?language=en#t-829880.
5. Reid L. Neilson and Scott D. Marianno, "True and Faithful: Joseph Fielding Smith as Mormon Historian and Theologian," *BYU Studies Quarterly*, volume 57 (no.1), 2018, 61
6. https://www.merriam-webster.com/dictionary/dogmatic.
7. Paul V. Johnson, "A Pattern for Learning Spiritual Things," Seminaries and Institutes of Religion Satellite Broadcast, August 7, 2012; emphasis added.
8. E. Frenkel-Brunswick, "Intolerance of ambiguity as an emotional and perceptual personality variable," Journal of Personality, 18 (1948), 108–23.
9. A. Furnham and J. Marks, summarizing Frenkel-Brunswik (1949), 718.
10. See T. Million, "Authoritarianism, intolerance of ambiguity and rigidity under ego- and task-involving conditions," *Journal of Abnormal and Social Psychology*, vol. 99 (1957), 29–33.
11. See A. Furnham and J. Marks, ibid., 725.
12. *Psychological Reports*, 26 (1970), 791–98.
13. *Psychological Reports*, 793.
14. See J. Budner, "Tolerance of ambiguity as a personality variable," *Journal of Personality* 30 (1962), 29–40; see also D. Mclain, "The Mstat-I: A New Measure of an Individual's Tolerance for Ambiguity," *Educational and Psychological Measurement* 53 (1993), 1:183–89.
15. For a good summary of these sources on the book of Abraham's production, see "Introduction to the Book of Abraham," Joseph Smith Papers, http://www.josephsmithpapers.org/intro/introduction-to-book-of-abraham-manuscripts.
16. See Heber C. Kimball letter to Parley P. Pratt, 17 June 1842, Parley P. Pratt Papers, LDS Church Archives, Salt Lake City, Utah. See also Willard Richards to Levi Richards, Letter, 7–25 March 1842.
17. See Steven C. Harper, "Freemasonry and the LDS Temple Endowment," in *A Reason for Faith* (2016), 148. See also Richard Bushman, Joseph Smith: *Rough Stone Rolling*, (New York: Knopf, 2005), 449–51; "Masonry," https://www.lds.org/study/history/topics/masonry?lang=eng
18. Historian's Office General Church Minutes, March 26, 1847, Church History Library, Salt Lake

City, spelling and punctuation modernized. Taken from LDS.org footnote #4, https://www.lds.org/topics/race-and-the-priesthood?lang=eng#4.

19. As cited in John Turner, Brigham Young: Pioneer Prophet (Cambridge, MA: Harvard University Press, 2012), 221.
20. Marta Harding, "3 Ways to Get Comfortable with Ambiguity," Apr. 13, 2018, https://www.ideo.com/blog/3-ways-to-get-comfortable-with-ambiguity.
21. Dennis Okholm, "Apologetics as if People Mattered," *Talking Doctrine: Mormons and Evangelicals in Conversation*, Richard Mouw and Robert Millet, eds., (InterVarsity Press: Donners Grove, Ill., 2015), 53.
22. Williams, Paulhus, Harms, "The Over-Claiming Questionnaire: Invulnerable to Faking and Warning about Foils," 3, 9, http://www2.psych.ubc.ca/~dpaulhus/research/OCT/PRESENTATIONS/APS.2001.poster_invulnerability.pdf.
23. "The Opportunities and Responsibilities of CES Teachers in the 21st Century," address given to CES Religious Educators, February 26, 2016.
24. Jennifer Brea, TED Radio Hour, "Getting Better," Feb. 10, 2017.
25. "History, 1838–1856, volume E-1 [1 July 1843–30 April 1844]," 1970, The Joseph Smith Papers, http://www.josephsmithpapers.org/paper-summary/history-1838–1856-volume-e-1–1-july-1843–30-april-1844/342.
26. *TIME*, August 4, 1997, 56.
27. Brigham Young, Discourse, 25 March 1855, Papers of George D. Watt MS 4534 box 3 disk 1 images 142–153. Transcribed by LaJean Purcell Carruth, punctuation and capitalization added.
28. Dieter F. Uchtdorf, "The Adventure of Mortality," Worldwide Devotional for Young Adults, January 14, 2018.

Chapter 6: Discerning Truth from Error

1. See Henry B. Eyring, "Gifts of the Spirit for Hard Times," *Ensign*, June 2007; see also D. Todd Christofferson, "The Power of Covenants," *Ensign*, May 2009.
2. *Preach My Gospel* (2004), 18.
3. *True to the Faith*, 2004, 144.
4. See D&C 21:9, 24:5, 28:1, 28:4, 31:11, 35:19, 36:2, 39:6, 42:16, 47:4, 50:14, 50:17, 52:9, 75:10, 75:27, 79:2, 90:11, 90:14, 124:97.
5. Richard G. Scott, "Helping Others Be Spiritually Led," CES Symposium on the Doctrine and Covenants and Church History, 1998, 4.
6. Transcript taken from "Elder and Sister Bednar—Recognizing the Spirit," https://www.lds.org/media-library/video/2015–05–2008-elder-and-sister-bednar-recognizing-the-spirit?lang=eng.
7. See, for example, "To Go or Not to Go," *New Era*, May 2010, or "My Big Decision," *Liahona*, June 2011.
8. See Shai Danziger, Jonathan Levav, and Liora Avnaim-Pesso, "Extraneous Factors in Judicial Decisions" Proceedings of the National Academy of Sciences of the United States of America 108.17 (2011): 6889–6892. PMC. https://www.ncbi.nlm.nih.gov/pmc/articles/PMC3084045/ Paragraph summarized from "The Science of Justice: I think it's time we broke for lunch . . . ," *The Economist*, https://www.economist.com/science-and-technology/2011/04/14/i-think-its-time-we-broke-for-lunch.

9. "History, 1838–1856, volume C-1 [2 November 1838–31 July 1842]," 1309, The Joseph Smith Papers, http://www.josephsmithpapers.org/paper-summary/history-1838-1856-volume-c-1-2-november-1838-31-july-1842/483.
10. *The Teachings of Howard W. Hunter*, 185.
11. "History, 1838–1856, volume C-1 [2 November 1838–31 July 1842]," 1305, The Joseph Smith Papers.
12. "Appendix 3: "Articles of the Church of Christ," June 1829," 1, http://www.josephsmithpapers.org/paper-summary/appendix-3-articles-of-the-church-of-christ-june-1829/1.
13. *The Joseph Smith Papers: Histories*, 1:424–27; also see Joseph Smith, History of the Church, 1:104–5.
14. See Russell M. Nelson, "Honoring the Priesthood," *Ensign*, May 1993.
15. John Sims Carter Journal, 10 March and 5 April, 1833, CHL.
16. "History, circa June 1839–circa 1841 [Draft 2]," 54, The Joseph Smith Papers, https://www.josephsmithpapers.org/paper-summary/history-circa-june-1839-circa-1841-draft-2/60.
17. Joseph F. Smith, Anthon H. Lund, Charles W. Penrose, *Improvement Era*, Sept. 1913, 1148–49; emphasis added.
18. *The Autobiography of Parley Parker Pratt*, 50.
19. "John Whitmer, History, 1831–circa 1847," 26, The Joseph Smith Papers, http://www.josephsmithpapers.org/paper-summary/john-whitmer-history-1831-circa-1847/30.
20. Joseph Fielding Smith, *Church History and Modern Revelation*, 1:201–2.
21. "Times and Seasons, 1 April 1842," 744, The Joseph Smith Papers, http://www.josephsmithpapers.org/paper-summary/times-and-seasons-1-april-1842/10.
22. See, for example, Dallin H. Oaks, "Balancing Truth and Tolerance," *Ensign*, February 2013.
23. Summarized from Luisa Dillner, "A Case of Mass Hysteria," *The Guardian*, July 6, 1999, and "Health Care Blamed on Mass Hysteria," *BBC News*, July 2, 1999.
24. Julie B. Beck, "And upon the Handmaids in Those Days Will I Pour Out My Spirit," *Ensign*, May 2010.

Part 3: Seeking Holiness

1. See Dallin H. Oaks, "The Challenge to Become," *Ensign*, November 2000.

Chapter 7: Obtaining Spiritual Gifts

1. Bruce R. McConkie, "What Think Ye of Salvation by Grace?," BYU Devotional, January 10, 1984.
2. James K. A. Smith, *How Not to be Secular: Reading Charles Taylor* (Eerdmans: Grand Rapids, Mich., 2014), 19, 28.
3. Dallin H. Oaks, "Truth and the Plan," *Ensign*, November 2018.
4. "U.S. Religious Landscape Survey: Religious Beliefs and Practices: Diverse and Politically Relevant," The Pew Forum on Religion and Public Life, June 2008, 54.
5. "Do Jehovah's Witnesses Practice Faith Healing?" *The Watchtower* (10), 10/1, 13.
6. https://www.gotquestions.org/Pentecostals.html.
7. If you are interested in a brief explanation of the gift of tongues in the Church, see Alan J. Clark, "'We Believe in the Gift of Tongues': The 1906 Pentecostal Revolution and Its Effect on the LDS Use of the Gift of Tongues in the Twentieth Century," *Mormon Historical Studies*, Vol. 14 (no.1), 2013, 67–80.

8. Joseph B. Wirthlin, "The Unspeakable Gift," *Ensign*, May 2003.
9. James E. Faust, "Lost Horizons," *Ensign*, August 1999.
10. See "Spiritual Gifts," *True to the Faith* (2004), 167.
11. See Larry Hiller, "Hope: The Misunderstood Sister," *Ensign*, June 2009, or Thomas Adams's 1847 classic work *The Three Divine Sisters* (various publisher's reprints available).
12. "Lecture 1," in *The Lectures on Faith in Historical Perspective*, Larry E. Dahl and Charles D. Tate Jr., eds.,(Provo, Utah: Religious Studies Center, Brigham Young University), 31.
13. David A. Bednar, "Seek Learning by Faith," Address to Religious Educators, February 3, 2006.
14. See C. S. Lewis, *Mere Christianity*, 122–24.
15. See Ronald A. Rasband, "Be Not Troubled," *Ensign*, November 2018.
16. See James E. Faust, "Be Not Afraid," *Ensign*, October 2002.
17. See David A. Bednar, "Therefore They Hushed Their Fears," *Ensign*, May 2015.
18. For a deeper elaboration on these six atoning powers of Jesus, see my book *Christ In Every Hour* (Deseret Book: Salt Lake City, 2016).
19. For a similar analogy, see Gary B. Sabin, "Stand Up Inside and Be All In," *Ensign*, May 2017.
20. See Bible Dictionary, "Charity," 632.
21. http://www.merriam-webster.com/dictionary/agape.
22. Credit to Mark Callister, BYU communications professor, for this metaphor from his October 7, 2014, BYU devotional, "Lost and Found."
23. See Ezra Taft Benson, "Beware of Pride," *Ensign*, May 1989.
24. See Dieter F. Uchtdorf, "In Praise of Those Who Save," *Ensign*, May 2016.
25. Ezra Taft Benson, "Beware of Pride."
26. See Dieter F. Uchtdorf, "In Praise of Those Who Save."
27. James K. A. Smith, *How Not to be Secular*, 2.

Chapter 8: Sustaining Modern Prophets

1. "The Sustaining of Church Officers," presented by Dieter F. Uchtdorf, April 2015.
2. See Terryl Givens, "Paradox and Discipleship," address at Harvard University, Oct. 28, 2006, 4.
3. J. Richard Clarke, "The Household of Faith," *Ensign*, November 1980.
4. See David B. Haight, "Heed the Prophet's Voice," *Ensign*, November 1994.
5. "5 Ways to Sustain and Follow the Prophets," https://www.lds.org/prophets-and-apostles/unto-all-the-world/5-ways-to-sustain-and-follow-the-prophets?lang=eng.
6. David B. Haight, "Sustaining the Prophets," *Ensign*, November 1998.
7. Carol F. McConkie, "Live According to the Words of the Prophets," *Ensign*, November 2014.
8. "History, 1838–1856, volume A-1 [23 December 1805–30 August 1834]," 228, https://www.josephsmithpapers.org/paper-summary/history-1838–1856-volume-a-1–23-december-1805–30-august-1834/234.
9. Russell M. Nelson, "Sustaining the Prophets," *Ensign*, November 2014; emphasis added.
10. Gary E. Stevenson, "Where are the Keys and Authority of the Priesthood?," *Ensign*, May 2016.
11. See "Who Knew: New Interview Guidelines," *New Era*, Oct. 2018.
12. LDS.org Gospel Topics, "Prophets."
13. "We Sustain Our Leaders," *Ensign*, March 2012.

14. Gordon B. Hinckley, "A Prophet's Testimony," *Ensign*, May 1993.
15. David B. Haight, "Sustaining the Prophets," *Ensign*, November 1998.
16. https://www.merriam-webster.com/dictionary/listen.
17. https://www.merriam-webster.com/dictionary/heed.
18. "Chapter 19: Following the Living Prophet," *Teachings of Presidents of the Church: Wilford Woodruff* (2011), 195–204.
19. LDS.org, "5 Ways to Sustain and Follow the Prophets."
20. *Teachings of Presidents of the Church: George Albert Smith* (2011), 64; emphasis added.
21. *Teachings of Presidents of the Church: Joseph F. Smith* (1998), 218–19.
22. Thomas S. Monson, "Hands," *Ensign*, November 1972.
23. Boyd K. Packer, "Parents in Zion," *Ensign*, November 1998.
24. LDS.org, "5 Ways to Sustain and Follow the Prophets."
25. "We Sustain Our Leaders," *Ensign*, March 2012.
26. "Chapter 19: Following the Living Prophet," *Teachings of Presidents of the Church: Wilford Woodruff* (2011), 195–204.
27. Gordon B. Hinckley, "This Work Is Concerned with People," *Ensign*, May 1995.
28. *Teachings of Presidents of the Church: Joseph F. Smith* (1998), 218–19.
29. https://www.lds.org/prophets-and-apostles/unto-all-the-world/sustaining-our-prophets?lang=eng.
30. David B. Haight, "Sustaining the Prophets," *Ensign*, November 1998.
31. Gary E. Stevenson, "Where Are the Keys and Authority of the Priesthood?," *Ensign*, May 2016.
32. Ronald A. Rasband, "Standing with the Leaders of the Church," *Ensign*, May 2016.
33. Janette Hales Beckham, "Sustaining Living Prophets," *Ensign*, May 1996.
34. See "Chapter 5: The Quorum of the Twelve Apostles," *Teachings of the Living Prophets Student Manual* (2010), 56–69.
35. "In the government of God's kingdom," said President Dallin H. Oaks, "questions are honored but opposition is not." "Opposition in All Things," *Ensign*, May 2016.
36. The Council of the First Presidency and Quorum of the Twelve Apostles, June 28, 2014.
37. See "Mormons free to back gay marriage on social media, LDS apostle says," Religion News Service, March 17, 2015.
38. *Handbook 2: Administering the Church* (Salt Lake City: Intellectual Reserve), 2010, 157.
39. Summarized from infantsonthrones.com podcast, "Who is #anyopposed?" (no transcript available) http://infantsonthrones.com/?s=any+opposed (see discussion from 13:00-16:00 mark).
40. As reported by Cami Cox Jim, "LDS grassroots group organizes shouted protests during conference broadcast," *St. George News*, April 5, 2015.
41. "The Sustaining of Church Officers," presented by President Dieter F. Uchtdorf.
42. See M. Russell Ballard, "Counseling with our Councils," *Ensign*, May 1994.
43. The Council of Fifty was organized by Joseph Smith in March 1844 to help establish the political kingdom of God on the earth. See https://www.josephsmithpapers.org/topic/council-of-fifty?highlight=council%200f%20fifty.
44. "Council of Fifty, Minutes, March 1844–January 1846; Volume 1, 10 March 1844–1 March 1845,"24, The Joseph Smith Papers, https://www.josephsmithpapers.org/paper-summary/council-of-fifty-minutes-march-1844-january-1846-volume-1–10-march-1844–1-march-1845/26.

45. "Council of Fifty, Minutes, March 1844–January 1846; Volume 1, 10 March 1844–1 March 1845," 81, The Joseph Smith Papers, https://www.josephsmithpapers.org/paper-summary/council-of-fifty-minutes-march-1844-january-1846-volume-1–10-march-1844–1-march-1845/83.
46. See Robert Millet, *Precept upon Precept: Joseph Smith and the Restoration of Doctrine* (Salt Lake City: Deseret Book), 2016.
47. Bruce R. McConkie, "All Are Alike Unto God" *BYU Speeches*, August 1978.
48. See, for example, "Introduction" to the Doctrine and Covenants, paragraph 6: "These revelations were received in answer to prayer, in times of need, and came out of real-life situations."
49. See the Church's 1981 guide to priesthood leaders, *Homosexuality, Second Edition* (Intellectual Reserve: Salt Lake City), 1.
50. "Church Teachings," on Mormonandgay.lds.org
51. See "LGBT People Who Live God's Laws Can Fully Participate in the Church" by Elder D. Todd Christofferson, https://mormonandgay.lds.org/videos?id=8476007148069176400&lang=eng.
52. See "Sexual Orientation & Homosexuality," *American Psychological Association*.
53. See "Sexual Orientation & Homosexuality."
54. Newsroom, "Interview With Elder Dallin H. Oaks and Elder Lance B. Wickman: 'Same-Gender Attraction.'"
55. See letter from the Council of the First Presidency and Quorum of the Twelve Apostles, June 29, 2015, released after same-sex marriage was legalized in the United States. See also "The Divine Institution of Marriage," Newsroom.
56. Dieter F. Uchtdorf, "Come, Join with Us," *Ensign*, November 2013.
57. Neil L. Andersen, "Trial of Your Faith," *Ensign*, November 2012.
58. Jeffrey R. Holland, "Lord, I Believe," *Ensign*, May 2013.
59. See Discourses of Brigham Young, 137; Wilford Woodruff, Notes following Official Declaration 1; M. Russell Ballard, "Stay in the Boat and Hold On!," *Ensign*, November 2014.
60. The Complete Discourses of Brigham Young (Salt Lake City: Smith-Pettit Foundation, 2009), 3:1418.
61. See Russell M. Nelson, "The Correct Name of the Church," *Ensign*, November 2018.
62. Revelation to John Taylor, April 14, 1883, "Book of Revelations, 1882–1884"; emphasis added. See also James R. Clark, comp., *Messages of the First Presidency of The Church of Jesus Christ of Latter-day Saints*, 6 vols. (1965–75), 2:352–54.
63. Russell M. Nelson, "Sustaining the Prophets," *Ensign*, November 2014.
64. Gordon B. Hinckley, "In Counsellors There Is Safety," *Ensign*, November 1990.
65. M. Russell Ballard, "Stay in the Boat and Hold On!," *Ensign*, November 2014.
66. See Russell M. Nelson, opening remarks, in Conference Report, October 2018. See also Russell M. Nelson, "Ministering," *Ensign*, May 2018.
67. Council of Fifty, Minutes, April 18, 1844, Joseph Smith Papers, Administrative Records: Council of Fifty, Minutes (Church Historians Press: Salt Lake City, 2016), 119–20.
68. Brigham Young, August 29, 1852, in *Journal of Discourses*, 6:281.
69. Patrick Mason, author of *Planted: Belief and Belonging in an Age of Doubt* (Salt Lake City: Deseret Book, 2015) in an online Q&A, https://rationalfaiths.com/qa-patrick-mason-answers-sundry-questions/.

70. Rachel Cope, "Hermeneutics of Trust vs. Hermeneutics of Doubt," *Journal for the Study of Spirituality*, vol. 3, no.1 (2013), 56–66; see also Steven C. Harper, "Suspicion or Trust: Reading the Accounts of Joseph Smith's First Vision," in *No Weapon Shall Prosper: New Light on Sensitive Issues*, ed. Robert L. Millet (Provo, Utah: Religious Studies Center, Brigham Young University; Salt Lake City: Deseret Book, 2011), 63–75.
71. George Q. Cannon, in Conference Report, 1896.
72. See Dallin H. Oaks, "Criticism," *Ensign*, February 1987.
73. David A. Bednar, "A Conversation on Leadership," February 24, 2010, 6.

Chapter 9: Inviting the Presence of God

1. See Russell M. Nelson, "Prepare for the Blessings of the Temple," *Ensign*, October 2010.
2. See Exodus 19:6; 1 Peter 2:9. Joseph Smith said to the Relief Society he was "going to make of this Society a kingdom of priests" ("Nauvoo Relief Society Minute Book," 22, The Joseph Smith Papers, http://www.josephsmithpapers.org/paper-summary/nauvoo-relief-society-minute-book/19). President John Taylor asked, "Have you forgotten who you are, and what your object is? Have you forgotten that you [are] clothed upon with the holy priesthood? Have you forgotten that you are aiming to become kings and priests to the Lord, and queens and priestesses to him?" (*The Gospel Kingdom* [1987], 229–30). See also Joseph F. Smith, *Gospel Doctrine*, 461.
3. Joseph Smith, Discourse, Nauvoo, Ill., 7 Apr. 1844; in *Times and Seasons* (Nauvoo, Ill.), 15 Aug. 1844, vol. 5, no. 15, 612–17.
4. These three covenant patterns have been repeatedly emphasized by the Church and the prophets in public discourse. For example, President Ezra Taft Benson said, "Celestial laws, embodied in certain ordinances belonging to the Church of Jesus Christ, are complied with by voluntary covenants. The laws are spiritual. Thus, our Father in Heaven has ordained certain holy sanctuaries, called temples, in which these laws may be fully explained, the laws include the law of obedience and sacrifice, the law of the gospel, the law of chastity, and the law of consecration" (Ezra Taft Benson, "A Vision and a Hope for the Youth of Zion," BYU devotional, April 12, 1977). Relief Society General President Bonnie D. Parkin taught: "So often we talk of making and keeping covenants, but exactly what are they? . . . In the temple, we further covenant to be obedient, to sacrifice, to keep ourselves worthily pure, to contribute to the spreading of truth, to be chaste, to pray, to live the gospel, and to be forever faithful" ("Celebrating Covenants," *Ensign*, May 1995). See also Bruce R. McConkie, "Obedience, Sacrifice, and Consecration," *Ensign*, May 1975; Robert D. Hales, "Stand Strong in Holy Places," *Ensign*, April 2013 "Stand Strong in Holy Places."
5. https://www.etymonline.com/word/obedience#etymonline_v_30944.
6. https://www.etymonline.com/word/faithful#etymonline_v_32950.
7. https://www.etymonline.com/word/keep#etymonline_v_1798.
8. *Preach My Gospel* (Salt Lake City: Intellectual Reserve, 2004), 62.
9. See Jörg Klebingat, "Approaching the Throne of God with Confidence," *Ensign*, November 2014.
10. Dieter F. Uchtdorf, "Forget Me Not," *Ensign*, November 2011.
11. See *Lectures on Faith*, 6:5.
12. "Praise to the Man," *Hymns* (1985), no. 27.
13. See *Teachings of Ezra Taft Benson*, 121.

14. See Casey Griffith, "A Covenant and a Deed that Cannot Be Broken': The Continuing Saga of Consecration," in Craig Ostler, Michael Mackay, Barbara Morgan Gardner, *Foundations of the Restoration: Fulfillment of the Covenant Purposes* (Provo, Utah: Religious Studies Center/Deseret Book), 2016, 121–38.
15. See "Lesson 14: The Law of Consecration," *Doctrine and Covenants and Church History: Gospel Doctrine Teacher's Manual* (1999), 75–80; see also Henry B. Eyring, "Opportunities to do Good," *Ensign*, May 2011.
16. Steven C. Harper, *Making Sense of the Doctrine and Covenants* (2008), 291.
17. Teachings of Gordon B. Hinckley, 639.
18. "Approaching Zion," vol. 9 of *The Collected Works of Hugh Nibley* (1989), 168; see also *Teachings of Ezra Taft Benson*, 121.
19. See Merriam-Webster, "Consecrate."
20. *Preparing to Enter the Holy Temple*, 35; see also *Teachings of Ezra Taft Benson*, 121.
21. Bruce R. McConkie, "Obedience, Consecration, and Sacrifice," *Ensign*, May 1975.
22. Steven Harper describes these as "Agency, Stewardship, and Accountability." Mine are a derivative of his, but I am indebted to his original breakdown. See "All Things are the Lord's: The Law of Consecration in the Doctrine and Covenants," *The Doctrine and Covenants: Revelations in Context*, Andrew H. Hedges, J. Spencer Fluhman, and Alonzo L. Gaskill, eds. (Provo and Salt Lake City: Religious Studies Center, Brigham Young University, and Deseret Book, 2008), 212–28.
23. Brigham Young, *Journal of Discourses*, 2:307.
24. Brigham Young University commencement exercises, Provo, Utah, 27 Apr. 1995. As cited in "Excerpts from Recent Addresses of President Gordon B. Hinckley," *Ensign*, Dec. 1995.
25. Ezra Taft Benson, "A Vision and a Hope for the Youth of Zion," BYU devotional, April 12, 1977.

Epilogue: Seeking Zion

1. Dieter F. Uchtdorf, "Are You Sleeping through the Restoration?" *Ensign*, May 2014.
2. See *True to the Faith*, "Atonement," (Salt Lake City: Intellectual Reserve, 2004), 14.
3. N. T. Wright, *Simply Jesus* (New York: Harper Collins, 2011), 202.
4. "History, 1838–1856, volume B-1 [1 September 1834–2 November 1838]," 680, The Joseph Smith Papers, http://www.josephsmithpapers.org/paper-summary/history-1838–1856-volume-b-1–1-september-1834–2-november-1838/134.
5. "Plat of the City of Zion, circa Early June–25 June 1833," 1, The Joseph Smith Papers, http://www.josephsmithpapers.org/paper-summary/plat-of-the-city-of-zion-circa-early-june-25-june-1833/1.
6. Jeffrey R. Holland, "Miracles of the Restoration," *Ensign*, November 2014.
7. *Handbook 2: Administering the Church* (2010), 2.2.
8. Gordon B. Hinckley, "Keep the Chain Unbroken," in *Brigham Young University 1999–2000 Speeches* (2000), 108–9.

INDEX

"Aaron, gift of," 44–46
Abraham, translation of book of, 75
Accountability, 143
Action, faith and, 106–7
Adam, 43, 47–48
Adamic language, 55
African men, priesthood restriction on, 75
Agapē, 110
Agency, 116, 123, 143
Age of reason, 99–100, 113
Alger, Fanny, 11
Alger, John, 7, 21–22
"All things in common," 140
Ambiguity, 71–72, 82–83; avoidance of, 73–74; intolerance of, 73–75; embracing, 74–77. *See also* Unknown
Andersen, Neil L., 35, 127
Answers, latter-day need for definitive, 72–73
"Articles and Covenants," 27
Atonement, 27–28, 109, 148

Ballard, M. Russell, 2–3, 34, 49, 69, 79, 128–29
Baptism, 30, 90
Beck, Julie B., 96
Beckham, Janette Hales, 121
Bednar, David A., 27, 68, 88, 107, 131–32, 155n13
Benson, Ezra Taft, 119, 145, 165n4
Bias, in historical sources, 14–16
Bible: weakness of, 56–57; translation of, 59; Joseph Smith Translation, 59–61, 68; King James Version, 67; New International Version (NIV), 67; New Revised Standard Version (NRSV), 67; substantiating scriptural renderings with, 67–68
Bold doctrine, 129
Book of Mormon: translation of, 16–18; weakness of, 56–57; as non-negotiable of faith, 76–77. *See also* Gold plates
Book of Mormon Central, 50
Bradford, M. Gerald, 29
Breastplate, 8, 22
Brethren Test, 91–93, 96
Bushman, Richard, 51, 56
BYU General Conference Corpus, 40–42
BYU Maxwell Institute, 50
BYU Religious Studies Center, 48–49
BYU Studies, 49–50

Cannon, George Q., 131
Celestial kingdom, 145
Celestial laws, 165n4
Charity, 105, 110–11
Chase, Willard, 8
Chastity, 95, 127, 165n4
Children, passing covenants to, 150–51
Christlike attributes, 94–95
Christofferson, D. Todd, 33, 34, 124
Church doctrine: tied to Church history, 9–10; types of, 23–31; as susceptible to change, 24–25, 31; expanding definition of, 25–26; sources of, 31–35; regarding Jesus's marriage status, 35–36; application of models concerning, 35–38; regarding Heavenly Mother, 36–37; defined, 155n13. *See also* Resources on Church history and doctrine
Church Educational System, 138–39
Church history: studying, 7–9; importance of, 9–10; factors for evaluating, 10–16. *See also* Resources on Church history and doctrine
Church History Library Catalog, 46–48
Church leaders. *See* First Presidency; General Authorities; Prophets; Quorum of the Twelve Apostles
Church publications, as source of Church doctrine, 32, 35
Church websites, on social and contemporary issues, 150
Circumcision, 29
Coca-Cola recall, 95
Commandments, 94–95

Consecration, 140–44, 145, 165n4
Contemporary accounts, 13–14, 20–21
Context, substantiating scriptural renderings with, 68–69
Coray, Martha, 8
Core doctrines, 26, 27, 30
Council of Fifty, 125, 163n43
Councils, voicing dissent through, 124–25
Covenants, 150–51, 165n4
Cowdery, Oliver, 44–46, 89–91, 108
Cultural Literacy: What Every American Needs to Know (Hirsch), 77–78
Culture, prophets operate within, 126

Dahl, Larry E., 29
Data, checking claims against known, 19
Databases, 39–43, 46–48
David (Michelangelo), 69
Deception, spiritual, 88–95
Deep doctrines. *See* Esoteric doctrines
Definitive answers, latter-day need for, 72–73
Degrees of glory, 130
Deseret Book, 50–51
Despair, 109–10
Disagreement: and sustaining prophets, 123–26; voicing, 131–32. *See also* Dissent; Opposition
Discerning truth from error, 84; and theology on Holy Ghost, 84–86; and fruits of Holy Ghost, 86–88; and spiritual deception, 88–95; and sociogenic error, 95–96
Dissent: voiced in General Conference, 115–16, 124–25; voicing, 131–32. *See also* Disagreement; Opposition
Divine healings, 101

Divining rods, 46
Doctrinal heresy, 99
Doctrine. *See* Church doctrine
Dogma / dogmatism, 73
Doubt, 106, 109–10

Edification Test, 93–94, 96
Emotion. *See* Feelings
Endowment, 75
Enlightenment, 85
Error. *See* Discerning truth from error
Esoteric doctrines, 26, 29–30, 36
Eternal doctrines. *See* Core doctrines
Evidence, faith and, 106–7
Evil speaking, against prophets, 131
External substantiation, 66–67
Eyring, Henry B., 121

Faith: and study, 53; as spiritual gift, 105–12
False spirits, 89, 93–94
Family scripture study, 63–64
Faust, James E., 101
Fear, 106, 107–8
Feelings: influence of Holy Ghost comes through, 86; and spiritual deception, 87, 88–89, 95–96
First Presidency, 32, 33–34, 128
First Vision, 7, 12, 14, 21–22, 55
Flexibility, and embracing ambiguity, 76–77
Freemasonry, 75
Frenkel-Brunswik, Else, 74

General Authorities: as source of Church doctrine, 32, 34–35; and Brethren Test, 91–93, 96. *See also* First Presidency; Prophets; Prophets, sustaining; Quorum of the Twelve Apostles
General Conference, dissent voiced in, 115–16, 124–25
Generosity, and sustaining prophets, 130–31
"Gift of Aaron," 44–46
Givens, Terryl, 116

God: seeking after, 4; becoming like, 81, 111; nature of, 81; trust in, 106, 107; love of and for, 110–11; metaphorical death of, 113; prophets as authorized agents of, 129; knowing, 134; alignment with will of, 135–37; plans of, for our lives, 138–39; Restoration and will of, 149
God, presence of, 134–35, 144–46; and law of obedience, 135–37, 145; and law of sacrifice, 137–40, 145; and law of consecration, 140–44, 145
Gold plates, 7–8. *See also* Book of Mormon
Grace, 40–41
Gratitude, in seeking spiritual gifts, 104

Hadley, Jonathan, 17
Haight, David B., 118, 119, 121
Hands, sustaining with, 120–21
Hardy, Grant, 57
Harold B. Lee Library collections, 50
Harper, Steven, 4, 14, 56, 141, 166n22
Harris, Martin, 18
Healings, divine, 101
Heart: Holy Ghost speaks to, 86; broken, and contrite spirit, 138
Heavenly Mother, 36–37
Heavenly Parents, 41. *See also* God; Heavenly Mother
Heresy, 99
Hinckley, Gordon B.: on role of prophets, 33; on prophetic unanimity, 34; on God once being man, 81; and global expansion of Church, 116; on sustaining prophet, 119, 120–21; on safeguards of prophets, 128; on laws of sacrifice and consecration, 141; on passing on covenant to children, 151

Hirsch, E. D. Jr., 77–78
Historical context, substantiating scriptural renderings with, 68–69
Historical source criticism, 11–23
Holland, Jeffrey R., 62, 127, 149
Holy Ghost: studying scriptures with, 62; theology on, 84–86; primary role of, 85; fruits of, 86–88; and spiritual gifts, 103. See also Discerning truth from error
Homosexual feelings and thoughts, 127
Hope, 105, 108–9
Humility, 104, 130
Hunter, Howard W., 62, 89
Hyde, Orson, 35

IDEO, 75
Ingersoll, Peter, 7–8
Intertextuality, 67

Jehovah's Witnesses, 101
Jensen, Marlin K., 9–10
Jessee, Dean C., 15
Jesus Christ: doctrines concerning, 27–28; marriage of, 35–36; Resurrection of, 76; promises of, 109; teaches in spirit world, 127; covenant relationship with, 144–46; as restorer, 147–48; millennial reign of, 148. See also Atonement
Johnson, Paul V., 73
Joseph Smith Papers, 44–46
Joseph Smith Translation, 59–61, 68
Journal of Mormon History, 50

Kimball, Spencer W., 68, 124
King Follett sermon, 81
King James Version, 67
Kirtland, Ohio, 93–94
Knight, Joseph Sr., 18
Known, splitting unknown from, 79–81

Language: weakness of, 55–57; translating, 58–59
Law of Moses, 29
LDS Scriptures Citation Index, 42–44
Lectures on Faith, 25
Lee, Harold B., 120
Lewis, C. S., 108
Lewis, Q. Walker, 75
Life plans, 138–39
Love: of and for God, 110–11; for prophets, 120; and sacrifice, 137

Marriage, and covenant relationship with Christ, 144–46
Marzano, Robert, 63
Mason, Patrick, 130–31
Matthews, Robert J., 68
McBaine, Neylan, 124
McConkie, Bruce R., 9, 72–73, 99, 126, 141
McConkie, Carol F., 118
McConkie, Joseph Fielding, 62
McLellin, William, 11
Meekness, 130
Memories, fallibility of, 13–14
Millennium, 148
Miller, Adam, 60–61
Mind, Holy Ghost speaks to, 85
Mindful reading, 61–62
Mistakes, made by Church leaders, 127
Monson, Thomas S., 116, 120
Mormon Historical Studies, 50

Neibaur, Alexander, 12, 14
Neilson, Reid, 72–73
Nelson, Russell M., 33, 116, 119, 128
New International Version (NIV), 67
New Revised Standard Version (NRSV), 67
Nibley, Hugh, 141
Non-negotiables, 76

Oaks, Dallin H., 66, 68, 99–100, 127, 163n35

Obedience, 135–37, 145, 165n4
Objective perspectives, 14–16, 20–21
Okazaki, Chieko, 53
Okholm, Dennis, 76
Opposition: against Church, 123–24; in God's kingdom, 163n35. See also Disagreement; Dissent
Order of Enoch, 140
Over-claiming, avoiding, 77–79
Ownership, and law of consecration, 141–42

Packer, Boyd K., 27, 29, 120
Page, Hiram, 91–93
Paraphrasing, 63–66
Parkin, Bonnie D., 165n4
Patience, 130
Penrose, Charles W., 36
Pentecostal churches, 101
Plan of salvation, 27
Plural marriage, 19
Policy doctrines, 26, 28–29, 30
Pratt, Orson, 35–36
Pratt, Parley, 93
Prayer(s): for prophets, 119–20; realignment with God through, 136
Pride, 106, 111–12
Priesthood, restriction on, 75
Priesthood keys, as non-negotiable of faith, 77
Primary sources, 12, 20–21
Prophets: as source of Church doctrine, 32, 33–34; substantiating scriptural renderings with, 68; and Brethren Test, 91–93, 96; disconnect between social ideas and teachings of, 116; studying teachings of, 118–19; listening to, 119; education of, 126; operate within culture, 126; change in teachings of, 127; fallibility of, 127; won't lead us astray, 128; safeguards on,

128–29; as authorized agents, 129. *See also* First Presidency; General Authorities; Prophets, sustaining; Quorum of the Twelve Apostles
Prophets, sustaining, 115–16, 131–33; understanding, 116–17; model for, 118–21; as continuum, 121–22; while disagreeing, 123–26; principles of, 129–31
Publishers, 50–52

Questions, unanswered, 71–72. *See also* Ambiguity; Dissent; Opposition
Quorum of the Twelve Apostles, 32, 33–34

Raphael, 77
Rasband, Ronald A., 121
Reason, age of, 99–100, 113
Rebellion, against Church, 123–24
Relationships of sources, 16–18, 20–21
Religious Educator, 49
Repentance, 135–36
Resources on Church history and doctrine, 39–40; BYU General Conference Corpus, 40–42; LDS Scriptures Citation Index, 42–44; Joseph Smith Papers, 44–46; Church History Library Catalog, 46–48; BYU Religious Studies Center, 48–49; BYU Studies, 49–50; publishers, 50–52
Restoration of all things, 147–52
Resurrection, 76
Revelation: and weakness of language, 56; and scripture study, 62, 66
Richards, Willard, 12
Rich young ruler, parable of, 137, 139
Roberts, B. H., 32–33, 66
Rough Stone Rolling (Bushman), 51

Sacrifice, 137–40, 145, 165n4
Salvation: policy doctrines affecting, 29–30; participation in work of, 149–51
Same-sex attraction, 127
School of the Prophets, 25
Scott, Richard G., 86
Scriptures: as source of Church doctrine, 32–33; weakness of, 54–55, 70; and weakness of language, 55–57; translation of, 57–69; personal interpretation of, 59–69, 70; seeking in, 69–70. *See also* LDS Scriptures Citation Index
Sealing keys, 129
Second Coming, 28
Seeking: avoiding, 4; need for, 4, 5
Seer stone: translation of Book of Mormon via, 16–18; of Hiram Page, 91–93
Selflessness, in seeking spiritual gifts, 104
Seminary, 138–39
Smith, Emma, 17–18
Smith, George Albert, 120
Smith, James, 113
Smith, Joseph: on seeking knowledge, 6; and gold plates, 7–8; Church doctrine tied to, 9; and Fanny Alger, 11; and translation of Book of Mormon, 16–18; and plural marriage, 19; on esoteric doctrines, 29; depiction of, in *Rough Stone Rolling*, 51; on limitations of language, 55–56; on correctness of Book of Mormon, 57; and translation of book of Abraham, 75; and ambiguity of life, 82; on false spirits, 89, 93–94; and Stewardship Test, 89–91; on seer stone of Hiram Page, 91–92; on studying prophetic teachings, 118–19; and diverging opinions in Church councils, 125; education of, 126; as Lord's agent, 129; on sealing keys, 129; commission of, 134; on knowing God, 134; on Zion, 148. *See also* First Vision; Joseph Smith Papers; Joseph Smith Translation
Smith, Joseph F., 36, 120, 121, 127
Smith, Joseph Fielding, 72–73, 94
Smith, Lucy Mack, 8, 22
Social issues, 149–50
Sociogenic error, 95–96
Source criticism, 10–11
Spirit, contrite, 138
Spiritual deception, 88–95
Spiritual gifts: obtaining, 99–101; seeking, 101, 103–5, 113; scriptural lists of, 102–3; and Holy Ghost, 103; of faith, hope, and charity, 105–12; belief in, 113
Spiritual phenomena, 88–89, 93–94
Spirit world, Christ's ministry in, 127
Split decisions, 79–81
Statistics, 19
Stevenson, Gary E., 119
Stewardship, and law of consecration, 142–43
Stewardship Test, 89–91, 96
Study: and faith, 53; of prophetic teachings, 118–19
Substantiation, external, 66–67
Summarizing, 63
Supporting doctrines, 26, 27–28, 30, 37
Supporting evidence, 18–19, 20–21
Sustaining, understanding, 116–17. *See also* Prophets, sustaining
Sweat, Calvin, 64
Sweat, Jane, 64, 106
Sweat, Lauren, 106
Sweat, Reagan, 106
Sweat, Vivian, 64

Taylor, John, 165n2
Temple endowment, 75
Temples, 134, 165n4

Temple sealer, mistaken memory about, 13
Tongues, gift of, 101
Tripod of Truth, 87, 88, 96
Trust: faith and, 106–7; and sustaining prophets, 130–31
Truth, seeking, 53. *See also* Discerning truth from error; Tripod of Truth

Uchtdorf, Dieter F., 82–83, 115, 125, 127, 138, 147–48
Unanimity, among General Authorities, 128–29
Unanswered questions, 71–72. *See also* Ambiguity
Uncertainty, 71–72. *See also* Ambiguity
United Firm, 140
Unknown: and over-claiming, 77–79; splitting known from, 79–81. *See also* Ambiguity

Walker, Charles, 7, 21–22
Wallace, Daniel, 66
Wheat and tares, parable of, 151
Whitmer, David, 17–18
Whitmer, John, 93
Williams, Brian, 13, 154n10
Wirthlin, Joseph B., 101
Witnesses, law of, 33
Woodruff, Wilford, 120
Woodworth, Jed, 51
Word of Wisdom, 29–30, 63
Wright, N. T., 148

Young, Brigham: on Jesus's marriage status, 35; researching, 43, 47–48; on JST, 59; on studying scriptures, 67, 70; and restriction on priesthood, 75; on ambiguity of life, 82; on prophets leading people astray, 128; on Joseph Smith as Lord's agent, 129; on degrees of glory, 130; on consecration, 142

Zion, 144, 147–52

ABOUT THE AUTHOR

ANTHONY SWEAT is an assistant professor of Church history and doctrine at Brigham Young University. He is the author of numerous best-selling books and a regular speaker at various events and conferences. He received a BFA in painting and drawing from the University of Utah and MEd and PhD degrees in education from Utah State University. He and his wife, Cindy, are parents of seven children and reside in Utah.